p63TT8T5

The Body as a
Medium of Expression

Essays based on a course of lectures given at the
Institute of Contemporary Arts, London

Edited by Jonathan Benthall and Ted Polhemus

ALLEN LANE

First published in 1975

Allen Lane
Penguin Books Ltd
17 Grosvenor Gardens, London SW1

ISBN 0 7139 0774 6 cased
ISBN 0 7139 0986 2 paper

Printed in Great Britain by
Richard Clay (The Chaucer Press) Ltd,
Bungay, Suffolk

Contents

List of Illustrations

Editors' Introduction

The forming of the five senses is a labour of the entire history of the world down to the present.   Karl Marx

---

This volume of essays is based on a series of lectures round which a programme called The Body as a Medium of Expression was built at the Institute of Contemporary Arts in autumn 1972. This programme also included a rich variety of supporting events of a less formal nature – from modern-dance demonstrations to encounter-group sessions. We have made no attempt to document these supporting events in this volume, which is already ambitiously wide-ranging in its sweep.

This is the fourth publication resulting from an I.C.A. lecture-series.[1] We have discovered that a many-pronged attack by a number of carefully chosen specialists on a major topic of human concern can lead to a most illuminating whole, by a process of 'creative interference'.

We regret that one entertaining and appropriate feature of the lecture-series cannot be reproduced in print: almost every speaker was criticized or praised by the audience for his performance-style – posture, gesture, clothing, intonation and so on. Only John Broadbent retaliated after his lecture by criticizing the audience's demeanour, and some aggressive cut-and-thrust ensued among the audience on the theme of sadism in everyday life.

In this Introduction we will explain as concisely and neutrally as possible the structure of this volume. A Prospectus for the Body Programme by one editor (at the time Secretary of the I.C.A.)

and an opening essay by the other editor serve as further prefatory material of a more personal and controversial kind.

Jonathan Benthall's original Prospectus is reprinted with virtually no alteration. He notes that, though there is a surge of interest in the 'body as a medium of expression' in many fields, the subject has not yet been studied seriously and comprehensively, and he outlines some of the approaches which are brought to bear on it in this volume. He closes with some speculations about the political relevance of the body in a society that is dominated by verbal language, but which also contains diverse minority groups who may perhaps focus on other channels of communication.

Benthall's Prospectus is followed by five essays (by Polhemus, MacRae, Poole, Hinde and Argyle) which suggest, at a fairly general level, what a number of different intellectual approaches can contribute to an understanding of the body. Four of them take Charles Darwin as their starting-point.

Ted Polhemus is a social anthropologist who has attempted to make a synthesis of what American and European anthropology can contribute to our understanding of the body as a system of socially constructed meanings. **Ray Birdwhistell**, the world's leading authority on kinesics – the study of the meaning of bodily gestures – contributes an essay reviewing the origins of his subject in the studies of Lavater and Darwin, and considers some of the theoretical implications that raise themselves after his many years of empirical research. **Donald MacRae** the sociologist considers the body as one of the richest sources of metaphor that we have. **Roger Poole** contributes a philosophical essay influenced by phenomenology and strikes a polemical position against what he sees as scientistic approaches to the subject of the body. (Since Dr Poole criticizes a book edited by R. A. Hinde, Professor Hinde is given an opportunity to reply.) **R. A. Hinde**'s own contribution follows, exploring what the study of animal communications can tell us about human communications. (Since Jonathan Benthall's 'Prospectus' is criticized in this essay, he is given an opportunity to reply.) **Michael Argyle** then contributes a social psychologist's view of bodily communication.

The book now comes to focus on a variety of rather more specialized approaches and topics. **David Crystal** writes on 'paralinguistics' – the study of intonation, tone of voice, hesitation and so on, what might be called the 'greasy' part of speech. This provides a kind of bridge between systematic linguistics and the study of non-verbal communication. **J. A. V. Bates** then analyses various ways in which hand-positions convey meaning, with illustrations from both art-history and present-day manners.

Continuing the theme of the expressive capacities of the non-verbal, **Aaron V. Cicourel** contributes an essay which relates deaf-sign languages to conventional verbal language. This will be found a demanding essay by some readers, since its frame of reference is both sociological and linguistic; but we believe it is both original and suggestive.[2]

At this point in the volume, there is a shift in emphasis from theoretical approaches to empirical studies and illustrative material.

Paul E. Willis shows how an English minority group – a club of motor-bike boys – compensates for its lack of verbal sophistication by finding forms of bodily expression which are usually un-appreciated by the middle class and which indeed oppose middle-class values. **John F. Szwed** investigates the social mechanisms whereby other minority groups, such as the blacks and the Irish, have been and are being oppressed by means of cultural stereo-typing and sometimes by racial theories, originating in the percep-tion of physical bodily differences and expressive behaviour, which deny the existence of the creative resources which these minorities supply to the alienated majority.

Philip Rawson contributes an essay on the body in Tantra – that cult diffused throughout India which attempts to reach the Divine through techniques which involve the whole body and its vital forces. It has attracted considerable attention in the West recently, no doubt because it is so different from the dominant Western tradition of bodiless spirituality. This essay may be read as spiritual education, but also perhaps as an ethnographic case-study.

In the two final essays, our subject explodes into politics and poetry. **John O'Neill** argues that the auspices of political know-ledge are challenged by contemporary rejections of the mind–body dualism underlying the politics of office, age, gender and race. O'Neill sees demonstrations, street art, sit-ins and the like as literally and palpably – though also falteringly and vulnerably – *embodying* arguments to challenge verbal mystification and lies.

4   *The Body as a Medium of Expression*

The concluding essay is by **John Broadbent**, the expert on Milton and seventeenth-century literature. Having been invited to take part in the series (he suspected) rather as an object of *virtu*, he impressed his audience greatly by his relating of seventeenth-century poets to such modern prophets of bodily liberation as Herbert Marcuse and Norman Brown – eluding the role of 'object of *virtu*' so successfully as to be the programme's most challenging internal critic. He sees the contemporary concern with the body as a symptom of our century's inability to make sense of larger entities such as the cosmos and society, and closes the book on a note of thoughtful ambiguity.

J.B. T.P.

Editors' Acknowledgements

The Editors wish to thank for their ideas or encouragement Roger Abrahams, George Banu, Alan Beattie, Jean-Marie Benoist, John Bodley, Mary Douglas, Annette Lavers, Julie Lawson, Alan Lomax, Jonathan Miller, José Sasportes, David Thompson and Peter Ucko; and also the tenacious and critical audience that took part in discussions following each lecture. Thanks are also due to Nancy Clark, Suzie Cussins, Gilly Hodson, Linda Lloyd Jones and Lynn Procter for administrative help; and most of all to the contributors themselves.

1. The others are as follows:

    N. Minnis, ed., *Linguistics at Large* (Gollancz, 1971; Viking Press, New York, 1971; Paladin Books, 1973).

    J. Benthall, ed., *Ecology, the Shaping Enquiry* (Longman, 1972; published in U.S.A. as *Ecology in Theory and Practice*, (Viking Press, 1972).

    J. Benthall, ed., *The Limits of Human Nature* (Allen Lane, 1973; Dutton, New York, 1973).

    In addition, Ted Polhemus has edited *The Social Aspects of the Body*, a reader of key texts (Allen Lane, 1975; Pantheon Books, New York, 1975), in association with the I.C.A.

2. For some speculations on wider implications of Cicourel's work (not commented on by Professor Cicourel himself) see J. Benthall's 'Prospectus', p. 8.

Jonathan Benthall

A Prospectus as Published in *Studio International*, July 1972*

An integrated programme on the Body will begin at the I.C.A. in September – the first of its kind to be attempted by any institution – consisting of lectures, performances, workshops, demonstrations and exhibitions.

The body is the first and the most natural instrument of man.
Mercel Mauss

The body ... the great central ground underlying all symbolic reference. *A. N. Whitehead*

It is not to the physical object that the body may be compared, but rather to the work of art. *Maurice Merleau-Ponty*

Nijinsky discarded the 'sauce' of the dance, according to the critic Jacques Rivière, and returned to the 'natural pace' of the body 'in order to listen to nothing but its most immediate, basic, etymological signs'. Modern interest in the body's expressive and symbolic resources has been strongest in the dance world, but also recurs in the cinematic tradition of Eisenstein and the theatrical tradition of Artaud and Grotowski. In the 'visual arts' context, too, the body has been a compelling aesthetic concern for painters and sculptors, even for the most 'abstract' artists; and recently, several artists have turned away from external instrumentation towards the body itself (their own or other people's).†

*This article expresses its author's views only. It is criticized in passing by R. A. Hinde in his essay, p. 107, which is followed by a reply from the author. This article was written with the help of a number of people, including Ted Polhemus.

†The diverse list includes Yves Klein, Manzoni, the Weiner Aktionismus, Lygia Clark, Vito Acconci, Gilbert and George, Nauman, Burgy, Oppenheim,

Outside the world of accredited art, physical games and sports are as popular as ever; the circus and variety entertainment have not been completely killed by the mass media; a host of cults to do with the body are flourishing, such as encounter groups, yoga and Reichian therapy. Bestsellers and newspaper articles are often published on clothing, cosmetics, sexual habits, funerary customs, etc.

But understanding of the Body as a Medium of Expression is rudimentary. Little serious research has been done in this field compared to the rigorous attention given to verbal language. This is because verbal language is widely and influentially regarded as *the* distinctively human capability. Linguists have recently ascribed great technical importance to what are assumed to be syntactic universals; but the extreme respect accorded to verbal language is by no means new in our culture. It appears in fact to be an entrenched orthodoxy; one which, as Julia Kristeva has pointed out, would seem to be much more a product of the 'Graeco–Judeo–Christian enclosure' than of cultures outside it such as the Egyptian, Chinese, Indian, Balinese and Japanese, where the body blossoms.[1] It is an orthodoxy, however, which the average reader of an art magazine presumably subscribes to much less than does the average reader of, say, *The Times Literary Supplement*.*

We do not mean to belittle the expressive capabilities of verbal language and literature. It is more a question, perhaps, of '*donner un sens plus pur aux mots de la tribu*'. The 'algebra' of verbal language is merely *one* means whereby the body's physical organs and energies are articulated to convey meaning. It is admittedly a very concentrated means – but when reflecting on its concentration it is sentimental to adduce merely Homer and Shakespeare.

We should also recall how verbal language enacts the stratification of social classes, the repression of deviant minorities, the rise of technological and professional élites, the marketing of commodities and the glossing of public cruelty. If verbal language no doubt contributed substantially to the evolutionary success of

---

Rinke, Dan Graham, Brisley, Michel Journiac. I approached the theoretical question of how the body is used as a medium in 'The inflation of art media', *Studio International*, October 1971.

*Moreover, many artists are averse to art magazines and criticism. In the literary world, a 'retreat from the word' has been described by George Steiner.

early man, it may now be a part of the over-specialization of industrial man. The majesty we now see in verbal language – our 'logocentricity' as Derrida has called it – may have caused us to neglect the expressive resources of the body as a totality, to crush certain potentials within ourselves in the same way that we have crushed certain other cultures that appeared to us to be deficient in civilizing values. (The word 'barbarian' is thought to have been derived from a Greek imitation of foreign gibberish.)

An alternative, Rousseauesque metaphor is suggested by the agronomist's term 'monoculture', which describes the process whereby man replaces the diversity of a 'natural' ecosystem by a single crop, till now agricultural production in some countries is highly intensified with new high-protein hybrid cereals that are more vulnerable to pests and diseases. In both his agriculture and his communications man's exploitation by enclosure has been overdone. The richness and diversity of the environment must be respected and restored where possible; so must the richness and diversity of the body.

An important source-book in this field is *Non-Verbal Communication* (edited by R. A. Hinde, recently published by Cambridge University Press), the result of a Royal Society study group. This contains invaluable material and references, especially on the linguistic and ethological aspects. But we claim respectfully to offer some new perspectives.

Ted Polhemus will argue in his opening lecture (see pp. 13 ff. that the very title of *Non-Verbal Communication* is a logocentric manoeuvre.* Most of its contributors assume that (in the words of one of them, Jonathan Miller) 'verbal communication takes precedence in human discourse and that non-verbal behaviour achieves most of its communicative significance in the context of syntactically organized utterances'. Our own working hypothesis is opposed to this. It is that verbal language, with its standardized

*Kristeva and the Tel Quel circle have persuasively argued that the notion of 'communication' should be discarded (since it reflects a society based on the economics of exchange, and an outdated metaphysic of the disembodied subject). I cannot consider this argument here except to comment that many of us have been too slow to question the idea of art as a form of communication. Tel Quel wish to substitute a vocabulary of terms such as production, *praxis*, *texte*, *signifiance*. I should also note here that, for reasons of space, the Tel Quel concept of logocentricity has been over-simplified in this article.

spelling and normative grammar, and its relative 'arbitrariness',* has achieved a very impressive efficiency, but that it should have no priority or precedence over other ingredients in the expression of meaning.

The most radical attack on the dominance of speech and verbal expression in our culture has probably been that of Artaud (see especially his essays on Balinese theatre). A similar argument has been more coolly put by Aaron V. Cicourel, a sociologist from San Diego who will lecture at the I.C.A. (see pp. 197 ff.). 'Everyday language is fascinating because subdomains of its rather awesome flexible structure permit us to construct other artificial languages like logical and mathematical systems or computer programs that can be set up in correspondence with objects, events and operations.'

But in all communication there is an 'irremediable indexicality'. To the linguist, an 'indexical' (or 'deictic') expression is, for instance, 'Look there!'† It draws the attention of the receiver to a particular situational context, not by naming it, but by locating it in relation to the source (*deixis* = pointing). Cicourel suggests that grammarians, having identified 'context-free objective statements' as the essence of language, must try constantly to 'repair' an indexicality which is in fact inherent in *all* expressions, verbal and non-verbal. Any expression, in his view, implies more contextual information than can be analysed out by the linguist; it builds on an inexhaustibly large substratum of tacit common experience and meanings. Cicourel concludes that: 'The interactional context, as reflexively experienced over an exchange, or as imagined or invented when the scene is displaced or is known through a text, remains the heart of a general theory of meaning.'[2]

The I.C.A. programme will explore the body's role in interactional contexts as a mechanical, topographic and symbolic

*The relative *arbitrariness* – or *opaqueness*, or *non-motivation* – of verbal language is illustrated by the existence of totally different names for the same object in various languages; e.g. book, *livre*, *biblos*, etc.

†'Indexicality' has two confusing senses, both deriving from C. S. Peirce. The sense meant here is that of 'deixis' (pointing). (The other sense of 'indexicality' refers to signals that give information about the sender or source, e.g. rash which is an indexical symptom of an illness. See J. Lyons's article 'Human Language' in *Non-Verbal Communication*.)

complex. A variety of specialists will cover the following aspects of the body:

(a) gesture, posture and the study of movement (kinesics)
(b) face-to-face behaviour and the means whereby everyone manages his 'personal front' (a field pioneered by Erving Goffman)
(c) proximity studies (proxemics)
(d) deaf-sign languages
(e) paralinguistics – the 'greasy' parts of speech such as hesitation, vocalization, etc.
(f) animal signal systems (mainly primates but also dolphins and whales as representing another branch on the evolutionary tree)

But this is just the start. The lecture-series will attempt to subject some of this specialist research to a sociological and anthropological critique.

Recent American sociological trends will be touched on,* but we have been more guided by European social anthropology: the *Année sociologique* school (Durkheim, Mauss, Hertz), Lévi-Strauss and particularly Mary Douglas.[3] These and other theorists have tackled the vast question of the possibility of consonance between all layerings of experience – the physical, the psychological,

---

*Cicourel belongs to a new school of sociologists called 'ethnomethodologists' who study the rational properties of everyday mundane experience and indexical practice. Such research necessarily returns frequently to the body as the source of such experience and practice. Harold Garfinkel's paper 'Passing and the managed achievement of sex status in an "intersexed" person' – the case-history of 'Agnes', a psychiatric patient of ambiguous sexual status – is a classic of sociological reportage, complete with a narrative twist at the end that makes most contemporary fiction seem pale. Garfinkel's experiments – which he prefers to call 'demonstrations' or 'aids to a sluggish imagination' – recall the practices of certain avant-garde artists today; for instance, 'Students were instructed to select someone other than a family member and in the course of an ordinary conversation, and without indicating that anything unusual was happening, to bring their faces up to the subject's until their noses were almost touching . . .' (H. Garfinkel, *Studies in Ethnomethodology* (Englewood Cliffs, N.J.): Prentice-Hall, 1967). If art seems to revert again and again to the body as a source of meaning and understanding, it is because no attempt to repair indexicality, to transcend the flesh, can ever complete itself. This argument was classically elaborated by Merleau-Ponty in *La Phénoménologie de la perception* (Paris: Gallimard, 1945).

the social and the cosmic. Douglas has suggested that 'the achievement of consonance between different realms of experience is a
source of profound satisfaction'. The body is perhaps the foremost
of all metaphors for a society's perception of itself, recurring
constantly in myths and cosmogonies, art and literature. One
lecture in the series will be given by Philip Rawson (see pp. 273 ff.)
on the Indian cult of Tantra, where the body becomes a metaphor
perhaps more explicitly all-embracing than in any other social
situation. The ambiguous attitude of Christianity to the body –
oscillating between glorification and mortification – is particularly
close to home and should not be forgotten.

Body behaviour and body imagery differ so widely from culture
to culture that it is impossible to unscramble those biological or
genetic constituents of any given behaviour which might fairly be
called 'culture-independent' or 'specific to the human species'. It is
doubtful whether any formal attempt to unscramble the biological–genetic dimension from the social and psychological dimensions would be a profitable exercise (since the notion of an
asocial human nature is an abstraction); but such ethnographic
field-data as exists – about such cultures as Bali, Navaho, Southern
Italy – is useful for testing all theories about the body.

We shall investigate various 'aids' to the body-medium such as
clothing, adornment, body-mutilation, hair-styling, bathing and
care of the body; and the use of the dead body as an art-form.
These 'aids' need to be studied in relationship to images and ideas
of the body.

But the most urgent and radical aspect of the subject is what
John O'Neill, author of *Sociology as a Skin-Trade* (Heinemann,
1972; New York: Harper & Row, 1972), calls 'body politics' (see
pp. 293 ff.). O'Neill refers to Marx and Freud, but also to Norman
Brown and the activists – such as Jerry Rubin, Cassius Clay,
Eldridge Cleaver and Frantz Fanon – who have between them
'taught us to understand the deep political structures of sex,
language and the body'. According to Rubin, 'Nobody really
communicates with words any more'. Demonstrations, street art
and sit-ins are literally and palpably *embodying* arguments to
challenge verbal mystification and lies. (Polhemus will speculate
that it is the 'arbitrariness' of verbal language which makes it the
most 'alienating' form of communication.[4])

O'Neill writes of the 'non-verbal rhetoric' of political dissidents. Developing his case, we are working on the hypothesis that, since our society uses words as its primary means of social control, all repressed groups will tend to find their most effective and confident expression through the body's wider resources rather than within the enclosure of verbal language, in so far as they opt for self-assertion rather than for integrating with the norms of the majority. There are three clear test-cases: blacks, male homosexuals, and the deaf. (Other test-cases – such as women, female homosexuals, artists, lunatics, children – are not so clear but could be brought into the argument at a later stage.)

Blacks

Any student of the history of white attitudes to the negro will be aware of the intense interest in the negro's body and his place in the Great Chain of Being.[5] Racial theory attempted to define scientifically how exactly the black body was set off from the white body. In reaction to stereotyping by the whites as a mindless brute, or a phallic symbol, the black has recently asserted his relationship with his body as different from that of the white. This is articulated in the ideologies of *négritude* and of Black Power.

Male homosexuals

Epithets implying unnaturalness or animality have been used in our culture to crush sexual deviance, as 'nigger' has been used to repress the blacks. Even in more sophisticated discourse, the homosexual is taught to regard himself as doomed to *miss* essential human experiences such as the procreation of children. The ethos of the Western homosexual sub-culture is celebrated today in the world of dance and ballet.

The deaf

Lacking a sense – claimed by the dominant speaking–hearing majority as essential to fully human communication – the deaf often communicate by manual signing which to the speaker–hearers is a crude – almost animal – version of verbal language. Cicourel has brilliantly criticized this logocentric view, reminding us that all the notations used to describe deaf-sign languages are invented by speaker–hearers. He imagines an anthropologist from another planet who can only make a field-study of the earth-people by using the deaf people as his informants. The anthropologist ends up feeling sympathy with the deaf for having to live with such a barbaric community as the speaker–hearers.

I have left to the end of this article the question which perhaps the reader is asking: why write an article on the subject? Why allow new jargon to proliferate on this subject, of all subjects? Why organize a series of lectures? This is a good objection; our answer is that, whereas the I.C.A. programme on the Body has been conceived by highly logocentric people, we are keen to hand on its direction to people with different qualifications as soon as possible, and from the start the lectures will be interleaved with performances, demonstrations, workshops and classes. The initial response to our proposals from dancers, choreographers and mimes has been most encouraging. We hope for similar participation from people working in the visual arts, theatre and film.

1. J. Kristeva, 'Le Geste: pratique ou communication?', *Semiotike: Recherches pour une Sémanalyse*, Du Seuil, Paris, 1969.
2. Aaron V. Cicourel, 'Ethnomethodology', to appear in T. A. Sebeok *et al.*, eds, *Current Trends in Linguistics*, vol. 12.
3. Especially Lévi-Strauss's *La Pensée sauvage* (*The Savage Mind*); and Mary Douglas's *Natural Symbols* (Barrie & Rockliffe, 1970) and 'The Social Control of Cognition: some factors in joke perception', *Man*, vol. 3, no. 3, September 1968.
4. See footnote p. 8.
5. See Winthrop Jordan, *White Over Black* (University of North Carolina, 1968; Penguin, 1971).

Ted Polhemus

Social Bodies

If the so-called 'primitive' people of the world decided to send anthropologists to make studies of Western civilization (which I should think they would have little interest in doing), it would not be surprising to find these anthropologists reporting back from the field about the Westerners' new religious cult: the cult of the human body. Horace Miner, taking things into his own hands, reports to us on the extraordinary 'Body ritual among the Nacirema' (Nacirema is 'American' spelled backwards);

> While much of the people's time is devoted to economic pursuits, a large part of the fruits of these labors and a considerable portion of the day are spent in ritual activity. The focus of this activity is the human body, the appearance and health of which loom as a dominant concern in the ethos of the people. While such a concern is certainly not unusual, its ceremonial aspects and associated philosophy are unique.
>
> The fundamental belief underlying the whole system appears to be that the human body is ugly and that its natural tendency is to debility and disease. Incarcerated in such a body, man's only hope is to avert these characteristics through the use of the powerful influences of ritual and ceremony. Every household has one or more shrines devoted to this purpose. The more powerful individuals in the society have several shrines in their houses and, in fact, the opulence of the house is often referred to in terms of the number of such ritual centers it possesses.
>
> (Miner, 1956, p. 503.)

Logically enough, this cult of the body has penetrated into the academic world and we find ourselves with a cult of *the study* of the social aspects of the human body – a cult which, like any other, ought to be studied as a socio-cultural phenomenon. To understand this recent upsurge of interest in body research would require something like an anthropology of the anthropology of the human body, and this is perhaps the real theme of the following essay. It is ironic that the academic world – that fantastic machine geared for the production of verbal jargon – should focus its 'logocentric' attention upon the movements, gestures, postures and expressions of the physical body.* Surely the subject of the human body is more suited for the dance-floor than for the lecturer's podium.

Why then has anthropology so persistently taken on this difficult subject? The obvious answer is that the peoples whom ethnographers have studied tend to emphasize the expressive capacities of the human body (in dance, bodily adornment, figure sculpture, sign 'language', etc.). But this is not a complete answer since ethnographers are famous for ignoring matters which are of great importance to the natives whom they study. The real answer, I suspect, will come only when we are prepared to turn our attention to an anthropology of anthropology and begin to raise the more fundamental question of the socio-cultural role of *anthropology* in Western society. Possibly anthropology in particular, and the social sciences in general, constitute an attempt to bring human behaviour – that constant source of surprise and mystery – into the bounds of Western reason and therefore (in a manner of speaking) into the bounds of Western control. We have always been at least a little frightened by what Lévi-Strauss has called the savage mind. Perhaps what worried Westerners most about these savages was that they were 'naked'; that they danced and communicated powerful symbolic statements with their tattooed bodies. The West responded to this 'threat', I would argue, with a two-pronged attack. First we sent out the troops of missionaries armed with the story of the fall of man, so that the native might have the sense to feel ashamed of his own nakedness. Next (and here I will be regarded as more heretical; a fact which is itself of interest) came

---

*The term 'logocentric' was coined by Jacques Derrida and is currently to be found in the writings of Julia Kristeva and the Tel Quel circle in Paris. My own use of the term does not imply an alignment with the somewhat complicated position of these theorists. Many studies of the body have reflected the logocentricity of the Western world: consider, for instance, the title of the Cambridge University Press's recent publication *Non-Verbal Communication*.

the troops of anthropologists, who (armed with their notebooks) were enlisted to bring home the good news that even such bizarre behaviour as that indulged in by the primitive could be made to fit into rational, empirical models of human behaviour. And it was clear from the start that if we were to render the savage understandable, we would have to understand his 'nakedness', his scarification, his tattooing, his dancing and his erotic appeal (to the young ladies back home). *If we were to render the savage world safe for Western, verbalizing man, we would have to bring the mysteries of the human body within the bounds of Western rationality.* Herein, I suggest, lies the answer to the question of why anthropology has so doggedly taken on the subject of the human body even though it was so ill-suited to the task.

In the following pages I will attempt to trace out the story of how anthropology has tried to cope with the problem of the social aspects of the human body. If the arguments and counter-arguments seem to you to be a bit dry and far from the subject, then I would suggest that you join with me in a private anthropology of the anthropology of the human body and at each stage pose the question, 'What kind of social values are expressed in these various theories, methods and assumptions about the human body as expressed by the anthropologist?' In this way a critique of anthropological research itself becomes a sample of ethnographic evidence, and we might thus begin to understand our own corporal and social predicament.

About 100 years ago, in 1873, Charles Darwin concluded his book *The Expression of the Emotions in Man and Animals* with the assertion that 'all the chief expressions exhibited by man are the same throughout the world' (Darwin, 1873, p. 359). Darwin was primarily concerned with facial expression but others have expanded his hypothesis to include a much wider range of bodily activity. The explanation offered by Darwin and the universalists to account for their findings is that bodily expression is universal because it is transmitted genetically. Darwin backed up his universalist conclusion with six different types of data. First, observation of infants, as in the following letter to Huxley:

I rejoice that your children are all pretty well. Give Mrs Huxley the enclosed queries and ask her to look out when one of her children is struggling and just going to burst out crying. A dear young lady near here, plagued a very young child, for my sake, till it cried, and saw the eyebrows for a second or two beautifully oblique just before the torrent of tears began. (Ward, 1927, pp. 355–6.)

Second, observations of the insane; third, galvanization experiments; fourth, observation of facial expressions as recorded in 'the great masters in painting and sculpture' (Darwin, 1873, p. 14); fifth, ethnographic data and sixth, observation of animals. With only minor exceptions, all of the types of evidence which Darwin collated pointed to the same conclusion: 'that the young and the old of widely different races, both with man and animals, express the same state of mind by the same movements.' (Darwin, 1873, p. 351.)

Since Darwin's writing, students working in various fields of research have unearthed what appears to be a great wealth of data which contradicts his evidence and his conclusions. This is not the place to examine the total range of this data, but I would like to consider two categories of evidence which have a direct bearing upon our subject of the social anthropology of the human body: evidence concerning the *learnt* nature of bodily expression and evidence concerning the *variable* nature of bodily expression.

Physiologists have for a long time been aware of medical cases of apraxia in which patients 'forget' how to perform various bodily expressions and movements. Physiological explanation did not seem justified, first because patients were usually able to 'remember' how to use their bodies in due time, and secondly, because no physio-pathological cause of the disturbance could be detected. The conclusion reached by many researchers investigating this problem was that at least some types of bodily expression were learnt in infancy and could be 'forgotten' in much the same way that aphasia patients 'forget' their names.

Furthermore, ethnographic field-workers have been able to observe occasions wherein bodily expression is taught either consciously or unconsciously. Marcel Mauss in his essay 'Les Techniques du corps' (written in 1936), insisted that the techniques of the body are learnt: that they are social and cultural phenomena and not 'natural'. Every kind of action, according to Mauss, carries the imprint of learning. The ethnographic data to back this claim was patchy and he had to resort to his own personal observations: 'A little girl did not know how to spit and this made every cold she had much worse. In her father's family in particular . . . people do not know how to spit. I taught her to spit.' (Mauss, 1935, trans. 1973, p. 84.)

Since the time of Mauss's writing, several anthropologists have supplied evidence that specific aspects of bodily expression are learnt: not only complicated, formalized and ritualized expressions, gestures, postures, etc., but also 'simple' bodily activities such as the rate of eye-blinking.*

Two specific studies, in particular, have been important. The first is by David Efron and the second is by Margaret Mead and Gregory Bateson. Efron (1941) demonstrated that as Jewish and Italian immigrants in New York City are assimilated into American culture they tend to forget their traditional gestures and learn new ones which comply with those of American culture *in general*. Bateson and Mead (1942) used the techniques developed by Gessel for the study of infant bodily expression in America in order to study infant development in Balinese society. In the course of this research they were able to isolate many instances of the education (or training, though not necessarily performed consciously by the Balinese parent) of bodily expression.

Darwin had gathered his ethnographic evidence of the universality of facial expression by sending a questionnaire out to government workers, missionaries, etc., who were living in various remote parts of the world. This questionnaire which Darwin had devised posed questions such as the following: 'When considering deeply on any subject, or trying to understand any puzzle, does he [the native] frown, or wrinkle the skin beneath the lower eyelids?' (Darwin, 1873, p. 15.) There were sixteen questions in the questionnaire and in 1867 it was sent to Englishmen and women residing in the four corners of the world. The result, as we have already seen, was in the affirmative – everyone in the world was observed to exhibit the same facial expressions as the British. Certainly Darwin should be given credit for his, perhaps, pioneering use of the questionnaire in ethnographic research, but then again, the questionnaire may not be a very reliable tool in

*For example: Belo (1935), Bailey (1942), Devereux (1951), Astrov (1950), Birdwhistell (1971), LaBarre (1947), etc.

ethnographic studies of this type, and, as we have seen, anthropologists working in *direct* contact with native informants (unlike Darwin) have unearthed a great deal of data contradictory to that which Darwin gathered via his questionnaire.

The first anthropological evidence supporting the view that bodily expression is learnt came from reports of specific, *single* societies. Hocart in 1927 reported on the sitting postures of the Mongolians, and Kroeber studied posture and expression in many of the tribes of the Indians of California. For example he comments on sitting postures of the Mohave Indians: 'Mohave men sit with their thigh on their calves and heels, or with legs bent to one side on the ground. These are women's fashions among the Indians of the western Plains.' (Kroeber, 1925.) Gradually the bits and pieces of ethnographic data were put together and cross-cultural surveys of bodily expression were assembled. The research of Hewes (1955 and 1957), Hall (1955, 1959 and 1963) and LaBarre (1947) are good examples of such comparative studies. Hewes's work is the most thorough, although he has found it necessary to limit himself to the study of posture only.

It is important to note that in many cases Darwin, on the one hand, and the ethnographers, on the other, were directing their attention into different aspects of bodily expression. Darwin (by and large) limited himself to facial expression and this is one aspect of bodily expression which has not received the full thrust of ethnographic research. LaBarre has commented on it, but his remarks are vague and impressionistic and the same could be said of Hall's work, especially *The Silent Language* (1959). Birdwhistell, however, a contributor to the present volume (p. 36) has studied facial expression intensively and he has concluded that, like other aspects of bodily expression, it is subject to socio-cultural variation (Birdwhistell, 1971). Unfortunately, Birdwhistell's research is concerned only with variation within the United States and we wait for someone with his sensitivity to variation in facial expression to examine less closely related socio-cultural systems. I can see no reason, however, why – if posture and simple motor habits, for example, exhibit cross-cultural variability – facial expression should be exempt from this pattern of variation. 'Neo-universalists' (if I may coin a term) such as Eibl-Eibesfeldt (1972), Van Hooff (1972) and Grant (1969) are currently theorizing that facial expressions which occur in situations of instinctual response (such as fright, extreme anger, etc.) are *not* culturally variable; and Eibl-Eibesfeldt has shown evidence for the universality of what he calls 'the eyebrow flash'. That a few specific facial expressions may be universal does not in any way erase the fact that other bodily expression has been found to be variable from one society to another. Even if only a limited range of bodily expressions were found to be cross-culturally variable (which is clearly *not* the case), the social sciences would still have to account for such variability *as does exist*. We can see that not only are the *social* sciences justified in concerning themselves with the study of the human body, but that by exposing cracks in Darwin's paradigm they have inherited the responsibility of positing an explanation. To demonstrate that bodily expression is not universal (that it is variable from one society to another) is not to explain such variability. And, in showing that bodily expression (or some types of it) is learnt, ethnographers have only provided us with an understanding of the *mechanism* whereby bodily expression is able to exhibit variability.

Some anthropologists studying the body have contented themselves with the task of compiling vast indexes of body behaviour variation. They have been *collectors* of data in a way, not very different from the collectors of artifacts who scoured the world for items of interest for museums. These anthropologists who have never put forth a substantial theoretical explanation of the variability of bodily expression I will call the *relativists*. The techniques of collection which they have employed have varied in both quality and scope. Most often they have had to restrict themselves to one particular aspect of the subject of the human body, and they have usually drawn boundaries to define the limits of their research according to arbitrary criteria. Neither in his article in the *American Anthropologist* (1955), nor in his article in *Scientific American* (1957) does Gordon Hewes bother to define his subject – namely, posture. Nor does he explain anywhere why he has selected this particular field of study. Nor does he explain how the study of posture relates to the study of other aspects of bodily expression, such as kinesic and proxemic behaviour. Thus not only has Hewes failed to offer much of a theory beyond his statement, 'Human postural habits have anatomical and physiological limitations, but there are a great many choices, the determinants for which appear to be mostly cultural' (1955, p. 231), but he has also failed to convince us that his subject is not a non-subject. (But as we will see, this would seem to be the most common problem of anthropological studies of the human body.)

Some of the relativists have made their collecting into a very *scientistic* enterprise. For example, Watson and Graves have scrupulously measured the proxemic distancing among groups of American students and among groups of Arab students. We are much impressed by all their graphs and statistics, but we do not feel any nearer to an understanding of *why* it should be that 'highly significant Arab–American differences emerged in the direction expected, with the Arab students confronting each other more directly than the Americans, moving closer together, more apt to touch each other while talking, looking each other more squarely in the eye, and conversing in louder tones'. (Watson and Graves, 1966, p. 983.) But while the relativists have not provided us with an explanation of the variability of bodily expression, they *have* presented us with even more data which, since it does not fit with Darwin's paradigm, begs for an explanation. It is, I think, time to cease debating with Darwin – he and the universalists are, after all, really interested in a different subject with different questions and different answers – and get on with the business of explaining the evidence which is sociologically relevant.

Sensing that bodily expression could not profitably be studied and explained in the same way that we study most of the social and cultural activities of man, some anthropologists have assumed that it could best be dealt with by the use of models and methods borrowed from linguistic research – language being that other activity of man which has never responded to traditional anthropological treatment. Increasingly anthropology is coming to use linguistic models for the study of all aspects of human behaviour. Also, the use of linguistic models and methods has precedents such as MacDonald Critchley's *The Language of Gesture* (1939). Apart from the possibility that this analogy between bodily expression and language may not be justified (a point which we will return to later), the use of linguistic models for the study of the social aspects of the body has suffered because, more often than not, students of the subject have failed to make it clear just *which* linguistic model they were using as a frame for their research.*

On the other hand, some students of the subject of the body *have* made it clear which linguistic model they were using, but have (in my opinion) misused or misemployed these models. Edward Hall, the well-known originator of proxemics or the science of personal space, has in all of his writings emphasized the analogy of proxemic behaviour (which, of course, includes the spatial aspects of the body) and language. His popular book on the subject he entitled *The Silent Language* (1959). In more academic publications, Hall has defended the analogy between body behaviour and language by relating proxemic behaviour to the 'design features of language' which were set down by the linguist Charles Hockett.†
In his article in the *American Anthropologist* (1968), Hall proceeds point by point through Hockett's 'design features' and at each point argues that proxemic behaviour fulfils the criteria that Hockett insists a language must satisfy. Hall concludes that proxemic behaviour 'parallels language, feature for feature'. (Hall, 1963, p. 1019.) On one of these points I think that critical comment is necessary – this concerns Hockett's design feature of *arbitrariness*. Hall remarks, somewhat obscurely, on the arbitrariness of proxemic behaviour as follows:

Proxemics lacks none of the . . . features of language listed by Hockett. Its arbitrariness is not obvious at first, because proxemic behaviour tends to be experienced as iconic – e.g., a feeling of 'closeness' is often accompanied by physical closeness – yet it is the very arbitrariness of man's behavior in space that throws him off when he tries to interpret the behavior of others across cultural lines. For example, the fact that Europeans name streets (the lines that connect points) and the Japanese name the points and ignore the lines, is arbitrary . . . American suppression and repression of olfaction in proxemic behavior is also arbitrary. (1963, p. 1018.)

Slightly later on in the same article he adds:

The iconic features of proxemics are exaggerated in the minds of those who have not had extensive and deep cross-cultural experience. In fact, when a subject stops treating proxemic behaviour as iconic and sees its

---

*This criticism could be lodged against Efron (1941), Messing (1960), Ruesch and Kees (1956) and also Critchley (1939).

† See, for example, Hockett (1960).

arbitrariness, he is beginning to experience the over-all arbitrariness of culture. (1963, p. 1019.)

Many of us may feel confused by Hall's use of this term 'arbitrary'. If we refer back to Hockett we find that he explains the term in the following fashion:

In a semantic communicative system the ties between meaningful message-elements and their meanings can be arbitrary or nonarbitrary. In language the ties are arbitrary. The word 'salt' is not salty nor granular; 'dog' is not 'canine'; 'whale' is a small word for a large object; 'microorganism' is the reverse. (1960, p. 4.)

Hall's use of the concept of arbitrariness does not – to my mind – follow closely to Hockett's explanation. Hall does not refer back from the 'meaningful message-elements' (observed proxemic behaviour, in this case) to the 'meanings' which these elements carry or refer to. While for Hockett the concept of arbitrariness has to do with the 'ties' that link these two factors, Hall has only, in his examples, compared different 'message-elements' for different societies (namely, the United States and Japan). It is unfortunate that Hall does not bother to define his use of this term – especially unfortunate since he is so convinced not only that proxemic behaviour is 'arbitrary' but also that there exists an '. . . over-all arbitrariness of culture'. (Hall, 1963, p. 1019.)

Hall does not seem to be alone in his assumption of the over-all arbitrariness of culture, nor in his use (or, I would argue, misuse) of the term 'arbitrary'. Philip Bock concludes his recent textbook for American students of anthropology with the statement:

Throughout the book I have stressed the *arbitrariness* of cultural phenomena: the criteria that we use in categorizing colors, sounds, kinsmen, or diseases, the ways in which we structure time and space, and the standards we use in evaluating 'goodness' or 'beauty' are all creations of our predecessors. They *could have been different*. In some other society they may be either ignored or reversed. (1969, p. 443.)

Earlier in his book, Bock explained the term 'arbitrary': 'To say that a cultural pattern is arbitrary means only that it *could be otherwise* under different circumstances, not that it is random or that it bears no relationship to human biology *or to the rest of the culture*.' (1969, p. 59; second italics are mine.)

It would appear that for some American anthropologists, the concept of 'arbitrariness' refers to the possibility of variation between societies and from one time to another within one society. Such a use of the concept (although quite different from the use of the term as found in either the linguistics of Hockett or indeed of de Saussure for example) might be justified if it was made clear that the use of the term differs from its more general linguistic usage. Hall is using the term 'arbitrary' essentially as a synonym for 'cultural relativity', since in both cases all that is meant is that things 'could be otherwise'. It is clear that Hall's research does not suggest an explanation of *why* bodily expression should be variable, relative, or 'arbitrary' (to use the term in Hall's sense). Any *explanation* of the variability of bodily expression must deal not with the relationship of differing bodily expressions in differing societies, but rather with the relationship of elements of bodily expression *to other aspects of the cultural and social environment within which they occur*. It is quite possible that bodily expression (or at least some forms of bodily expression) is arbitrary, in the more general linguistic sense of the term, and it will be of considerable interest to see in what social circumstances bodily expression is arbitrary and in what social circumstances it is not. But we will determine this only by examining the ties between bodily expression 'message-elements' (to use Hockett's terms) and their 'meanings' within the same socio-cultural context.

One possible way in which this might be done would be by using a linguistic model of the semiotic type. Semiology has always been especially concerned with the problem of the arbitrariness of sign systems and for this reason it might be better suited than Hockett's model for exploring the arbitrariness of bodily expression. When the Swiss linguist Ferdinand de Saussure was confronted with the question of whether or not language is arbitrary, he found it necessary to formulate a model or frame of study wherein language-like, arbitrary signs would constitute only a subset of the total range of possible signs. By distinguishing a conceptual *signified*, on the one hand, and an expressive or material *signifier*, on the other, de Saussure was able to precisely examine the *relationship* of these two factors.*

*This distinction of signified–signifier is perhaps not really very different from Hockett's distinction between 'message-elements' and their 'meanings'.

Employing a Saussurian framework for the study of the human body would permit us to contrast *bodily expression* on the one hand, with *body imagery*, on the other: the former being the material signifier, the latter being the conceptual signified. The new factor which emerges when such a linguistic model is used is body imagery, something which is ignored in most linguistic–anthropological studies of the body, but which has a long history in psychological studies. It was, in fact, the neurologist Henry Head (back in 1920) who 'theorized that each person constructs a picture or model of his body . . .' (Fisher, p. 114.) Head called this picture or model the *body schema* and Seymour Fisher converted Head's term into the phrase *body image*. (Fisher, 1968.) Fisher also suggests the phrase *body concept* as a synonym of both body image and body schema, and for our purposes this third phrase is helpful since the term 'concept' contrasts nicely with the term 'expression', thus completing Saussure's famous dichotomy.

Having distinguished our terms in this way we could now begin to consider the *relationship* of the two terms and from this we might come to an understanding of whether or not the social aspects of the human body are (or can be) language-like in the sense of being arbitrary or unmotivated. But any who would attempt this (and I think that someone schooled in linguistics *should* attempt it) ought to be aware that this model (see Figure 1)

$$\frac{\text{Bodily expression}}{\text{Body imagery}} \equiv \frac{\text{Signifier}}{\text{Signified}} \equiv \frac{\text{material expression}}{\text{concept}}$$

Figure 1 Application of Saussure's model to body studies

like any other involves the student in several special problems. To begin with, there is the question of *which* semiotic model to use, since Saussure has been interpreted in many different directions. It is also true that following the wave of the recent popularity of

---

But Saussure's preciseness of terminology may help us to avoid Hall's mistake of comparing differing signifiers in differing societies instead of (as must be done if we are to move beyond cultural relativism) relating the body signifieds and signifiers *of one society* to each other.

semiology has come a second wave of criticism – especially from a phenomenological perspective.

Another problem with the Saussurian model is that it may focus too much of our attention on the *specific* relationship of the signifier (bodily expression) and the signified (body imagery) so that we would neglect the larger question of the relationship of *both of these* to the social system that generates them. Some students with a particularly linguistic preoccupation might argue that a semiotic model could be of use in dealing with this larger problem, but I personally think that it would stretch the Saussurian model beyond all recognition since *all* the social system would have to be taken as the Saussurian signified and *all* body activity (including both expression and imagery) would have to be taken as the Saussurian signifier. The question really is: should anthropology become a sub-science of linguistics, or can we not draw on the traditional resources of social science?

Before moving on to examine some non-linguistic approaches to the subject, we ought to mention that some students of bodily expression have managed to side-step the problem of the arbitrary or non-arbitrary nature of bodily expression by turning to communication models. Such an approach, of which the work of Ray Birdwhistell is the most distinguished example, does not depend – at least to begin with – upon answering the question of whether or not bodily expression is language-like in the sense of being arbitrary. For Birdwhistell there is a channel of communication of language and there is also a channel which pertains to kinesic, 'body-motion communication'. (Birdwhistell, 1971.) Whether or not this kinesic channel of bodily expression is similar to the linguistic channel is of only secondary importance for Birdwhistell. The important point, for him, is that this kinesic channel is seen as distinct and separate from the verbal channel and that bodily expression is not seen merely as a *modifier* of the verbal–oral channel. Thus Birdwhistell's approach is not only distinct in its method, but it is also distinct in the particular problem to which it addresses itself, namely, 'What is the relationship of bodily expression *to the other channels of communication* which occur side by side with it?' Birdwhistell (unlike Hall) does not try to squeeze bodily expression into the verbal–linguistic channel.

While it would appear that Birdwhistell began his research from the perspective of individual psychiatric communication, he moved his research into the sociological or anthropological domain when he began to insist that person-to-person communication (on any and all channels) occurs with, and depends upon, a *social context*. The problem of the relationship of this social context to the *content* of the bodily communication which occurs within it is a second stage of the problem, which Alan Lomax (a student of Birdwhistell) has inherited. The preliminary results of Lomax's computerized Choreometrics Project (1968), a world-wide study of dance movement,* suggest a high degree of correlation between dance styles and certain features of the socio-cultural context within which they occur (especially features related to the techniques of subsistence such as styles of hoeing).†

Studies of the body which have been based upon linguistic and communication models have had such an impact upon the social sciences (and in some cases, upon the public) that many students of the subject have ignored the long tradition of body studies whose models and methods might be defined as more strictly '*sociological*'. Marcel Mauss (1935) and Robert Hertz (1909), both students of Émile Durkheim and both contributors to Durkheim's *Année sociologique*, were early to recognize the importance of studying the social significance of the human body. Their models and methods were neither linguistic nor involved (directly) in theories of communication. Like others who have used the Durkheimian model, they assumed that a society constitutes a whole which is greater than the sum of its parts (its individual members), in so far as the various individual members of the social community share a *cognitive consensus*, or in Lévi-Strauss's phrase, a 'socio-logic'. (1968, p. 76.) Therefore, those who use a Durkheimian model to study the human body assume that the members of a particular society will share certain attitudes towards, and understandings of, the human body – that there will be a com-

*The relationship of dance movement and kinesic movement should, perhaps, be explained. Lomax argues that dance movement represents highly redundant and repetitive forms of kinesic activity (Lomax, in seminar, University of London, 1971).

†The preliminary results of Lomax's research are found in his book *Folk Song Style and Culture* (1968) but he has also completed several films which demonstrate the relationships of dance, kinesic movement and subsistence techniques in more dramatic form.

munally shared knowledge of how a 'healthy', or a 'beautiful', or an 'erotic' body is defined – by the members of a particular society (or a group of people within a society).

Robert Hertz and Marcel Mauss were, as sociologists, interested in the human body less for its own sake than as a reservoir of the cognitive consensus or 'socio-logic' of a society. For them (and for those who have followed in their tradition, in which category I would include myself), the physiological raw material of the human body is of interest in so far as it is transformed by its social environment and 'embodied' with social meaning. In short, Hertz and Mauss were interested in *social* bodies.

Robert Hertz focussed his attentions upon the specific problem of right–left body symbolism and showed how societies play upon the (apparently) slight physiological predominance of the right hand and via education, ritual and etiquette *transform* the right and left hands into potent manifestations, metaphors and symbols of social and cultural duality and hierarchy. In short, Hertz suggested that we ascribe our social values to the attributes of the two sides of our bodies. In Hertz's words, 'The difference in value and function between the two sides of our body possesses therefore in an extreme degree the characteristics of a social institution; and a study which tries to account for it belongs to sociology.' Hertz's hypothesis, far from attempting to contradict the physiological evidence, managed to find a point of cross-fertilization between the physiologists and the social scientists. His concern as a sociologist was to show how social meaning is grafted on to the physical medium of the human body. Is it not amazing that so many years later the physiologists and the social scientists are still bickering over this same issue? The point that Hertz made was simply that societies take raw objects and transform them into artifacts pregnant with social meaning; and, of course, the body is the object *par excellence* for such an exercise for obvious reasons.

Marcel Mauss (1935), following after Hertz, zeroed in on the mechanism and processes by which the body object is transformed into an artifact: namely, the processes of the training and education of 'The Techniques of the Body'. He concluded that 'in every society, everyone knows and has to know and learn what he has to do in all conditions', the techniques of the body being assembled by and for social authority'. (1935, trans. 1973, p. 85.)

Building upon the work of Mauss and Hertz, Professor Mary Douglas has continued the tradition of examining the human body via a Durkheimian model of society. Douglas begins with the assumption that 'the social body constrains the way the physical body is perceived'. (1970, p. 65.) That is, the physical body *as we perceive it* (and of course there is no such thing as an unperceived body) is a segment of our 'social construction of reality'. Furthermore, Douglas suggests that far from being just like any other segment of this socially perceived reality, the body occupies an especially important place since 'the physical experience of the body, always modified by the social categories through which it is known, sustains a particular view of society. There is a continual exchange of meanings between the two kinds of bodily experience so that each reinforces the categories of the other.' (1970, p. 65.)

Thus Douglas (like Mauss and Hertz before her) extends a Durkheimian analysis of society to include physiological experience and finally to suggest that for any society there will be a drive to achieve *consonance* between these two levels of meaning: social meaning, on the one hand, and socio-physical meaning on the other. Professor Douglas has provided us with two excellent examples of her hypothesis that 'the body communicates information for and from the social system in which it is a part'. (1971, p. 387.) In *Natural Symbols* (1970), she uses the example of trance behaviour, suggesting that 'as trance is a form of dissociation, it will be more approved and welcomed the weaker the structuring of society'. (1970, p. 74.) And in her more recent paper 'Do dogs laugh? A cross-cultural approach to body symbolism' (1971), she uses the example of laughter to discuss further the implications of the relationship of bodily and social control.

If Douglas is correct that 'the human body is always treated as an image of society' (1970, p. 70) then it follows that by examining a people's attitudes to the human body, and their definition of its boundaries, we should gain some understanding of the native informant's *other* body – his social body, his society. Because of this suggestion that the study of the social aspects of the human body can provide us with an understanding not just of the physical body and its own communication, but also of the social context *itself*, we ought to recognize a special value in a Durkheimian approach to the study of the human body. The body is not just another subject for the field-worker to make note of, but, if Douglas is right, it is a tool – a native-made model or image of society – which the social scientist cannot afford to ignore.

It is also important to note that the raising of Douglas's question of the 'Two Bodies' is a separate and distinct aspect of research into bodily expression which can exist side by side with (and not in opposition to) other types of research on bodily expression – such as that of Birdwhistell, which concerns itself, primarily, with the problem of the relationship of the various channels of communication to each other. And as we have seen, Birdwhistell's former student Lomax, in testing his hypothesis that 'body movement can be regarded as a communication of the mores, customs, and role relationships found in a particular culture' (Lomax, 1968, p. 228), is posing a very similar question to that raised by Douglas concerning the drive to achieve consonance between the social and the (socio-)physical levels of experience. Lomax and Douglas are both interested in the relationship of the two bodies, the two systems which every man possesses. This ideal of the correspondence of bodies, systems and societies is also noted by Lévi-Strauss in *The Savage Mind*:

The Australian tribes of the Drysdale River, in Northern Kimberley, divide all kinship relations, which together compose the social 'body', into five categories named after a part of the body or a muscle. Since a stranger must not be questioned, he announces his kinship by moving the relevant muscle. In this case, too, therefore, the total system of social relations, itself bound up with a system of the universe, can be projected on to the anatomical plane. (1968, pp. 168–9.)

And, of course, the same metaphor is found in St Paul's first letter to the Corinthians: '. . . the body is one, and hath many members, and all the members of that one body, being many, are one body . . . For the body is not one member, but many.' (I Corinthians xii, 12, 14.)

Concluding remarks

I suggested at the start of this essay that the real value in our looking into these sometimes tiresome debates of anthropologists is as a kind of ethnographic exercise. Just as the myths and theories of magic in the primitive world may be assumed to reflect the social environments within which they develop, so too the theorizings of anthropologists might be assumed to reflect *their own* social environments. By and large, anthropology has found itself at a loss to bring to bear the models and methods developed in the study of primitive and peasant peoples upon our own problems (i.e. the problems of the middle-class, university-educated fraction of the Western world). But in our debates about 'them', 'out there', we reveal much about *ourselves* and it might just be that an anthropology of anthropology would be instrumental in helping us to understand ourselves, since we are still awaiting a report on our own way of life as written by an ethnographer from 'out there'.

Even a cursory glance at the anthropological research concerning the human body which I have tried to summarize in this essay reveals two principal preoccupations of anthropological debate. First, a preoccupation with the problem of communication and, second, a more limited, but intense preoccupation with a Durkheimian model of society as a holistic beast: that is, with the organismic form of society, the social 'body'. In both cases, I would argue that these academic preoccupations reflect our own 'social facts'.

The anthropologist's concern with bodily expression as communication reflects, I think, a communication crisis in middle-class, educated Western peoples. We are rapidly coming to realize that by our excessive dependence upon verbal–arbitrary language, oral and written, we have allowed to atrophy our resources of bodily communication. I recall Zorba the Greek's remarks about his English friend's communicative abilities: 'While you are talking I watch your arms and chest. Well, what are they doing? They're silent. They don't say a word. As though they hadn't a drop of blood between them.' (Kazantzakis, 1961, p. 226.) And we realize that we are indeed a sadly 'silent majority'. Unlike some of the minority groups in our own culture such as the blacks, we are deaf and dumb to the powerful symbols of bodily expression.* Our initial response as anthropologists to this crisis of communi-

---

*It may be speculated that verbal language, which according to some linguists is a basically arbitrary sign system, is an appropriate means of communication for Western industrial society, which is based on a separation of mental activity from bodily labour, and which results in the condition which some Marxian social theorists describe as 'alienation'. It is, I think, in this context that John O'Neill's essay later in this volume (p. 293) should be considered.

cation was the defensive action of arguing that bodily expression was 'language-like' (in the narrowest sense of the term), thus bringing the naked savage's gesture, expression and dance within the bounds of our own would-be supreme achievement. Anthropology should now reconcile itself to a task of helping us to dance like the natives, so that we may regain our full complement of communicative powers.

A second preoccupation of anthropological and sociological debate, on this and other subjects, is Durkheim's (and his followers') devotion to that hulking god which he called 'Society'.* Essentially this represents a search for *social form* in an age of anomie or formlessness. If Douglas's assumption concerning the 'Two Bodies' is correct – the assumption that the form of the social body is reflected in the form of the physical body and vice versa – then we are close to answering the question which I began with, namely, 'Why are we experiencing a cult of the body and a cult of the study of the body?' Sociologists and anthropologists have for a long time contrasted the organic wholeness and formfulness of the primitive world with the anomic disintegration of form in the West. We look to our bodies (and admiringly to the bodies of our primitive friends) in the hope that we might rediscover in the corporal form, the integration of our *two* bodies.

Two factors would seem to contribute to this disintegration of form and the subsequent disintegration of the consonance of physical and social levels of experience. Firstly, we are faced with social change so rapid that the physical body cannot catch up so that consonance might be retained (or regained) and so that we might look to our bodies as a model or image by which we as individuals might contribute to the maintenance of our social system.† Cosmetics, plastic surgery, artificial hair and fashion

---

*The preoccupation of the ethnomethodologists in arguing against a Durkheimian model of society ought to also be considered here.

† As Durkheim pointed out, societies only exist because of individual activity: men (not to mention women) create, maintain and change society. But in order that some continuity be maintained (since humans have the habit of dying and being born) individuals born into society must be taught what society is. Because every individual in a society has a physical body and because the education of that body can begin from babyhood (if not before) I suspect that 'the body' (that is the socialized body) is *the* fundamental and universal guide by which human beings understand that they are social beings. I further suggest

itself all aim at increased rapidity of physical change. Scarification and tattooing – the permanent body arts – are aggressively conservative, and *un*fashionable, for typically they are the bodily expression of small social enclaves which are being swallowed up in the overall wave of social change and in what seems to be a general trend towards social impermanence.* Fashion, a phenomenon of Western consumer economies, is aimed at no fixed point, but rather at the process of change itself.

A second factor which is contributing to the inability of the physical body to maintain consonance with the social body is

---

that it is for this reason that (as Douglas has pointed out) there is a drive to achieve consonance between the physical and social bodies. If consonance is not maintained, then the future of the social order is in jeopardy, unless some other image of society can be found which is individual in the sense that it can be imprinted on to the individual by the society, and 'social' in the sense that it is learned and generates meaning in communication according to collectively shared criteria. Perhaps primitive man does not need to have anthropologists to tell him what society is because he has his body to tell him.

* Tattooing and scarification have always been popular subjects with anthropologists and the public. They are interesting because they are extremely social and extremely anti-social acts at one and the same time. They are social because they can reflect allegiance to small social groups which the individual member would like to believe are permanent but which are threatened with being swallowed by larger social groups and the social change of these larger groups. Tattoos and scarification are a kind of declaration of belief in the permanence of a particular small social group be it a group of prisoners, soldiers, or the members of an isolated Indian village. On a recent B.B.C. programme about the Hell's Angels a member of the motor-cycle group remarked: 'I have "Hell's Angels" tattooed on my chest and on my back – that's on there for life. I guess that explains how I feel about the Angels.' In Western cultures these permanent body arts become anti-social with reference to the larger social group. Permanent types of clothing such as leather jackets, metal bracelets which cannot be removed from the wrist, nose-rings, etc., also fall into this classification. A few years ago some underground magazines reported that tattooing was becoming popular among American hippy groups (Janis Joplin, the pop star, was tattooed, for example) but this never caught on. Apparently few were really willing to gamble on the permanence of the hippy revolution. Nose-rings are said to be on the rise among members of the British underground at the present, but perhaps these persons know that it would be possible to have such a hole in the nose covered up by plastic surgery if it should ever become necessary to 'go straight'. At any rate, I put out the hypothesis that among small social groups which are threatened with the collapse of social form (for whatever reason) there will be an increase of the permanent body arts as an attempt to stave off the threatened social disintegration.

simply that there is a multiplicity of social systems which our bodies are called on to reflect. This second factor might be called the Politics of the Body and it suggests that if there is confusion of corporal form it is because there is confusion of socio-political form. Each set of social values is embodied in corporal form via a corporal model or icon. The values of the American businessman are appropriately represented in the 'well-endowed', mammothly breasted *Playboy* 'playmate'; the values of the British 'Undergound' are appropriately embodied in the pale, emaciated face of the girl on the masthead of *International Times* (*I.T.*) who literally looks as if she lives under the ground. Corporal resolution awaits political resolution and in the meantime we must depend on cosmetic magic to allow us (or our women) to switch allegiances from day to day and from hour to hour.

It is not, then, so surprising that ethnography (always an escapist preoccupation) should search 'out there' for a form, a shape, a healthy primitive body to hang above the mantelpiece like a moose-head. Nor is it surprising that this project has been fraught with difficulties. The principal problem with most anthropological studies of the human body conducted thus far is that they have dealt with only bits and pieces of the body instead of the *whole* body. We have studied the body and its 'aids' of adornment and clothing as separate media and not as a total and complete body system. We have tended to supply *our own* would-be objective definition of the boundaries of the body and its peripheral media; we should in the future be more sensitive to *native* definitions of the body as a system of meaning.

While we have studied body styles, feather head-dresses, penis-sheaths, smiles, postures, ear-rings, tattooing, cranial deformation, gestures, etc. – we have studied each of these on its own. We have allowed our own condition of social anomie, of formlessness, to creep into our research and we have not given definite organic form and structure to the limits and definition of our subject. If we have failed to gain an understanding of the body as a whole system of meaning, then we have also failed to utilize the study of *corporal* form as a tool for the understanding of *social* form and hence we have failed to further our understanding of social systems and social bodies.

Astrov, M., 'The concept of motion as the psychological leitmotif of Navaho life and literature', *Journal of American Folklore*, vol. 63 (1950), pp. 45–56.

Bailey, F., 'Navaho motor habits', *American Anthropologist*, vol. 44 (1942), pp. 210–34.

Bateson, G., and Margaret Mead, *Balinese Character: A Photographic Analysis*, Special publications of the New York Academy of Sciences, 1942, vol. 2.

Belo, J., 'The Balinese temper', *Character and Personality*, vol. 4 (1935), pp. 120–46.

Birdwhistell, Ray L., *Kinesics and Context: Essays on Body-Motion Communication*, Allen Lane, The Penguin Press, 1971; University of Pennsylvania Press, Philadelphia, 1971.

Bock, P., *Modern Cultural Anthropology: An Introduction*, Knopf, New York, 1969.

Critchley, M., *The Language of Gesture*, Edward Arnold, 1939.

Darwin, C., *The Expression of the Emotions in Man and Animals*, 1872; republished 1965, University of Chicago Press, London and Chicago, ed. Francis Darwin.

Devereux, G., 'Mohave Indian verbal and motor profanity' in G. Roheim, ed., *Psychoanalysis and the Social Sciences*, International University Press, New York, 1951, vol. 3, pp. 99–127.

Douglas, M., *Natural Symbols: Explorations in Cosmology*, Barrie & Rockliff; The Cresset Press, 1970, also Penguin, 1973.

Douglas, M., 'Do dogs laugh? A cross-cultural approach to body symbolism', *Journal of Psychosomatic Research*, vol. 15, (1971), pp. 387–90.

Efron, D., *Gesture and Environment*, King's Crown Press, New York, 1941.

Eibl-Eibesfeldt, I., 'Similarities and differences between cultures in expressive movements' in R. A. Hinde (ed.), *Non-Verbal Communication*, Cambridge University Press, 1972, pp. 297–312.

Fisher, S., 'Body image', *International Encyclopedia of the Social Sciences*, vol. 2, 1968.

Grant, E., 'Human facial expression', *Man*, vol. 4, no. 4 (December 1969), pp. 525–36.

Hall, E., 'The anthropology of manners', *Scientific American*, vol. 192, no. 4 (April, 1955) pp. 84–90.

Hall, E., *The Silent Language*, Fawcett World Library, Greenwich, Conn., 1959.

Hall, E., 'A system for the notation of proxemic behavior', *American Anthropologist*, vol. 65 (1963), pp. 1003–1026.

Hertz, R., 'La prééminence de la droite: étude sur la polarité religieuse', *Revue philosophique*, vol. 68 (1909), pp. 553–80 (trans. Rodney and Claudia Needham, in R. Hertz, *Death and the Right Hand*, Cohen & West; Aberdeen University Press, 1960).

Hewes, G., 'The anthropology of posture', *Scientific American*, vol. 196 (February 1957), pp. 123–32.

Hewes, G., 'World distribution of certain postural habits', *American Anthropologist*, vol. 57 (1955), pp. 231–44.

Hocart, A., 'Methods of sitting', Letter to the editor, *Man*, no. 66 (May 1927), pp. 99–100.

Hockett, C., 'The origin of speech', *Scientific American*, (September 1960) (reprint no. 603).

Kazantzakis, N., *Zorba the Greek*, Faber & Faber, 1961.

Kroeber, A., *Handbook of the Indians of California*, Washington, D.C.: Smithsonian Institution (Bureau of American Ethnology), Bulletin 78, 1925.

LaBarre, W., 'The cultural basis of emotions and gestures', *Journal of Personality*, vol. 66 (1947), pp. 49–68.

Lévi-Strauss, C., *The Savage Mind*, Weidenfeld & Nicolson, 1968.

Lomax, A., *Folk Song Style and Culture*, Washington, D.C.: American Association for the Advancement of Science (publication no. 88), 1968.

Mauss, M., 'Les Techniques du corps', *Journal de la psychologie*, vol. 32 (March–April 1935) (trans. as 'Techniques of the Body', *Economy and Society*, vol. 2, no. 1, 1973, pp. 70–88).

Messing, S., 'The nonverbal language of the Ethiopian Toga', *Anthropus*, vol. 55, nos. 3–4, 1960, pp. 558–60.

Miner, H., 'Body ritual among the Nacirema', *American Anthropologist*, vol. 58 (1965), pp. 503–7.

Ruesch, J., and Kees, W., *Nonverbal Communication: Notes on the Visual Perception of Human Relations*, Berkeley and Los Angeles: University of California Press, 1956.

Saussure, F. de, 'On the Nature of Language' in M. Lane (ed.), *Structuralism: A Reader*, Jonathan Cape, 1970, pp. 43–56.

Van Hooff, J., 'A comparative approach to the phylogeny of laughter and smiling' in R. Hinde (ed.) *Non-Verbal Communication*, Cambridge University Press, 1972, pp. 209–41.

Ward, H., *Charles Darwin: The Man and His Warfare*, John Murray, 1927.

Watson, M., and Graves, T., 'Quantitative research in proxemic behavior', *American Anthropologist*, vol. 68 (1966), pp. 971–85.

Ray L. Birdwhistell

Background Considerations to the Study of the Body as a Medium of 'Expression'

The power of communication between the members of the same tribe by means of language has been of paramount importance in the development of man; and the force of language is much aided by the expressive movements of the face and body . . . Nevertheless there are no grounds, as far as I can discover, for believing that any muscle has been developed or even modified exclusively for the sake of expression.
(Charles Darwin, *The Expression of the Emotions in Man and Animals*, 1872)

A century has passed. Psychology, sociology, linguistics, anthropology and ethology have emerged as sciences, and literally thousands of papers, theses, dissertations and books have been written that are related directly or indirectly to these summary sentences. However, I know of no serious student of the relationship between body activity and human interaction who is convinced that the issues touched upon within these two sentences have been fully explored, much less settled.

Certainly a factor in our present difficulties is derived from the tendency to read into Darwin knowledge he could not have had in his time. Terms which had common vocabulary value in the nineteenth century can be misread as containing their twentieth-century content. A hundred years of research have radically modified 'language', 'communication', 'expression' and 'emotion' for the specialist, if not for the general public. However, let us be clear from the outset. The fact that these terms have gained some degree of technicality among specialists should not mislead us into assuming that there is general agreement as to the basic assumptions underlying their appropriate usage, even within fields of specialization. A review of even the last five years of the literature indicates that although many scholars have become uneasy about using such terms without special definition, these definitions have not achieved extended acceptance. Ancient epistemological ghosts continue to inhabit these words in technical as well as in everyday usage. It is my feeling that, notwithstanding even the most rigorous attempts to purify or to operationalize these concepts, these ghosts cannot be exorcised by definition, because they are so important to our unrecognized conceptions of man and of society. It is likely that until we can comprehend the implicit assumptions immanent in their usage, the hidden assumptions in these concepts inevitably will contribute to non-creative disagreement, spurious and genuine. We need perspective upon the power of their sustaining preconceptions. Hopefully, some preliminary discussion of them will contribute to this perspective.

Darwin's discussions of communicative processes remain interesting today, not because he solved particular interactional problems or because of any single finding which he made in this area, but because he recognized the importance of such processes to a naturalistic and unified description of man and nature. He deserves our continuing attention, not because he solved communicational problems but because he realized that, in order to understand man, it was also necessary to understand the means by which man gathered and transmitted knowledge in ways similar to and differing from his animal forebears. And he is particularly important to us because of the model he provides as a natural historian who did not shrink from the lessons he learned through disciplined observation of both animal and human behaviour in naturalistic settings. Darwin did not, of course, originate the idea that man was and is an animal, nor was he original in the conception that evolution was a matter of continuous and ongoing processes. However, the mechanisms of natural selection, as presented in *The Descent of Man*, laid the groundwork for the recognition that central issues of inheritance were and are determined in the behavioural relationships *between* animals. And it was in the attempt to understand this behaviour, these relationships and their transmission, that *The Expression of the Emotions in Man and Animals* was written.

Darwin himself was a rigorous and relentless observer and the modern ethnographer and ethologist can read his careful descriptions with pleasure. His uses of secondary information are less persuasive. The naïveté of his questionnaires and his organization of the responses in his search for cross-societal and cross-speciational material were congruent with and no better than the field methods of his day. However, he took every opportunity to recheck the reports of his informants, was critical of intuitionist interpretations of the data and was sensitive to the problem of false homologies and pseudo-differences. The social science student of today should not be critical of Darwin on the grounds that, in his isolation of bits of behavioural sequences, he tore a social fabric which he could not have known existed. Darwin was writing in a period when sciences concerned with man were still largely branches of philosophy. His reading of Spencer, Lubbock and Morgan, for example, could give him little assistance at the behavioural level and he was wise enough to recognize it. To say it simply, Darwin observed, thought and wrote in a period before the discovery of society, or, perhaps better stated, in a period when the conception of society, either animal or human, precluded any comprehension of the nature of social behaviour. If, despite his attempt to avoid it, he was dualistic in his assignment of social behaviour to either physical or to mentalistic sources, he cannot be justly criticized from a more modern perspective.

Darwin paid close attention to the extent to which animals and humans modified their behaviour in response to the behaviour of others within the group. He was fully cognizant of the extent to which his conception of natural selection was dependent upon the behaviour of individual animals in relation to others within the group. Variable success within the membership, for Darwin, gave shape to selection. He spent much thought upon – and, in fact, a good proportion of his research energies were employed in – the attempt to determine the specific behaviour and its genesis which gave selective precedence to one animal over another in conflict or in courtship. Insofar as I have been able to determine, he remained concerned but less than satisfied with his explanations of the mechanisms whereby non-physiologically determined adaptive behaviour was incorporated into the behaviour-patterns of successive generations. He fully recognized that adaptations (information?) had to be stored and transmitted within and between generations. These processes are obviously central to his thesis. He struggled with the evolutionary shift from 'social instinct' to social learning. Yet, consistent with his times, Darwin could comprehend neither society nor social relationships as stored in or immanent to and regulated by social organization. It is unlikely that he could have conceived of language or communication as behaviour-ordering systems. This deficiency reinforced (or occasioned) the implicit dualism in his conception of *communication* by means of language as differing from *expressive* corporeal behaviour, which he saw as supportive to rather than integrated with language behaviour.

Natural selection, in the forms of sexual selection in competitive situations, seems to have led Darwin, as it has his followers, into a focus upon the behaviour of interacting pairs. Obviously, he did not ignore other social behaviour, but the shape of his problem and the nature of his solutions centred attention upon competing males, mating pairs and the parent–child engagement. The dyadic shape of these relationships, and the isolation of these from the social situation of which they are an aspect, conditioned his understanding of basic interactional processes and their organiza-tion. For example, following his discussion of the fact that he saw no instances of special adaptation of the muscles for the 'sake of expression', he says,

The vocal and other sound-producing organs, by which various expressive sounds are produced, seem to form a partial exception; but I have elsewhere attempted to show that these organs were first developed for sexual purposes, in order that one sex might call or charm the other. (op. cit., p. 355.)

I concentrate upon this point, not because I would deny the importance of the mating situation nor the conditions which lead particular males or females to select one another from potential partners, but because exclusive methodological preoccupation with isolated events can obscure the larger social conditions which are necessary to and contain many of the ingredients necessary to these particular encounters. Perhaps the point can be made by analogy. The 'double-play' in baseball, the assist and shot in basketball or hockey, or, even, the pitcher–batter relationship in baseball are all critical incidents within their respective games.

However, there is absolutely no way by which even the most careful observer can understand these plays or the games in which they occur if they are seen as microcosms containing all the conditions and processes of the larger social situations from which they have been isolated.

It is my contention that the underlying assumption that the basic social unit is the mating or mated pair, an assumption at least as old as the Adam and Eve myth, is derived from *a priori* definitions of society and cannot be supported by the systematic observation of either animal or human social organization. Moreover, because the dyad has been so generally accepted as *the* primary social form, as *the* basic building-block of social organization, it has too often been used as the ideal situation for the investigation and measurement of interactional processes. In the dyad, the pair, or the couple situation, interaction inevitably becomes action–reaction for the observer, the investigator is prevented by his focus from gaining any larger comprehension of communication as a social phenomenon. To say it explicitly, social relationship, social organization and communication cannot be understood by the analysis, however exhaustive, of the encounter. Regardless of how repetitive the shape of a particular event may seem, and regardless of how automatic the performance of the participants may seem, the encounter does not contain the data governing its occurrence – unless that performance is seen as merely the outcome of forces *inside* the participants. Reductionism in communicational studies may be the inevitable result of the assumption that the dyad is *the* basic and fundamental social unit. To repeat, since much of the data relevant to social interaction cannot be observed in the activity of an isolated pair, the investigator, unaware of the violence to the data occasioned by the isolation of the situation and unaware of the social regulation which orders even the most temporary pairing, turns for his data *and explanations* to the internal, the mental or to the anatomic or the physiological processes of the individual animals.

Parenthetically, I am not at all sure that I am not in the above discussion making Darwin responsible for the sins of his more experiment-minded descendants. While his critical observation situations, i.e. those of fighting and mating, are dyadic, I can find no explicit statement on his part supporting a multi-dyadic model of society. His thesis demanded no such simplification and, in the final analysis, he had no need for an explanation of the social group. Incidentally, I have some of the same sense of hesitation when I attempt to understand Darwin's conception of 'instinct'. Darwin recognized that within his theoretical frame he had not only the task of explaining the individual animal's transmission or expression of his emotions, but also that of dealing with the source of the reacting animal's interpretation of or reaction to the actor's behaviour. He asked the salient question in as clear a manner as possible then.

Although most of our expressive actions are innate or instinctive . . . it is a different question whether we have any instinctive power of recognizing them . . . the question is, do our children acquire their knowledge of expression solely by experience through the power of association and reason?

As most of the movements of expression must have been gradually acquired, afterward becoming instinctive, there seems to be some degree of *a priori* probability that their recognition would likewise have become instinctive. (op. cit., p. 358.)

Thus, if we interpret him narrowly and literally, and treat 'instinct' and 'innate' as physiologically grounded concepts, 'expression of the emotions' becomes largely a physiological matter with social consequences. From this interpretation the meaning of a major proportion of expressive behaviour is inevitably physiologically stored. On the other hand, if we interpret Darwin's 'instinct' and 'innate' to refer to those regular behaviours which could not be explained as derived from the observable experiences of the individual, he could have seen meaning as stored in the social system. In the latter case we would make a very different appraisal of the Darwinian position. He explicitly rejects the explanations of Lemoine, whose *La Physiognomie et la parole* was an early suggestion of the associationally learned nature of communicational phenomena. However, again it is unfair to demand that even such a genius as Darwin could anticipate what was to be learned later about language, kinesics and communication as social phenomena. In my best judgement Darwin had, in the final analysis, an essentially rationalistic, mentalistic interpretation of language and a physiologically deterministic view of the emotions and their expression and recognition. This, I believe, left him in a basically dualistic position, dependent upon one variation of the mind–body dichotomy and with the nature–nurture dichotomy left unresolved. Darwin possibly would have rejected this description of his theoretical underpinnings. But modern research in his name maintains these bifurcations of behavioural genesis.

Although the discussion above has centred around Darwin, this is not intended in any way as a critical review of him. Because his name is in common currency in animal and human communication studies today I have used certain selected passages as points of departure. And any student of Darwin may justly complain that I have taken liberties with his thought in this discussion. However great Darwin was, he was a man of his century and of his culture. It is not to belittle him to say that he would not overcome a metaphysics of which he was unaware or that he did not possess knowledge yet undiscovered.

There is no easy way to order the discussion of human body behaviour, sustaining or variable, as it functions in communicative processes. In fact, it is difficult even to locate the central problems for investigative analysis. The young scholar who attempts to review either the research or the prevailing opinion on these matters finds the data files choked with particular facts, categorized by loose generalization and replete with pseudo-pregnant theory. More seriously, the investigator finds the very approaches to his problem hidden in semantic confusion and guarded by jealous proponents of special methodologies justified by disciplinary preconception. It would be feckless, however, to dismiss relevant issues as hopelessly lost in the usual mire of academic provincialism. The interstices between established disciplines have always contained lodes of information left undiscovered or unassayed while the miners fought for exclusive mineral rights. I feel that there is thus little point in reviewing at this time the special claims of particular modern disciplines (my own or others) to the explanatory rights of animal and human communication. The old dictum – to locate the phenomenon and it will dictate its investigation – seems relevant here. Unfortunately, nature can hide in the open and a myopia induced by preconception can leave her undiscovered.

In our search for perspective upon the conceptions which governed the thought about facial expression and body motion –

and which in altered form are still relevant today – it would be a mistake to treat Darwin as if he were the founding father of such studies. His was but a particular adaptation of more than a century of intense interest in the study of the face and the body as conveyers of meaning. But this is not to discount his sustaining influence. There is no way of overstating his importance to modern studies, anthropological or ethological, concerned with the study of animal and human social systems, and particularly to those now concentrating upon the behavioural aspects of animal and human communication. My personal debt to Darwin is immeasurable. Long hours of argument with myself and with him as I first read and re-read his works led to my conviction that social organization and communication are interdependent. From these hours of argumentation, moreover, came my conviction that society as an organized system preceded man by thousands of species, that man did not invent society but, rather, society invented man. Perhaps, most importantly, I was forced to realize that a knowledge of behavioural biology is necessary for the understanding of the history of society. Darwin and his naturalist descendants freed me from social contract theory and its inherent mentalistic pre-suppositions. However, regardless of his importance in these matters, much of the present interest in the role of the body in the form of gestures and facial expression has had a history quite apart from him.

There was nothing particularly novel, even for his day, in Darwin's recognition of the importance of language as central to human communication and thus to human development. Nor was his recognition that 'the force of language is much aided by the expressive movements of the face and body'. A hundred years before Darwin wrote, the physiognomists were preoccupied with the study of gestures and facial expression as both indicative of personality and as of absolute importance to human intercourse. The doughty Calvinist cleric, Lavater, if we disregard his rhetoric, sounds modern when he writes in defence of a science of physiognomy:

. . . Nothing more is necessary, than to pay attention for a few days to what we hear, or read, respecting the human character, in order to collect Physiognomical decisions pronounced by the very Adversaries of the Science. 'I read that in his eyes – It is sufficient to see him – He has the air of an honest man – I prognosticate good from that face – These eyes promise nothing good – Probity is painted in his looks – I would trust him merely on his Physiognomy – If that Man deceive me, I will trust nobody hereafter – He has an air of candor, an open countenance – I distrust that smile – He dares not look you in the face.' Even Antiphysiognomical decisions confirm, as exceptions, the universality of the sentiment for which I contend. 'His physiognomy is against him – I could not have suspected that from his look – He is better, or, he is worse than he appears, etc.' (1789, vol. I, p. 94)

Lavater (1741–1801) was widely read and of consequence in his day if for no other reason than he was widely and competitively published throughout Europe. The new technology of engraving made possible the clearer reproduction of graphic art and Lavater's publishers from a variety of European nations vied with one another in the beauty of the volumes they produced. The early English edition, for example, contained engravings by Blake, Trotter, Hall and Thomas Holloway among others. In these volumes, Lavater analysed a wide variety of drawings taken either from life or from the old masters as exercises in physiognomical character analysis. He wrote with certainty about the various facial characteristics as indicants of basic character. His language is eighteenth-century, but I am not at all sure that it is not preferable to that used today by those who analyse particular expressions as diagnostic of particular personality characteristics.

Lavater is not easy to read. His discussions are little more than an assemblage of what he terms 'fragments', notes, and testimonial bits taken from earlier authorities and his supportive contemporaries. But he is worth reading carefully despite his ponderous and often ecclesiastical rhetoric, for, notwithstanding his controlling preconceptions, he is determined to make his work scientific. And, he is convinced that the world he observes is sufficiently regulated to make it subject to study.

Who would not exclaim against the affrontery of affirming, that joy and sorrow, pleasure and pain, love and hatred, are characterized by the same signs; which amounts to an affirmation that they are not marked by any man whatever in the exterior of Man? . . .

It cannot be too often repeated: To ascribe every thing to arbitrary causes, to blind chance, without rule and without law, is the philosophy of madmen, the death of sound Physics, sound philosophy, sound

Religion: To proscribe this error, to attack it wherever it appears, is the business of the true Naturalist, of the true Philosopher, of the true Theologian. (op. cit., p. 30)

Although he seemed sure of his own ability as a diagnostician, he had no illusions that physiognomy was likely to become a science during his lifetime. In fact, regardless of the importance of his own work, he did not feel that when it became a science he should be regarded as its originator. He says,

... my chief aim is to encourage the Reader himself to engage in the career of observation ... Let us begin only by collecting a sufficient number of observations, and endeavoring to characterize them with all the precision, all the accuracy of which we are capable ...

The principal point in question is, to discover what is evidently determined in the features, and to fix the characteristic signs, the expression of which is generally acknowledged.

Lavater sees his books as training instruments. He presents a series of profiles, discusses them briefly and instructs the trainee:

Here are five profiles, very different from one another but not so much, by a great deal, as they might be. Every connoisseur will at once see that they are copied after nature; but he will likewise perceive that they are sensibly deviate from nature. However, to consider these faces just as they are, is it possible to doubt that they may be determined and classed scientifically? You have only to compare the outline, the situation, and the obliquity of the foreheads; to compare the eyes, and particularly, the under contour of the upper eyelid; the angles formed by the exterior contour of the point of the nose, and of the upper lip; and finally, to compare the chins. – Observe, and account to yourself for the characters of this difference; substitute other features in their place, and then ask yourself, if they would not at once produce a different impression? (op. cit., p. 72)

I vividly recall when I first encountered these passages from Lavater. I had just returned from my office at the University where I had been reading a dissertation proposal from a young graduate student in psychology who was interested in facial expression. The proposal contained only two additions to Lavater's methodological suggestions: the student planned to use six of his fellow students as evaluators and to use some statistical procedures to evaluate their judgements. He was convinced, as

Lavater had been, that the manipulation of variables to be correlated with *a priori* categories would reveal the meaning of expression.

Lavater anticipated future developments in other ways as well. Although he was primarily concerned with the indelible traces of character represented in facial form and expression and with its study by physiognomists, he suggests that there must also be a study of what he calls pathognomy. Physiognomy, he says, is 'the science which explains the signs of the faculties' and pathognomy, 'the science which treats of the signs of the passions'. In his 'Fragment Fourth', he makes distinctions here which are still made although without the same explicitness.

> The one [physiognomy] considers the character in a state of rest; the other [pathognomy] examines it when in action. ... Physiognomy points out the fund of human faculties, and Pathognomy the interest or revenue which it produces. The one considers man such as he is in general; the other what he is at the present moment ...
> Physiognomy is the mirror of the Naturalist and the Sage.
> Pathognomy is the mirror of Courtiers, and men of the world. Of it everyone knows something, but few understand Physiognomy. (op. cit., p. 24)

Lavater was convinced that there is a basic set to each man's character which is displayed in his facial and gestural behaviour, that there is in the skin, the musculature and in the bone structure a composite which can be read by the talented and experienced observer. However he was explicit in his position that the individual could change, that the countenance could be shaped by an individual's life experiences, that a good life or one of evil was reflected in the countenance and behaviour of the person. Moreover, a clever person could 'dissimulate', could modify his behaviour and appearance in such a way as to fool those with whom he came into contact. Perhaps the most important aspect of Lavater's thought for us, however, rests in his certainty that not only does every body set or position, and every facial set or expression have a meaning, but also that meaning could be read in whatever setting it might appear by a sufficiently talented observer. In modern terms we might describe him as a semantic universalist. That is, behaviour might be modified and sophisticated individuals could convincingly pretend a feeling they are not experiencing.

However, good or evil, beauty and ugliness, anger, cupidity, jealousy, love or rage are not only universal feelings (or states) but are universally and identically expressed. From this point of view a particular body set or facial expression stands for or represents a particular feeling or character component, regardless of the society in which it appears.

Lavater is optimistic about the potential of physiognomic research and his methodology, perhaps because of his certainty about human nature. He sees man as the perfect combination of three 'sorts of life', the animal, the intellectual and the moral. Man is 'a physical, moral and intellectual Being'. The human figure 'bears a greater resemblance to the brute in those parts which are the seat of animal force; as it has a more obvious dissimilitude where the faculties of a higher order reside, where the active and physical powers of Man predominate'. (op. cit. p. 16)

Stern Calvinist that he was, Lavater paid little attention to society or even to primary social relationships. The individual dominated his focus; man as Mankind conditioned his thought. And, while he includes extensive sections upon the measurement and the analysis of animal, bird and insect physiognomies, he disclaims any real knowledge of biology and directs the reader to Buffon. However, he finds in the faces and skulls of animals evidence of many of the same character traits and of the same passions as occur in man. His essential belief in physiognomy as expressing the central forces in nature precludes the necessity of his taking any position on the question of evolution, of which as a widely read and unorthodox thinker he must have been aware. In a very interesting section he speaks of the threefold composition of man:

This threefold life of man, so intimately interwoven through his frame, is still capable of being studied in its different appropriate parts; and did we live in a less depraved world we should find sufficient data for the science of physiognomy.

The animal life, the lowest and most earthly, would discover itself from the rim of the belly to the organs of generation, which would become its central or focal point.* The middle or moral life would be

* This section is taken from the Thomas Holcroft translation from the German. In the earlier translation by Henry Hunter, D. D., Minister of the Scots Church, from the French, this sentence reads, 'The animal life, the

centered in the breast, and the heart would be its central point. The intellectual life, which of the three is supreme, would reside in the head, and have the eye for its centre. If we take the countenance as the representative and epitome of the three divisions, then will the forehead, to the eye-brows, be the mirror, or image, of the understanding; the nose and cheeks the image of the moral and sensitive life; while the eye will be to the whole its summary and centre. I may also add that the closed mouth at the moment of most perfect tranquillity is the central point of the radii of the countenance. (*c*. 1892, p. 10)

Although Lavater was primarily concerned with Man and with the fact of absolute individuality of men, he was not blind to social – or perhaps local concentrations of characteristics would be a better way of saying it. In another methodological section, Lavater warns travellers not to restrict their attention to famous men even though there is much to be learned from their analysis.

Yes, scholars of nature, you have much to learn from the countenances of famous men. In them you will read that the wasp will dare to alight on the face of the hero . . .

I would rather mix unknown with the multitude; visit churches, public walks, hospitals, orphan houses, and assemblies of ecclesiastics, and men of the law. I would, first, consider the general form of the inhabitants, their height, proportion, strength, weakness, motion, complexion, attitude, gesture, and gait. I would observe them individually; see, compare, close my eyes, trace in imagination all I have seen, open them again, correct my memory, and close and open them alternatively; would study for words, write and draw, with a few determinate traits, the general form, so easy to be discovered. I would compare my drawings with the known general form of the people. How easily might a summary, and index of the people be obtained . . . I would next examine the forehead; then the eyebrows; the outline and the colour of the eyes; the nose; and especially the mouth, when it opens, and the teeth, with their appearance, to discover the national characteristic. Could I but define the line of the opening of the lips, in seven promiscuous countenances, I think I should have found the general physiognomical character of the nation, or place. I almost dare establish it as an axiom that, what is

---

lowest and most terrestrial of all, having its seat in the belly, would extend to, and comprehend the organs of generation, which would be its focus.' I prefer this translation but inasmuch as the Holcroft was more widely influential than the more expensive and limited Hunter rendition. I quote it first.

common to six or seven persons of any place, taken promiscuously, is more or less common to the whole. (*c.* 1892, p. 407)

Again, Lavater sounds quite modern and many young ethnographers could profit from his observational cautions. This insistence upon rigour and discipline prevails throughout his work, and he is contemptuous of either proponents or adversaries of his system who would rely on easy or intuitionistic generalization, or upon anecdotal accounts which he justly terms 'rumour'. Lavater, however, is not simply relevant for us today because, as a tough-minded investigator, he insisted upon the possibility of a science of facial expression, nor simply because he insisted that extreme caution and methodological rigour should be exercised in the development of this science. Many of his successors in the area of physiognomy, as it developed into phrenology and later contributed to the development of modern psychiatry,* paid little attention to his observational strictures. I find him useful because, in spite of his rigour and in spite of insistence upon an inductive methodology, neither he nor his followers succeeded in their attempts to utilize the study of facial expression to further the understanding of man and his behaviour. In fact, it seems fair to say that – to judge by the popular press, or by the spate of paper-back books on sale today which purport to instruct the general public on the diagnosis of their neighbours – we have regressed from Lavater's position of two hundred years ago.

It is true that no discipline or science has a history which is marked by steady progress. Interest wanes in areas of investigation. Subject-matter as well as methodology fall into disrepute, only to be revived later as new information forces attention to or reveals errors of earlier studies. For example, to return for the moment to Darwin, not only was his importance as a student of behaviour and as an investigatory innovator obscured by the drama of his evolutionary position, but the emergence of Mendelian inheritance and the scholarly excitement engendered by the idea of the conditioned reflex – both of these subject to study in the

---

*Lavater has a deserved place in this development. He was quite interested in mental illness and in mental hospitals. In fact, he got into serious trouble with the ecclesiastical authorities of his time because he was so impressed with the work of Mesmer. He felt that 'animal magnetism' deserved investigation and objective evaluation as a therapeutic tool.

comfort of a home-based laboratory – drew attention away from the naturalistic observation of human and animal social behaviour. Only as the laboratory failed in its promise did investigators begin to be willing to return to the field and to naturalistic situations. And even the fact that many of these sought to take their laboratories into the field with them has not totally eliminated the possibilities inherent in the naturalistic observational technique.

The last two decades have certainly marked more progress than all the intervening years. But the fact remains that after over two hundred years of interest in these matters, we still have but little sure knowledge in this area. This is not to depreciate the importance of recent discoveries in psychology, ethology and anthropology. I am excited by and delighted with the developments in, for example, modern structural linguistics and kinesics. I think that we know a great deal more about the nature of human communication from this perspective than could have been known before. However, I think that we are still a long way from being able to hand the psychiatrist a sure and reliable diagnostic instrument. And we are not close to providing the educator with a set of instructions on how to reach and edify his students. Certainly, we have not developed a method which would make an electorate certain of the morals or probity of its chosen representatives. Fortunately, perhaps, our studies have not advanced to the point that these same legislators can learn methods which would enable them to be convincing to their constituents. More importantly, as I said above, it is still difficult to structure critical situations for analysis, to develop clean hypotheses for test, or even to be sure as to the appropriate training necessary for the young scholar who would make a career of investigation in these areas.

There is no intention in the above paragraphs of seeming pessimistic about the study of animal and human communication. We do have in the sound camera and the video recorder, and in the slow-motion analyser, a hitherto unavailable technology for recording and for replay. We have a large number of students willing to invest their futures in such research and both the academies and the general public seem ready to support this interest. This volume and the set of lectures upon which it is based testify to this interest. On the other hand, my optimism engendered by all of these factors is dampened by the feeling that there are serious epistemological problems which if left unresolved will lead to much of the present energy and enthusiasm being expended with little return.

In the discussion above, I alluded to what I felt was an essential dualism which emerges in the work of Darwin and which is a given in the thinking of Lavater. In the case of Lavater one of these dualisms is explicit; his position was that external behaviour is a direct expression of the interior of man. Lavater *knew* in an absolute manner the nature of the basic character components and he had no doubt as to the composition of the basic passions. Once these were accepted as a given he had only to analyse the external behaviour and Lavater was satisfied that his was an efficient instrument for character or feeling assessment. Lavater never provided his reader with a catalogue of the basic character components or passions which he uses in his diagnoses. A perusal of his works reveals that he was extremely concerned with the descriptive language he uses in each analysis. Even his admiration of Aristotle does not make him an Aristotelian in this area. Furthermore, although intentionality is seen by Lavater as possible in certain cases of facial expression, intentionality is not central to his discussion. Neither is Lavater particularly troubled with the effects of an expression on others. Not only is the expression or basic anatomic characteristic natural, but so is its recognition. Misconception on the part of the observer or reactor is possible but this is due to defective internal processes, to lack of attention or to trickery on the part of the actor.

Darwin, with his task of explaining the social situation as the crucible of selection, deals with expressive behaviour in part functioning to give shape and force to language in the process of communication. Communication *per se* is of little interest to Lavater, who is concerned primarily with character analysis. Lavater attends to the nature of the actor. He is interested in the participant in the interaction, rather than in the interactional sequence. The interaction itself, except as influenced by the passions or character of the participants, is a function of mental processes. He makes no attempt to relate these processes. However, from my point of view the epistemological underpinnings of the positions of Darwin and Lavater, if we disregard Lavater's preliminary nod to the Deity, are the same: a human being contains within him activities, structures or forces which operate to express attitudes, feelings or passions that are recognizable and reacted to by other members of his species. The behaviour conse-quent to these basic feelings is separate and different from that which is performed in language usage.

My own research has always centred upon social relationships as behaviourally constituted. This led to my concern with com-munication. At the outset I searched for biologically based uni-versals which would constitute core behaviour upon which com-munication behaviour was constructed. But as an investigator of the role of body behaviour in human interaction, and as one who has avidly followed the developments in ethology and compara-tive psychology, I have been forced to the conclusion that I cannot understand communication and social interaction if I attempt to sub-divide the behaviour which I observe, record and analyse into two distinct types: one, socially coded, the other, physiologically coded. This may well be because I have never been able to develop an observational stance which permitted me to view simultan-eously, or in comparative sequences, interactional behaviour in a manner which would permit such subdivision. While my anthro-pological training, my recognition that man constituted but a single species, and my distaste for racist interpretations left me eager to discover basic and universal human behaviour which had the same consequences from its performance in all the societies I have had the opportunity to observe in depth, I have been unable to do so.

My files from my earliest explorations contain a large number of homomorphs, that is, of descriptions of common body articula-tions which I observed in every population I studied. Head-nods, wags and swivels appear everywhere; tense and lax brows seem universal; lids narrow and the corners of the eyes crinkle in every population I have observed; the record from every group contains smiling and crying; blushing and blanching is recorded even for heavily melinized skin. I could use all of my allotted space here in reporting neck, mid-section, arm, hand, finger and toe movements which were seen in all groups or in all films I have studied. How-ever, homomorphs are not the point. The human or the animal body, in spite of its fantastic malleability, can engage in only a limited number of positions, articulations or movements. Moreover, while it is true that every group I have observed has positions and expressions which do not appear in others, and while every human being whose movement pattern I have intensively analysed has a number of idiosyncratic positions, expressions or movements, for me this is not the point either. The recognition of the fact that there are universal, locally specialized and idiosyncratic performances is obviously interesting and of relevance to the description of man, to the recording of special groups and, particularly, to the descriptions of particular individuals. Such observations are of considerable interest to the physical anthropologist who would demonstrate both the conservatism and the malleability of the human soma. For the student who would understand human social relationships, social learning, social organization and communication, the mere fact of the distributions of similarity or difference in articulatory form is interesting but, in the final analysis, trivial to his problem.

When I use the term 'consequences' above, I am talking about *meaning*. And I wish to be clear here. When I use the word 'meaning' I am not using the term to stand for the set of responses that I receive from an informant or even from all my informants in response to the question 'What does this or that expression, gesture or word mean?' Such responses I regard as no more than further data elicitable by this technique, contributory but nondefinitive. I certainly would not regard such a response as any more valid or complete than I would any other description of any other aspect of his behaviour or performance. The informant is a member of, not an expert on, his behaviour. His descriptions of his behaviour are aspects of the very phenomena I wish to understand and can be no less mythic or conventionalized than any other of his descriptions of his behaviour or that of his societal mates. Such information is data but not evidence (unless explicitly so operationalized). Neither would I assign meaning, as I would use the term, to the agreements of however large a set of judges. With my use of meaning as measured by social consequence, I am to a large degree concerned with behaviour whose descriptions are not yet stored in words. Thus, the use of words for the elicitation of words and the tests which would categorize words standing for behaviour into further categories of words are methodologies, which (however useful they may be for the elicitation and analysis of reactive behaviour) often produce little information of relevance to the study of human communication, other than that done through words. Furthermore, by 'social consequence' I am not talking about the observable reaction on the part of subjects when the experimenter introduces bits or sections of behaviour, vocalic or otherwise, as variables in the experimental situation. For me, the meaning of any act or action rests in the difference its presence *or absence* makes in a customary interactional sequence.

Charles Hockett, the anthropological linguist, has made a telling distinction in his definition of the vocalic events which have linguistic and, by extension, communicational consequence. He says that there must be duality of patterning. The particular event must have an articulatory identity; it must be subject to abstraction and manipulation but it must also have a structural identity. That is, it must operate in a patterned position. Thus any isolatable particle or assemblage of behaviour, to be observed as of structural (or in this case of communicational) consequence, must have not only articulatory but also structural identity. This is perhaps over-technical for this essay. Let me try to say it in another way. In the paragraphs above I said that in my early research I collected many homomorphs and a number of expressions, postures and movements which seemed locally bound or even idiosyncratic. I indicated that their universality or rarity was not cogent to our discussion of communicative activity. The organs of breathing and swallowing can be observed to produce, by the passage or impedance of air, what seems to be an almost limitless variety of distinct sounds. Some of these sounds (depending upon the measuring instruments) appear to be universally utilized by all human societies in their language behaviour. Others seem to be extraordinarily rare. A bi-labial fricative (M) seems to appear throughout the world, for example, while a particular click (?) might have an exceedingly limited range. The anthropological linguist might be tempted to assign 'primitiveness' to the bi-labial fricative because of its distribution, but he would scarcely fictionalize it as having a *basic* meaning. The nature of the linguistic conditions under which it appears precludes such an interpretation. I would maintain that the same situations prevail for all body-behavioural articulations which I have been able to isolate and study.

The question, then, about expression, gesture, position or movement is not one about the occurrence of articulatory isolates, universal or specialized. The question is, is there any piece of body behaviour which is such a specific isolate that it overrides all conditions of its appearance? That is, is any facial expression or gesture so powerful and exclusive that its appearance (or its absence in a situation calling for its appearance) has but a single consequence and this consequence cannot be modified by surrounding behaviour? If such can be discovered – and I know of none which has so far been isolated and tested in context – then and only then would I be willing to distinguish between that behaviour at present called expressional and that which is termed communicational. I wish to be clear about this point. I am not for a moment saying that the physical state of any participant of any interaction is not of consequence to that interaction. Neither am I suggesting that all physiological states are of equal consequence. What I am saying is that the consequence of these states is patterned and codified by the culture because the states of consequence to interaction themselves are codified by the culture. Idiosyncratic and specialized local variations of this patterning can and do occur, but they are just that – specialized and localized.

Clearly, any communicative activity can provide a site for the isolation of physiological behaviour. The articulatory aspect of blushing and blanching is necessarily accompanied at the physiological level of capillary activity. But the blush or the blanch is not circulatory or physiological; it is social. Enunciation of the word 'dog' requires adjustments in the oral apparatus. But the word 'dog' is not physiological; it is social.

In summary, let me say what I have discussed elsewhere at greater length.* By and large, I think that the present discussion concerning expression as separate from communication is a pseudo-controversy. There can be no dispute over the widespread distribution of a limited number of facial expressions or body positions. The only question which is cogent is whether these and their consequences, structural and social, are modifiable and patterned by particular cultures or not. It is my position that they are

*'The Language of the Body: The Natural Environment of Words', in *Human Communication: Theoretical Explorations* (in press, 1974).

and that this matter can only be tested conclusively in the social situations in which they occur. Ethnocentric and anthropocentric methodologies can only elicit data supporting the implicit assumptions of the investigator and each methodology must be examined in depth to determine the extent to which the results are but artifacts of the investigatory technique.

The word 'ethnocentric' is applicable not merely to those easily discovered conventionalized and parochial prejudices which condition our thought, but can be extended to include the logics inherent in the language we use to talk about a subject and, even, to the very logics which condition those logics. It should not be surprising that any investigator is ethnocentric nor should it be any more surprising that any student of man's behaviour is anthropocentric. The fact that it is not surprising does not make it any easier to penetrate our epistemologies and to discover that there are deeply rooted conceptions about man and his relationship to animals which control our investigation of him. To personalize, my investigations and their explication have always been hampered by deep-seated convictions which I am unable to control except by methodological tactics. It has been my experience as a teacher that I, my students and my colleagues have considerable difficulty in really accepting a continuous development from social animal to social man, whatever our protestations about our beliefs in man as natural and about society as the natural condition of man, or about animals as natural and about society as the natural condition of animals. I have a faith that the distance between man and his nearest animal progenitor will be demonstrated to be qualitative. I have no certain evidence to the contrary. But I have little or no evidence for the concept of asymmetrical evolution that provides the shape for the origin myth I carry, and which out of my awareness conditions my capacity to think about such matters as we have touched on above. Deep within my belief structure there is a central conception that evolution really happened to man's nervous system and not to his gut. This myth is shaped by my membership in a western European society, conditioned by my speaking and thinking in an Indo-European language and deeply structured by my early religious and later academic training. In this myth, man's head evolved but his soma remained animal. At some level of my thought I twist man as animal into man with the beast left in him. The basic dichotomies of my thought-processes make the upper part of my body better than the lower part against all evidence of my studies and explicit conviction. I, in spite of training in physiology which would deny any validity to the assumption, am inclined to see the nervous system as more modern and more amenable to training than the more 'primitive' gut and reproductive system. I may talk about this as a 'matter of degree', but in my incautious moments I mean it as absolute. In fact, it is only when I am consciously engaged in being an investigator or speaking as a scientist that I can overcome a series of interrelated dichotomies. It seems natural to think of man as split into a nervous system and an endocrine system, the first modern and civilized, the second primitive and brutal. The brain and the upper portions of the body are the source of good; the lower the source of evil. The upper part is human; the lower part animal. The upper part is subject to learning and is the source of reason; the lower is controlled by instinct and is the source of passion. It is only a step from these morphological conceptions to an explanatory mythology by which, unless I consciously struggle against the temptation, I subdivide behaviour. The upper part of man is the source of that behaviour which I will call 'thought' and describe as mentation or cognition; the nether region of man is the source of behaviour which I will call 'feeling' and describe as emotion or affect. I must struggle with the conviction that I would be rational if I could but control the juices which leak upward from the more brutal regions to control my thought. But, perversely, I am often tempted to see the upper regions as adulterated by social prejudice and thus unreliable and only those aspects of the body which are untampered with by the brain as capable of telling the truth. During these careless moments I am attracted to those who believe that it we could but 'read the body' we would know when men are really truthful or when women are really ready. Perhaps it is in reaction to all of these temptations, as much as it is the results of more than a quarter of a century of research, that I am persuaded to believe that 'expression' is a word we use for those aspects of human and animal communication behaviour that we have not yet investigated.

In short, the customary distinction between 'expression' and 'communication' seems an inadvisable one to me. It may be a useful bifurcation for the psychiatrist or the artist. It confuses the issue for the student of *social* communication.

Darwin, Charles, *The Descent of Man and Selection in Relation to Sex*, 2 vols., D. Appleton & Co., New York, 1871.
—*The Expression of the Emotions in Man and Animals*, John Murray, London, 1872.
Lavater, John Caspar, *Essays on Physiognomy, Designed to Promote the Knowledge and the Love of Mankind* (translated from the French by Henry Hunter, D.D.), 5 vols., London, 1789.
—*Essays on Physiognomy*, 18th edn (translated from the German by Thomas Holcroft), also *One Hundred Physiognomical Rules*, etc., London and New York, Ward, Lock & Co., n.d., (*c.* 1892).

Suggested further readings

Bateson, Gregory, *Steps to an Ecology of Mind*, Chandler Publishing Co., San Francisco, California, 1972.
Birdwhistell, Ray L., *Kinesics and Context: Essays on Body Motion Communication*, University of Pennsylvania Press, Philadelphia, 1970; Allen Lane The Penguin Press, London, 1971.
— 'The Language of the Body: The Natural Environment of Words', in *Human Communication: Theoretical Explorations*, Albert Silverstein (ed.), Lawrence Erlbaum Press, Potomac, Md (in press, 1974).
Duncan, Starkey, 'Non-Verbal Communication', *Psychological Bulletin*, vol. 72, no. 2, pp. 118–37, 1969.
Ekman, Paul, Wallace V. Friesen and Phoebe Ellsworth, *Emotion in the Human Face*, Pergamon Press, New York, 1972.
Hall, E. T., *The Silent Language*, Doubleday, New York, 1959.
Hewes, G. W., 'World Distribution of Certain Postural Habits', in *American Anthropologist*, **57**, pp. 231–44, 1955.
Hockett, C. F., 'Animal "Language" and Human Language', in *The Evolution of Man's Capacity for Culture*, arr. by J. N. Spuhler, Wayne State University Press, Detroit, 1959.
LaBarre, Weston, 'The Cultural Basis of Emotions and Gestures', *Journal of Personality*, **16**, pp. 49–68, 1947.
Lenneberg, E. H., *Biological Foundations of Language*, Wiley, New York, 1967.
McQuown, N. A., 'Linguistic Transcription and Specification of Psychiatric Interview Material', *Psychiatry*, **20**, pp. 79–86, 1957.
Osgood, C. E., and Heyer, A. W, jr, 'Objective Studies in Meaning: II The Validity of Posed Expressions as Gestural Signs in Interpersonal Communication', *American Psychologist*, **5**, p. 298, 1950.
Scheflen, A. E., *Stream and Structure of Communicational Behavior: Context Analysis of a Psychotherapy Session*, Commonwealth of Pennsylvania: E.P.P.I., Behavioral Studies Monograph, No. I, 1965.

Donald G. MacRae

The Body and Social Metaphor

Let me begin by being very positive and very brief, partly because I am saying what I believe to be true but cannot as yet display and prove to even my own satisfaction; partly and to a large extent because if I am not brief I will get nowhere with my subject in the space at my disposal. All reflection, thought and criticism begins in comparison, analogy and metaphor. Faust was wrong: in the beginning was not the act. St John was right: in the beginning was the word. We are concerned with man, and the world can only exist for man as man knows or imagines it.

Metaphor is the root of reason, science and art. It is the root of feeling as understood beyond the immediate sensations of the self and of all expression of feeling. Metaphors are social because speech is social, because all symbolism is social, because mind is social to an overwhelming degree. (I am not saying here that there is a social mind, a mistake of some past entomologists writing about bees and ants, and of historians, sociologists, ethnologists and psychologists writing about men – a mistake ultimately traceable to the early romantic concept of a *Volksgeist*, a transcendent unity to which actual people either are or ought to be subordinate. Nor am I denying a physical basis to mind although I would strongly oppose a reductionism of mind to its physical necessities, to the brain.) To recapitulate: in human feeling, reason, imagination, play, experiment, judgement and decision, metaphor is embodied, for these exist primarily in and through symbolization, symbolization which is social.

There is so far no satisfactory grammar of metaphor, although I think that structuralist analysis is beginning to suggest what such a grammar might look like. I think the lexicon of metaphors is far smaller than anyone familiar with poetry, representational art and science might at first think. It is not the place to argue it here but I hold that there is in existence probably only some small number of root metaphors, perhaps as few as fifteen or twenty, deployed by the human race, and that from these all other metaphors derive and are secondary. Think of root metaphors metaphorically as being like a theme in music, capable of almost endless variation, and my usage may be clearer. New metaphors, particularly root metaphors, are rare inventions, but in principle there is no obvious reason as to why their total number should have any limit. New arrivals may be rare, but they are to be expected. On the other hand any root metaphor is likely to be so powerful, so generative, so rapidly embodied in myth and thought and language, that I would think it exceptional for a major metaphor to vanish although one may lose its potency as social, historical and intellectual circumstances change. Certainly many archaic metaphors are still powerfully alive. Everyone can feel this in the familiarity, rather than surprise, with which we encounter either the temporally archaic world of, say, the Gilgamesh epic which may be in part more than 5000 years old, or with which we recognize items in the socially archaic mythologies of primitive and historically alien peoples in South America or the Siberian steppes as described by such diverse writers as a Lévi-Strauss or an Eliade.

In discussing these matters there is a puzzle and a disappointment as to what we mean by archaic. People such as us may well have had biologically only a very short history of much less than 100,000 years, however long the total hominid record. Our documentation of human culture however is limited to our interpretation of artifacts, figurines, murals, inhumations and middens until a period of not much more than 6000 years ago. What we call archaic therefore is not very old even in the short human perspective. In the perspective of a biological history of our species as tool-using hominids, 6000 years are nothing, for that perspective now certainly extends backward for a period of tens of millions of years. Tools are part of what we call material culture, but there is in fact no merely material culture. (Tools for example are *shaped*: consciously to shape, mould or pattern is to have culture in a very wide sense.) The history of metaphor is therefore for most of its story unknown, even unknowable. Things, then, which we take to be archaic may be relatively modern; matters which we neglect as trivial may be significant and very old. Again, and I come back to this, the frontiers of the cultural and biological are not fixed: they interpenetrate, and in the last decade or so we have been changing them.

Metaphors and similes are the small change of speech. We use them so often and so freely as to be unaware at any conscious level of their presence. In my first sentence of this section I employ a metaphor to indicate both the extent and triviality of metaphor: reader or listener, correctly taking in my meaning, would normally pay no attention, be unaware of the worn image I used. Yet the meaning is in the metaphor, or is nowhere. Verbal discourse without metaphor is very rare, even in one sense impossible. For example, the language of parliamentary draftsmen, of lawyers, or of engineers seems strange and difficult, inhuman and contorted, just because in any ordinary usage, it is unmetaphorical. Yet at another level even such technical, deliberately unmetaphorical kinds of usage are full of metaphors embodied in the history of the terms they employ. *Action, cause, implementation, torque, cycle, latent,* to take six words at random which belong to lawyers and engineers, are all – from the philologist's point of view – words embodying metaphors. Take an ordinary work like 'examination' which is used medically, scientifically, critically, pedagogically and as a term for any close scrutiny in our ordinary usage. The root metaphor is Latin, not English, for an *examen* is the tongue of a balance. To examine, then, is to weigh, hence metaphorically to assess. The root has no association in English. The metaphor is truly dead.

Yet it was once living. The idea of a balance having a tongue is by analogy with bodily form and the speech of justice. The idea of balance involves two elements: the balancing of the human body, upright against gravity, and the use of the arms extended bilaterally to assess different weights or tensions. Already the body is giving us metaphors. And other usages that seem quite dead are in fact actively operative. We talk about the body politic, about legislative, executive and administrative bodies, and so on. I was told in the United States Senate, 'this is the greatest deliberative

body in the world'. It is I think clear that that metaphor controls
to some degree the thinking and the acting of those who use it. We
ascribe qualities of the actual organic body to such assemblies:
they can be understood and treated *as if* they were people, and
people are quite certainly bodies, if not bodies only. Many metaphorical words and phrases that look stone-dead are in fact quick
with life and derive specifically and primarily from our experience
of the human body. (In that last sentence there are three such
metaphors, one of which, the central one, is concealed.)

Now all this is banal and obvious enough. Unfortunately it is
unavoidable for what follows, and it must be looked at further.
Take, for example, one of the central works of European political
thinking. Thomas Hobbes's *Leviathan, or the Matter, Form and
Power of a Commonwealth, Ecclesiastical and Civil* was published
in 1651. Leviathan itself is the sea monster of the book of Job – we
shall come to monsters later on – and 'None is so fierce that they
dare stir him up'.[1] So the state is a living body, huge, fierce, not
human. He has matter and form, which are the twin ingredients of
the Aristotelian universe. He is other than human, perhaps superhuman. The state is doubly dual: form and matter; ecclesiastical
and civil. The state is a creature, i.e. something created. Now I shall
suggest that the duality of form and matter derives from our
experience of the body and that the idea of duality in unity as a
fundamental mode of being also, but differently, derives from our
bodies.

But Hobbes, despite his chosen title, is a very non-Aristotelian
philosopher. He is a materialist, a mechanist. The frontispiece of
Leviathan is one of the most striking things in the iconography of
the seventeenth century. It shows not a sea monster but a giant
crowned figure of a man *whose body is made up of men*. The state,
society is itself, therefore, in some way a big and terrible man, a
giant if you like, composed of people. The image seems to belong
to some unfamiliar and terrible mythology of power. In a sense
then both the title and the frontispiece, in opposition one to the
other, are also in opposition to the actual content of the book. Yet
this opposition is *formal*. True the content is mechanical and
materialist, but the spirit of *Leviathan* is the spirit of the title –
'Will he make a covenant with thee? Wilt thou take him for a
servant for ever?'[2] – and also the spirit of that frontispiece. Once

again we meet duality in unity, once again we meet the body as hidden, operative metaphor. What is also becoming clear is that the body and its metaphors are neither simple nor unambiguous.

For our purposes the body exists only in so far as it is known and experienced. I suppose that to most people in our culture, at this time, and of what is usually classified as a fairly high level of education, the body is thought of in the first place visually and statically. It is perceived as an image, an image either male or female and belonging to quite specific representational conventions. It is Greek like the Venus of Milo, or Renaissance Italian like Michelangelo's David. It is stone, not flesh. Secondarily it is the body of science or medicine, reduced often to static, schematisized images drawn from modern, post-Leonardo anatomical science and then animated by a physiology which is curiously timeless in that all its processes are seen more as cycles than as histories. Only after these images do we admit the body which is the self, vulnerable, loving and flinching, ingesting and excreting, perishing, and only after that selfhood comes the body of another or the bodies of others. Just as the metaphors are neither simple nor unambiguous, so also is the body none of these things. And, like the metaphors, it has its being in society and history. This last point has one elementary and important aspect: metaphors of the body tend to antedate modern biology, a creation of our culture less than 500 years old. Remembering that let us look at some of these complexities and duplicities.

The human body is basically bilaterally symmetrical. This external symmetry is imperfect but dominant. The posture we regard – and I think this universal – as typical of the body in all societies is upright. This is to contradict experience: during most of the time we are, even in very physically active societies, as a matter of fact slouched, twisted and recumbent in sleep or rest, or crouched or seated or bent in action. Yet being upright seems a general convention of thought about being human. From the symmetry of this erectness we derive our categories of direction – up–down, left–right, before–behind, over–under, and beside. Our concepts of relations in space come not only from our binocular vision but above all from our experience of a fixed eye-level above a fixed ground. (How do birds, or arboreal creatures like gibbons *see*? How far can sight be said to be the same sense for such unstable observers as for us?) Certainly our ideas of dominance are all connected with the visual dominance of our erect postures. Both our categories for classifying and dealing with space manipulatively and organizationally, and our emotions about space and the values we attach to direction in space, derive directly from our body form. We begin with a *Kore*.

For example, what is superior is up or high and what is inferior is down or low. (Low is often dirty, but high is not necessarily clean.) Right is law, morals, the holy and the strong; left is sinister, profane, weak and (often) feminine.[3] Backward and behind are slow, hence stupid. Forward and in front are active, oriented and intelligent. Beside is confederate or paranoid: it is an ambiguous category of place. And I could continue this listing and give it an ethnography for pages. What is clear is that these aspects of space derive from our conception of the body and would not hold for an intelligent bilateral but horizontal animal, far less for a radially symmetrical one like a clever starfish, or for spherically symmetrical beings like those of the fable in Plato's *Symposium*. To understand ourselves we should do far more science fiction.

Being bilateral and erect but also balancing and swaying creatures we derive from this situation intimations of physical weight and mass which lead to our ideas of opposed forces and therefore of all opposition, and also of assessment and justice as derivatives of these experiences. We saw something of this earlier in the etymology of 'examine'; we also speak of 'even-handed' justice, and I suggest that in this iconography it is not just for reasons of impartiality that a personified Justice is shown blindfold. If you want to assess accurately the relative magnitude of two small weights in your hands you will do well for good physiological reasons to shut your eyes. From the body as balancer and weigher to the making of beam-scales and thence to social and specifically politically metaphors is a series of very short steps.

The body – despite the false images of stillness which are among the recurrent consolations of its symbolic representation, from archaic figurines of the fertile female body to the academic nude of the day before yesterday – is dynamic, and never more so when sustaining an erect posture or moving against gravity. To move is to measure. I spoke above of a 'short step': we can measure either through the movement or by the dimensions of the body. Very often, as Hunter Dupree has shown, measuring involves the doubling and redoubling of a human dimension, and this doubling I would suggest is bound up with the bilateralism of the body and the duplication of limbs. Ideas of measure, of proportion, of due restraint come from the body as well as ideas of scale: we talk of 'human scale' in our environment and also in our social relations. Man, in more than the classic Greek sense, but also very much in accord with that sense, really is the measure of all things if only because we have nothing and no one else through which to experience the world from inside outwards.

As such the body is at once unity and diversity, a diversity of which the primary experience is duality in unity. The experience of the dynamic body contains its own agonies, its struggles and utilizations of part against part in work or contest, in leverage and counter-pressure. The unity is in kinaesthetic oppositions, not just spatial relationships. The body in itself is a source of those disjunctions, oppositions and strains which we can transfer to our interpretations of both nature and society.

Thus far our discussion of the body has been very abstract and schematized: a fairly featureless minimal representation in fixed space and essential movement. Yet we have taken one thing for granted: the body is bounded. This is not so simple as it seems. There is, certainly, the envelope of the skin. The body is the skin and what it contains – and about its contents other societies without our science have had other ideas – but its boundaries are not merely skin as frontier, there is the ambiguous and psychologically and socially rich fact of hair, of both head and body, which is, unlike the skin and its contents, not shaped or moved by musculature. Boundary and measure are of the skin: their ambiguity is in the hair. (Logically we might also concern ourselves at this point with the smells of the body, varying in their nature and location, intermittent, and transcending the boundaries of visual and tactile space, but odours are not I think ever relevant to social metaphors and concepts of society except when associated with corruption, carrion and decay – matters to which we return later.)

The body of oneself is not completely accessible to the self, even in cultures possessed of mirrors. There are areas and regions of our bodies that we can see not at all or only with difficulty, nor can we touch ourselves all over with perfect ease. There are secret places and those not easily knowable – even without regard to the body as an internal system. In this the body is like and conforms with the worlds of nature and society. The body, indeed, is analogous to a landscape, explorable but not exhaustible. To anticipate: Donne's apostrophe to the body of his beloved as his America, his new found land, is representative of a metaphor, essentially erotic and worked out in detail by the minor poets of the European baroque. It connects directly with the metaphor of the body politic. The idea of the earth itself as the scene for social action, the world implicated by a pathetic fallacy in society, is involved here: the earth in many societies and all continents has a navel, and is nearly always feminine. The world is body, *terra mater* and *terra genetrix.*

To discuss this further we have to consider gender as characteristic of the body, sex as an activity, and procreation as a function. To my mind the theme of the female nude in art is never only erotic, but it is a metaphor of the world conceived – as our physics and astronomy lead us to forget – primarily as the human place, the world of humankind in undivorced nature and society.

The idea of gender in things is made unfamiliar to us by the habits of the English language. A few nouns in English, such as ships, have gender – masculinity or femininity without the specificity of active sexuality – but the permeation of the world of objects and concepts by gender is lost to English. The associations of the body as generalized in both male and female, in objects of love, comfort, nourishment and strength, work in many cultures to reinforce social, national or provincial loyalties. To conceive the natural and, especially, the political orders through gender is also to act by analogy and metaphor in terms of gender. The primary and secondary sexual characteristics are of course necessary to such modes of conceptualization but they are parts of a transcendent totality rather than conceived and considered separately in this kind of thinking.

Sexuality itself yields obvious experiences and fantasies of duality and unity – not forgetting as we saw the hermaphrodites of Aristophanes in Plato's *Symposium*. Male sex, by the largely involuntary mechanism of erection, is one source of ideas of possession, of unwilled force and power, of action as a distance, all of which have relevance to social as well as to physical conceptualizations. The quasi-autonomy of the genitals, in particular the male genitalia, is associated with and reinforces other ideas of autonomy and a power that is not rationally controlled deriving from the body. Nor is the recurrence of menstruation irrelevant here. Intercourse as reciprocal action is a pattern for physical, behavioural and social reciprocities. The association may be simply mechanical as in the making of fire and the nature of fire, hearth and forge, but it extends into all ideas of connection as action.[4] Bodily intercourse is social and one pattern of the social.

The relation of sex to generation is not necessarily obvious. It has been disputed as to whether any peoples are ignorant of this relation. Whether any now are, no doubt this ignorance once was. The discovery of this power in the body, the mysteriousness of this action over time, its enormous consequence for mankind, for beasts, for nature, form a complex of immense richness for all thought. Bodies as creators, creation as a work of time, are basic conceptual categories. They reveal that action is not force and is not instantaneous. They give rise to the idea of acts having unintended consequences, the central concept of all history, most of economic science, much of sociology. W. B. Yeats was right:

> A shudder in the loins engenders there
> The broken wall, the burning roof and tower
> And Agamemnon dead.

Troy and the house of Atreus belong in the limbo between myth and history. Such a limbo is a good place in which to find a paradigm of historicity and social knowledge through so elementary, so strange, an aspect of the body.

With sex and generation we come to a point touched on earlier. If we are to understand the body as metaphor, and as source of metaphors derivable directly or by transformation rules from it, we must remember that our own experience of our bodies is pre-scientific. We *learn* anatomy and physiology often in contradiction to our experience of them. We touched on this point earlier: our science in these matters is overwhelmingly an affair of the last few centuries of our culture, and only a few of our body metaphors derive from this recent achievement. So far we have considered the body, passively or actively, essentially from without. But the body is interior: mouth, gut, lungs, belly, womb, bowels are interiors, internal spaces, hidden agencies. Inside is labyrinth. To eat and to digest is to transform into energy and action. It is also to transform into urine and faeces. These are patterns of behaviour both economic and moral, virtuous and repulsive. (Even though urine and, more rarely, faeces may have magic potency, I do not think that this potency is usually thought to redeem bodily wastes. They are not just profane, but pollutant – on all this see Mary Douglas[5] – and bound up with concepts of status and worth. *Inside* the body, of course, saliva, urine and so on are neutral.) It is socially approved to produce economically, to have bodily energy, but it is social good at a cost: the body is simultaneously, interdependently involved, in good and bad production.

Interestingly breath is good, even sacred. It, too, is absorbed but not apparently transformed. The body as 'insides', absorbing, transforming, emitting, is surely a source of another duality of opposites, a cosmic and social balance or accounting, in that from it we derive categories of higher and lower functions, good energies and bad matter, the spiritual and the base. Breath is associated with spirit and with speech. The mouth is, all in all, good – the exceptions are obvious – but the physically lower cavities are neutral and/or bad. Their orifices are perilous; their products dangerous or grotesque, useful figuratively for the purposes of insult and the invidious ranking of social statuses. In social ranking the lower ranks are often described as being in some sense more 'animal' than the higher – an ascription that is much wider than its use to describe servile ethnic groups, such as black slaves in Islam or in the American South, or low castes in India. The digestive, excretory and – sometimes – the reproductive organs in several languages are the 'animal parts', their uses the 'animal functions'. Shakespeare is particularly ingenious with such body-social status metaphors. The analogies of the body thus yield extreme Manichaean dualism of spirit and flesh, and a rationale and an account of social status as contempt directed down a ranking system.

In all this we are in the world of mythical thinking which is not specifically archaic but to my belief a normal constituent in vary-ing proportion of all our thought and life. In it incompatibilities and contradictions, double-meanings, puns, ambiguities and dup-licities are normal. Social psychologists have made much of what they call 'cognitive dissonance', the felt strain of two or more modes of knowing, conceiving and believing, particularly when this dissonance is forced on the individual in society by his having to play plural social roles. In fact this seems to me a rationalistic error, a transference of the psychologists' own desire for lucid, consistent rational order and perhaps also of their guilt at not possessing this simplicity and this alone. Nothing is easier, more necessary even, than the flexibility of ambiguity, and few sources of this flexibility richer than mythical thought. Thus we find – as well as the associations of the evil and the base with the image of the body – also the image of its splendour: its exposure as Truth – the naked truth, the bare truth, *nuda veritas*, the confronter of veiled calumny and deceit as in Botticelli's allegory. Now truth is also social, public and not solitary, a need of society if action and co-operation are to take place.

It would be logical to go on from here to a consideration of the body as container of blood and blood as life, to the metaphors of the heart and other organs and their social analogues. In a short piece one cannot do so, for as well as the body as thing, as activity, as container and paradigm of the pairing of appearance with reality, something must be said of the body in time, that is the body as cyclical and the body as a history. The cycles of the body are not all obvious: for example, the cycle of the circulation of the blood is a recent discovery. Others are constant, obvious, im-pressive and yet mysterious. We have said something of the cycles and transformations of nourishment and of breathing. The cycle of menstruation, cosmic in its association with moon, tides and the creation of life, of fertility, is surely involved with all theories of temporal cycles. Analogy can associate it with the seasons, the return of life after winter, the fertility of nature as *mater genetrix*. This rhythm of the body and its correspondences in nature extend into conceptions of society from the sophisticated cycles of history of Danilevsky, Spengler or Toynbee to the most technical theories of cycles of social and economic activity, and to elementary social ideas of an eternal return in human affairs. In all this the starry heavens, the fecund earth and the human body seem to point the same moral of cyclical recurrence.

The cycles of day and night, of sleep and wakening – not that sleep is institutionalized similarly in all societies – are, perhaps oddly, less central than these other rhythms to metaphors deriving from the body as process. Sleep, swoon, trance, all stillness of the body which involves an estrangement of conscious and wary attention, are images of death. The body dies: each body is a history, a subject for narrative, and connected narrative is perhaps the primary form of social understanding. Narrative must begin and end: must societies, countries, peoples, tribes, kindreds not do the same? The body, which is sensible matter and bounded organization, dies and is corrupt, carrion, liquid, stench, a return to nature not as mother but as devourer of things, *edax rerum*. Social thought is haunted by such things, most of all in their manifestation as history, but also elsewhere. I know we often find an identity in opposites, that by specific operations we transform opposites into each other: I wonder if the curious atemporality of so much economics, anthropology and sociology is not in part a denial that the destiny of the body is an accurate metaphor of society. I wonder also if, in those times and places where society is studied, one reason for this study is not, as was certainly true of the 'father' of sociology, Auguste Comte, a desire to find reassurance in a human, even if not individual, continuity and permanence. Under one aspect it is possible to take the social sciences as an attempt to evade the implications of the body as social metaphor.

At night the body dreams, and dreams of itself. It is no longer limited by incapacity, but desire and fear are indulged without apparent frontier. Combinations of elements are made into monsters of delight, horror or indifference. In dreams giants and dwarfs occur as in legend: our images of the body are not just the images of day but of the freedom and irrationality of the night. This too affects our conceptions of the social, and the thought that social life perhaps is, perhaps will be, monstrous. We make our monsters out of bodily parts. We find our monsters in caves, in interior dangerous and uncontrolled places. We find the terrors of social living in bodily metaphors of the least harmonious kind.

There are so many aspects of this subject that we might develop beyond what I have touched on. For example: the body is the earth; the earth is active female nature; between active nature and society there is no distinction; kings contract cosmically significant holy marriages; these hierogamies sustain both natural and social order. What follows for conceptions of society ramifies into the arts: European romanticism in its cosmology, its social metaphors, its political aspirations is involved in all this in both its revolutionary and its conservative modes.[6] Out of that shorthand description one might make a book.

At the other extreme we could return to the body as expressive and consider such involuntary but apparently or actually expressive manifestations as tics, tremblings, convulsions, certain manifestations of madness. Society is the body: society is constraint. Constraint in these bodily afflictions is internal, involuntary, but also a signal – to whom? Again the reflexivity of body and society are amalgamated, and the metaphorical consequences both dense and complex.

No doubt I have expressed these last points too cryptically, but I use them to illustrate, by selection from many other possibilities, the richness and the oddities that await exploration in this subject. I want now to come to the social sciences more directly. We are concerned with the body in social metaphor – we should not forget that it has also a role in the metaphorical components of the natural sciences and technology – and in our time the social sciences are major modes of our expression and our self-consciousness. In sociology and social anthropology as they have grown up historically from˝the sixteenth century we find, I think the following metaphors for society, some of which are archaic, some modern: society is like a big man; society is like a net; society is like a balance; society is like a clock; society is like a market; society is like a battle. These sound as though they were the remarks of children. They are perhaps child-like stated thus, but they are very far from empty.

Ambiguously we met the idea of society as a big man, a kind of giant when we talked of Hobbes whose Leviathan is God's monster, sovereign individual man, humankind as collectivity, all at once. This is in its most naïve form a root metaphor of society in general and political society in particular. If (as has been argued) the tripartite categorization of this world into nature, society and the individual is a comparatively late product of historic times, accomplished only in the first millennium before Christ, certainly in many archaic cosmogonies we find the totality of things conceived either as forming, or as originating from, a single giant body. (The creation is frequently represented as the re-arrangement or transformation of dismembered parts of a single body.) Once however the world is categorized into three orders of nature, society and individual, then this big man becomes specifically a metaphor for society.

Social order is there represented in terms of the divisions of gross anatomy – the sovereign head, the noble heart, the base gut, the labouring hands and so on. The division of labour in society and hence the facts of social ranking and stratification are both explained and justified by such metaphors. What is more important is that from this metaphor we derive the idea of things being *organically* related – that is related not by a mere summation of parts but by their interdependence. Such a recent arrival on the intellectual scene as cybernetics with its concepts of positive and negative feedback formulates one form of the concept of organic relationship, even though the operational vocabulary of cybernetics derives from such mechanical metaphors as that of the rudder or that of the steam engine governor. It is, I believe, impossible to find any of the social sciences to which a concept of organic relationship, ultimately arising from the big man metaphor, is not central.

All this turns on what I called gross anatomy; but since Vesalius we have had access to a fine anatomy, a scientific cartography of the body, and also to a scientific physiology. The metaphor of the big man was transformed by this. Herbert Spencer elaborated the sociological and anthropological vocabulary of structure and function by a deliberate analogy of the social and biological bodies. Analogy is, of course, nothing but systematic and extended metaphor – which is not to discredit either analogical fancy or analogical reasoning. The sociology and social anthropology developed down to the 1960s was dominated by this vocabulary and by the sense that social relations were organic relations. Even what is called 'conflict theory' in the hands of Coser[7] or Gluckman[8] depended on these modes of thought, though I think that

Simmel, who was a source of this current of thought, was not much burdened by these metaphors.

In political theory, however, the metaphor is both conservative, as in Burke, and liberal and progressive (these adjectives are not ascriptions of value) in social Darwinism. So far as I can judge the metaphor is still operative here, along with a number of modern mechanical analogies from balances, clockwork and computers. One could indeed classify political scientists with rough accuracy in terms of their metaphorical prejudices, unconscious though they may be of these. In general, however, I would claim that as a source of social metaphors the body is on the whole a conservative (note the small c) influence on conceptualization and thought.

I suppose, given our culture, a follower of Wilhelm Reich – if any such still exist – would say, what else? He would then offer us, by way of an alternative culture, an alternative body and therefore alternative metaphors – not I suppose unlike those that occur in William Blake. But that is to embark on another theme. The body undoubtedly is conceived as structure in one way or another: it belongs properly to nature, not culture. Perhaps one reason why the social sciences have been so bad at analysing culture is because of the role of body metaphors. Equally however one could go on to the almost unexplored area of the body as cultural fact and see where that led us. But that would be to start writing again.

1. *Job*, 41:10.
2. *Job*, 41:4.
3. R. Hertz, *Death* and *The Right Hand*, translation, London, 1960.
4. M. Eliade, *The Forge and the Crucible*, London, 1962.
5. M. Douglas, *Purity and Danger*, London, 1966.
6. M. Abrams, *Natural Supernaturalism*, New York, 1971.
7. L. A. Coser, *The Functions of Social Conflict*, London, 1968.
8. M. Gluckman, *Custom and Conflict in Africa*, Oxford, 1956.

Roger Poole

Objective Sign and Subjective Meaning

Can Time come to a stop?

In 1872 Sir Charles Darwin published *The Expression of the Emotions in Man and Animals*.

In 1972, exactly a century later, another massive work on the same subject appears: *Non-Verbal Communication* – a collection of papers from various hands edited by R. A. Hinde.

Is there any noticeable advance, in assumptions, theory, content or level of methodological understanding, between the first and the second? I think none. 'Everyone who has had much to do with young children must have seen how naturally they take to biting, when in a passion. It seems as instinctive in them as in young crocodiles, who snap their little jaws as soon as they emerge from the egg.'[1]

This comes in fact from Darwin. Darwin does not conceive of any difference of *level* between the 'meaning' of animal expressions and human ones, the latter being only more sophisticated and evolved instances of the former. Darwin also assumes that the expression of the emotions is basically a physiological matter, the 'meaning' of all emotional expression being judged in terms of the evolution of the individual from baby to adult. Darwin assumes, thirdly, that most expressive gestures in man are universal and innate, only a few being modified or transmitted culturally.

It is on the question of the meaning of expressive gestures, both in Darwin and in the papers in the Hinde collection, that the sceptical reader has to call a halt. At least Darwin does refer to the problem of meaning, even if he naïvely assumes that once an instinctive–evolutionary 'cause' for the expression has been found, we have found its meaning. But in the new collection, the problem of meaning seems to have been abrogated altogether.

The second case was that of a Hindustani man, who from illness and poverty was compelled to sell his favourite goat. After receiving the money, he repeatedly looked at the money in his hand and then at the goat, as if doubting whether he would not return it. He went to the goat, which was tied up ready to be led away, and the animal reared up and licked his hands. His eyes then wavered from side to side; his 'mouth was partially closed, with the corners very decidedly depressed'. At last the poor man seemed to make up his mind that he must part with his goat, and then, as Mr Scott saw, the eyebrows became slightly oblique, with the characteristic puckering or swelling at the inner ends, but the wrinkles on the forehead were not present. The man stood thus for a minute, then heaving a deep sigh, burst into tears, raised up his two hands, blessed the goat, turned round, and without looking again, went away.[2]

I do not know what sort of 'meaning' you attach to this passage. Here is Darwin's reaction:

On the cause of the obliquity of the eyebrows under suffering. During several years no expression seemed to me so utterly perplexing as this which we are here considering. Why should grief or anxiety cause the central fasciae alone of the frontal muscle together with those round the eyes, to contract? ...

We have all of us, as infants, repeatedly contracted our orbicular, corrugator, and pyramidal muscles, in order to protect our eyes whilst screaming; our progenitors before us have done the same during many generations; and though with advancing years we easily prevent, when feeling distressed, the utterance of screams, we cannot from long habit always prevent a slight contraction of the above-named muscles; nor indeed do we observe their contraction in ourselves, or attempt to stop it, if slight ... The result which necessarily follows, if these fasciae contract energetically, is the oblique drawing up of the eyebrows, the puckering of their inner ends, and the formation of rectangular furrows on the middle of the forehead.[3]

Later Darwin tells how he was sitting in a train, when a lady opposite him suddenly attracted his attention:

Whilst I was looking at her, I saw that her *depressores anguli oris* became very slightly, yet decidedly, contracted; but as her countenance remained as placid as ever, I reflected how meaningless was this contraction, and how easily one might be deceived. The thought had hardly occurred to me when I saw that her eyes suddenly became suffused with tears almost to overflowing, and her whole countenance fell. There could now be no doubt that some painful recollection, perhaps that of a long-lost child, was passing through her mind. As soon as her sensorium was thus affected, certain nerve-cells from long habit transmitted an order to all the respiratory muscles, and to those round the mouth, to prepare for a fit of crying.[4]

Luckily for the don in the railway carriage, the lady restrains herself from the impropriety of tears in time. Darwin concludes:

In this case, as well as in many others, the links are indeed wonderful which connect cause and effect in giving rise to various expressions on the human countenance; and they explain to us the meaning of certain movements, which we involuntarily and unconsciously perform, whenever certain transitory emotions pass through our minds.[5]

'They explain to us the meaning of certain movements.' Do they, though? The gap between explanation in terms of physiological–muscular cause, and 'meaning' in any adequate sense, is too vast. Darwin talks here of 'the meaning of certain movements' just as Frazer talked of the 'meaning' of myth and later Malinowski talked of the 'meaning' of primitive religion and magic. We are in the presence of the old distinction between effective cause and final cause, and no nearer a solution for Darwin's efforts.

The intervention of behaviourism in the period between Darwin and the Hinde collection has only made that distinction more painfully obvious. 'Behaviourism', the *Encyclopedia Britannica* informs us, 'is first and foremost an extension of the methods of animal psychology to the study of man.'[6]

And indeed the papers in the Hinde collection are laid out in such a logical pattern, those dealing with the nature of communication as such being followed by those dealing explicitly with communication in animals, and these are followed in their turn by papers dealing with non-verbal communication in man.

The phylogenetic and ontogenetic hypotheses which fill the conceptual area between Darwin and the most modern exposition on the subject of human expressivity find themselves as a significant transition-means between the second and the third sections of the book. Indeed, Van Hooff's paper, 'A comparative approach to the phylogeny of laughter and smiling', which forms the bridge between Parts B and C, does several conceptual jobs at once.

For the larger pattern of the volume as a whole is given microcosmic expression in Van Hooff's study of the phylogeny of laughter and smiling. There, as in Darwin, are the diagrams of animals engaged in expressive behaviour. There are the sketches of chimpanzees with bared-teeth displays, and there is the end-product: photographs of smiling children at play. And just in case there should remain the slightest lingering doubt that Van Hooff might be mentally reserving to himself a difference of *level* between signifying activity in apes and humans, there is a diagram entitled 'Interspecific social play', which actually shows a chimpanzee with a '*relaxed open mouth* display' and a human boy who is obligingly providing a '*wide-mouth laugh*'.[7]

Reading the Hinde collection is an uncanny experience. There is of course tremendous methodological expertise in every kind of formalization, from linguistics to information theory. But on nearly every page (there are of course honourable exceptions to the conceptual norm) the reader comes across one of three basic implicit assumptions, every one of which is in fact as naïve and as unexamined (in any adequate sense) as the methodological apparatus is complex and impressive.

It is assumed, then, that human expressivity is 'meaningful' in so far as it is derivable from, related to, or comparable to animal instinctual behaviour and 'communication patterns'; or, that it is 'meaningful' according to its deployment and variation within a merely 'cultural' or 'cross-cultural' set of structures, and that these can and should be compared and interrelated indefinitely; or, that it is 'meaningful' in so far as it can be formalized in terms of some pre-existent linguistic assumptions and grids, including the assumptions and grids of information theory.

Whichever of the three assumptions is in question (sometimes all three are) one thing is for sure: the whole subject has been reduced to a merely epistemological, to a merely formalizable, to a merely scientific exercise. There is no suggestion anywhere in the book that human expressivity might be important as a subject of inquiry in its own right, that it might be significant in the wider pattern of life itself, that it might even attain the signifying level of ethical and political intellection.

Nor would it be fair to single out Van Hooff's paper. Nearly everywhere, there is evidence of this easy fashionable swing from discussion of hairy ape to naked ape and back again. The Darwinian assumptions are implicit, but unquestioned and almost unquestionable. Scientifically, with reference to the expression of emotion in man and animals, time stopped in 1872.

What grates most is this double evasion of the concept of *meaning*. One does not need to be a bishop, fearful for the faith of his flock, to feel that the subsumption of the concept of *meaning* under the classification of *effective cause* is facile. Nor is a moralistic standpoint necessary to perceive that analogies between animal expression and human expression are soon exhausted.

There is no widening, for instance, of the concept of 'context' when man's expressivity is in question. The important influence of 'context' upon cross-cultural expressive variation is allowed, of course, even emphasized, but only social, gestural or cultural context. The idea of ethical or political context is never considered, and it is in these contexts that man's expressivity is most clearly qualitatively different, as sign, from animal expressivity. This failure is important, for it means that the concept of 'context' is entirely behavioural.

It also carries a severe impoverishment with it. The distinction, the qualitative distinction, between man and animal as signifying agents can never be developed, nor even approached, since animals do not, so far as we know, have ethical or political contexts to signal in. Meaning in a full sense can only emerge in a context which is an existent temporal reality, and not merely a formal cultural convention. The Darwinist–behaviourist school thus fails to intersect the area in which the problem of meaning as such exists. In the Hinde collection, this evasion is implicit, but there is a new theory in which the evasion is explicit.

Ninety-nine years after Darwin's book, in 1971, Ray Birdwhistell brought out in this country a collection of essays called *Kinesics and Context*. Kinesics has recently taken its place as the Hussar regiment of the behaviourist army. And, true to form, the evasion of the question of meaning is noticeable on nearly every page. There is one long *tour de force* in which a lady smoking a cigarette and saying a banal little phrase is subjected to an exhaustive kinesic analysis. But Birdwhistell writes at one point:

The Problem

In this exercise, our focus is upon what Doris *says* in this situation. It is not our present problem to determine what she *means*. At the same time, operating upon the assumption that description approaches explanation as it deals with a greater proportion of the available data, it should be profitable to describe our corpus more adequately. [8]

The methodological naïveté of that assumption is only matched by the philosophical naïveté of the opening distinction. Adequacy of explanation does not automatically increase with a greater and greater accumulation of evidence.

But worse still is the overtone of the modesty of George Washington and the cherry-tree. Absolutely *no* meaning-grids are being fitted over this sequence, asserts Birdwhistell – as if this were even possible. For Max Weber here has the last laugh: just as the meaning found in any classification of phenomena will be the meaning that has been imposed upon it by the analyst, so the kind of explanation you eventually give of a set of observed phenomena is obviously a function of the kind of expectations you deployed in selecting the evidence.

Bertrand Russell once remarked that American rats in mazes seem to rush round with tremendous drive and energy, finally achieving the correct result by sheer chance, while German rats seem to sit still and to evolve their answer from reflective meditation. And if you set out to exclude (as Birdwhistell claims he does) *any* meaning-expectations from your survey of Doris smoking her cigarette and drawling her phrase, then the expectations that you *do* inevitably bring to bear go unnoticed, they are not consciously taken account of in analysis, and you therefore end up by falsifying the evidence. When this is allowed to happen, your work is circular and self-defining. You will notice more and more of what you decided to put in at the beginning.

But Birdwhistell says: 'In this exercise our focus is upon what Doris *says* in this situation. It is not our present problem to determine what she *means*.'

Well, what does she say? She says: 'I suppose all mothers think their kids are smart, but I have no worries about that child's intellectual ability.'

And what might she *mean*? For me, the words that Doris utters, the context in which she utters them, and the general setting in which the scene is filmed and recorded are significant to the highest degree. One would have to refer to the whole chapter in Bird-whistell's book to illustrate the point; but what is *meant* by Doris in her few words is in fact the *meaning* of the whole of her existence. She lights a cigarette and, with the weariness of a whole civilization in her voice, has her *meaning* discounted by the kinesicists, busy with their camera and tape-recorder.

It is true, no doubt, as Kristeva has pointed out, that Bird-whistell conceives of meaning in purely structural, purely relational, terms.[9] In the preceding chapter of his book he writes: 'I have tried to make it clear that the question "What does X mean?" is nonadmissible unless the system within which X operates has been subjected to sufficient analysis so that X in its multiple of transforms can be described.'[10]

Again, the assumption that *quantitative* increase of information will suddenly magically be transformed into a *qualitative* change in the level of explanation (possibly, one day, even 'meaning'). He ends his chapter: '*The final answer to "What does X mean?" can only be arrived at when all of the other social systems interacting in any situation are equally thoroughly analyzed.*'[11]

One is reminded of Kierkegaard's genial observation when describing the frustration of being lectured at by Hegelians:

When a man writes or dictates paragraphs in a running stream, promising that everything will be made clear at the end, it becomes increasingly difficult to discover just where the confusion begins, and to find a fixed point of departure. By means of 'Everything will be made clear at the end', and intermittently by means of the category, 'This is not the proper place to discuss this question', the very cornerstone of the System, often used as ludicrously as if one were to cite under the heading of misprints a single example, and then add, 'There are indeed other misprints in the book, but this is not the proper place to deal with them' – by means of these two phrases the reader is constantly defrauded, one of them cheating him definitely, the other intermediately. In the situation of the dialogue, however, this whole fantastic business of pure thought would lose all its plausibility.[12]

The greatest difficulty in the kinesic approach to bodily expressivity is one which has been deliberately built into the method by the practitioners themselves. For, by setting out to study Doris and her companions with the deliberate intention of setting aside the question of meaning, the practitioners have no means of ascertaining or isolating those movements and expressive gestures which have a meaning to the agent himself or herself, and segregating those which do not. Both at the level of practice, and of theory, it is thus impossible for Birdwhistell to distinguish acts which have a high *subjective* significance for his individuals from those which are *subjectively* insignificant to them.

With this distinction between acts considered as meaningful to the *observer*, and acts considered as meaningful in the context of the subjective experience of the *agent*, we leave the comfortable certainties of what Weber calls 'observational understanding' and find ourselves in front of the massive problem of 'explanatory understanding'. We face the Other as signalling to us about something that is meaningful to him in terms of his own rational universe. How do we start deciphering? How to achieve what Weber calls *sinnhafte Adäquanz* – 'adequacy at the level of meaning'? How do we begin to make sense of what the Other is signalling to us about, in terms of the concepts and aims which he is himself deploying, as opposed to those which we force down over him?

The first thing, of course, is a change of methodological stance. The clinical observer has to go, and the intersubjective world must be acknowledged. Meaning involves an agent, and an observer who is himself intersubjectively in communication with the agent, be it ever so distantly. There must be some mutual point of reference. There must be at least two in the situation: one as emitting agent the other as receiving agent. What is common to them is their *agency*: they are both in a cultural or ethical *place*, they are both situated in it *vis-à-vis* certain subjective realities of its intersubjective constitution, they are both *acting*.

The difficulties are daunting. One looks round for some kind of philosophical help. The search for meaning in this adequate sense left Oxford with Zuleika Dobson. As usual, therefore, we have to look elsewhere for philosophical guidance. And the only major philosophical attempt to study bodily expressivity has been phenomenological.

But Husserl, as early as 1900, was extremely discouraging about this possibility of intersubjective interpretation, and his depressing unhelpfulness seems to have affected the whole phenomenological enterprise. In his *Logical Investigations*, concerned as he was to establish pure meaning in the realm of logic and mathematics, he brushes aside *in one paragraph* the possibility of establishing such pure meanings in the realm of human physical expression:

5. *Expressions as meaningful signs. Setting aside of a sense of 'expression' not relevant for our purpose*

... Such a definition excludes facial expression and the various gestures which involuntarily accompany speech without communicative intent, or those in which a man's mental states achieve understandable 'expression' for his environment, without the added help of speech. Such 'utterances' are not expressions in the sense in which a case of speech is an expression, they are not phenomenally one with the experiences made manifest in them in the consciousness of the man who manifests them, as is the case with speech. In such manifestations one man communicates nothing to another: their utterance involves no intent to put certain 'thoughts' on record expressively, whether for the man himself, in his solitary state, or for others. Such 'expressions', in short, have properly speaking, *no meaning*. It is not to the point that another person may interpret our involuntary manifestations, e.g. our 'expressive movements', and that he may thereby become deeply acquainted with our inner thoughts and emotions. They 'mean' something to him in so far as he interprets them, but even for him they are without meaning in the special sense in which verbal signs have meaning; they only mean in the sense of indicating.[13]

The warning of the last sentence could not be clearer. The meanings which we intuitively ascribe to bodily expression are never pure, verifiable, universal meanings. If we attribute meaning to them, we should do so in the awareness that we are doing no more than following a personal hunch. To attribute any other sort of meaning is methodologically naïve.

A life-time later, when Husserl, deeply concerned for the human world we live in in all its social, historical and political exposedness and danger, wrote his fifth *Cartesian Meditation*, he could do no other than to repeat his earlier verdict. One may intuit what the embodied Other thinks, sees and communicates by various *ad hoc* procedures – Analogical Apperception, 'Pairing', Transcendental Intersubjectivity – but the terrible, brutal fact remains: I shall never know the inner experience of the Other as *he* knows it. I shall never know how it feels to be him, nor will he ever know how it feels to be me. *Hic* and *illic* are two totally disparate worlds. Before the meanings emitted by the Other we are, ultimately, helpless.[14]

This helplessness is evident in the history of phenomenologizing itself. Max Scheler, in his essay on sympathy published in 1913, avoided the hard necessity of choosing between analogy and empathy theories of understanding the behaviour of the Other only at the cost of introducing a *deus ex machina*, love, which in his view allows the closed period of 'egocentrism' to be transcended. It is doubtless true, as Scheler asserts, that the difficulty of understanding other people's behaviour is largely a false one, since it is only in terms of other people that I have understood myself at all during the first decade and a half of my life. Yet 'egocentrism' is an enduring and untranscended state for most people in later life, and has to be taken as the normal state in which one person sets to work to understand and interpret another's behaviour. In cases where one can't 'love' in Scheler's magnificent sense, one is still bound helplessly to one or other of the two theories he rejects, analogy or empathy. One cannot call upon Love as an instrument of *Verstehen* (adequate understanding) at will, neither is it a generalizable instrument of analysis.

Heidegger, in his famous torso of 1927, *Being and Time*, leads the phenomenological enterprise even further into the personal. Heidegger seems content to describe the expressive reality of others in the world entirely within categories that he has himself invented and which, while they reflect a vast and luminous intelligence, are ultimately self-referring. 'Idle Talk', for instance, 'Curiosity', 'Ambiguity', 'Falling and Thrownness', while doubtless forms of everyday *Dasein* which strike Heidegger as particularly significant, are neither verifiable nor falsifiable. One cannot give a specific content to any act which exists within these categories. They cannot be used again. They cannot be used by any other analyst than Heidegger.

The others in the world, too, are totally abstract, deprived of any historical features.

Dasein, as everyday Being-with-one-another, stands in *subjection* to Others. It itself *is* not; its Being has been taken away by the Others ... These Others, moreover, are not *definite* Others. On the contrary, *any* Other can represent them ... The 'who' is not this one, not that one, not oneself, not some people, and not the sum of them all. The 'who' is the neuter, *the 'they'* (*das Man*).[15]

This web of metaphorical categories is powerful enough to isolate the human subject completely within it – the human subject as individual disappears from sight. There is no comprehension of the Other in Heidegger, and no attempt towards it. Indeed, the only speech is that of the poets, and they are dead.

As it progresses, phenomenology seems to recognize that its ultimate fate will have to be silence. Alfred Schutz, writing at almost the same moment that Husserl was constructing his fifth Meditation, ruefully has to agree with Husserl that the problem, as then posed, was insoluble:

> Thus I am always interpreting your lived experiences from my own standpoint. Even if I had ideal knowledge of all your meaning-contexts at a given moment, and so were able to arrange your whole supply of experience, I should still not be able to determine whether the particular meaning-contexts of yours in which *I* arranged your lived experiences were the same as those which *you* were using.[16]

Later on, he puts it even more strongly, in an example which we may even find pitiful in its intellectual exhaustion:

> Let us illustrate this with an example. Suppose that you and I are watching a bird in flight. The thought 'bird-in-flight' is in each of our minds and is the means by which each of us interprets his own observations. Neither of us, however, could say whether our lived experiences on that occasion were identical. In fact, neither of us would even try to answer that question, since one's own subjective meaning can never be laid side by side with another's and compared.
>
> Nevertheless, during the flight of the bird you and I have 'grown older together'; our experiences have been simultaneous.[17]

In fact, check mate. There is an almost Beckett-like despair in the conclusion Schutz draws:

> I make no pretence to any knowledge of the content of your subjective experiences or of the particular way in which they were structured. It is enough for me to know that you are a fellow human being who was watching the same thing that I was. And if you have in a similar way co-ordinated my experiences with yours, then we can both say that *we* have seen a bird in flight.[18]

The mention of 'growing older together' is not as puerile as it may seem, as this idea of 'growing older together' in mutual attentiveness is a category which Schutz uses to substitute structure for time.[19] Nevertheless, the emptiness of Schutz's hands is disconcerting – and significant. It begins to look as if Husserl was right.

Sartre, like Heidegger, examines bodily expressivity in terms of categories invented by himself, and which reflect much light on Sartre's way of interpreting the actions of his counter-subjects, but which, like Heidegger's, cannot be used again, or used by any other analyst. Sartre's analyses of the body of the Other are intensely personal to Sartre, indeed he acknowledges this himself, and makes it a methodological necessity: 'The point of view of pure knowledge is contradictory; there is only the point of view of *engaged* knowledge . . . A pure knowledge would be a knowledge without a point of view; therefore a knowledge of the world but on principle located outside the world. But this makes no sense.'[20]

Of course Sartre is right to stress that there is no pure scientific knowledge, only a human point of view. But the language of metaphor he employs to convey the salient characteristics of that point of view is a hindrance to any kind of generalization. Readers of Sartre will not need reminders of what I mean: 'The Other is first the permanent flight of things towards a goal which I apprehend as an object at a certain distance from me but which escapes me inasmuch as it unfolds about itself its own distances.'[21] Or 'Rather it appears that the world has a kind of drain hole in the middle of its being and that it is perpetually flowing off through this hole.'[22] Or 'Thus the notion of the Other cannot under any circumstances aim at a solitary, extra-mundane consciousness which I can not even think. The man is defined by his relation to the world and by his relation to myself. He is that object in the world which determines an internal flow of the universe, an internal haemorrhage.'[23]

The Other is all this and more. There are two sentences in *Being and Nothingness* which fix the exact quality of Sartre's scrutiny of the Other in the world: 'Conflict is the original meaning of being-for-others.'[24] And 'The essence of the relations between consciousnesses is not the *Mitsein*; it is conflict.'[25]

For Sartre, one does not *observe* the Other in his expressive activity, nor is one oneself *observed* by the Other in one's own expressive activity. That is a loose and flaccid view of things. For Sartre the Other and the self are locked in a massive struggle for power, a tremendous encounter of wills, each of which is straining to the utmost to dominate and enslave the freedom of the other. The whole expressive activity of the Other is an attempt on my freedom, mine is an attempt upon his. Even in love, especially in love, the Other attempts to take us over, to possess us, by the Look. It is all power politics, a cold war, a vast series of takeover bids.

And the bodily expressivity of the Other is seen systematically through the grid of the *en-soi/pour-soi* distinction, which distinction carries with it the necessity of Bad Faith. Sartre remorselessly, undeviatingly erects arguments to show that comprehension of the Other, from the inside, is impossible. Bad Faith and the objectifying activity of the *pour-soi* imprison and mistreat the freedom of the Other by the Look, masochism, indifference, desire, hate, sadism and the other horrors of 'Concrete Relations with Others.'[26] Every consciousness is imprisoned like a goldfish in its glass bowl, and swims helplessly round in it, having no form of intuitive access to the element in which the other *pour-soi* is imprisoned. There is not a trace of helpfulness in Sartre about how to analyse what the Other, in the closed bowl of his own intentional life, might be meaning – how could there be, since this has been made systematically impossible by Sartre's own philosophy of isolated individual existence?

The bodily expressivity of the Other is always, in Sartre's early work, a matter between him and me – there is no reference to an intersubjective world in which ethical and social criteria might influence the interpretations we make of each other. It would appear that Sartre has repented of this. His penance is a long one: seven and a half hundred pages. In the *Critique de la raison dialectique*, there is indeed a Group in terms of which the individual's activities are interpreted, and usually with dire consequences for the individual. Whereas before one blushed when caught by the Look of the Other in an undignified posture, in the *Critique* one is liable to be lynched by one's loving fellow-politicians in the Group for the slightest deviance or act of free thought.[27] It could be that in this new political setting the interpretation of physical behaviour is achieved, in a crude and diagrammatic way, by Sartre, but, even in spite of the distinctions between *process* and *praxis*, and between the *series* and the *group*, I do not think that much has been added to our interpretative apparatus. Terror may be present in human society, and much behaviour may be made more explicable in terms of it, but I think that R. D. Laing has, in the uses he has made of Sartre's distinctions, made a purse from a sow's ear.

Phenomenology by the middle 1940s was, then, at the limits of its credibility. It had sunk in a morass of solipsism and metaphor. It was only Maurice Merleau-Ponty who seized its last semantic property, analogy, and made a final heroic effort to save the enterprise.

It is not as if Merleau-Ponty does not agree with Husserl that analogy is the fundamental fact, the brute datum beyond which there is no going – he does agree. But he does not regard this, as Husserl did, as a sufficient reason for rolling up the carpet and going home.

Just as I can be mistaken concerning myself and grasp only the apparent or ideal signification of my conduct, so can I be mistaken concerning another and know only the envelope of his behaviour. The perception which I have of him is never, in the case of suffering or mourning, for example, the equivalent of the perception which he has of himself, unless I am sufficiently close to him that our feelings constitute together a single 'form' and that our lives cease to flow separately. It is by this rare and difficult consent that I can be truly united with him . . . I communicate with him by the signification of his conduct; but it is a question of attaining its structure, that is of attaining, beyond his words or even his actions, the region where they are prepared.[28]

This seems to me one of the most beautiful passages of philosophy ever penned, and I have spent much time in meditating upon it. But finally, although this 'rare and difficult consent' may on extremely rare occasions be partially attained, it remains, like a Spanish doubloon washed up by the tide, only a beautiful and evocative suggestion of another world. *It cannot be used again.*

That passage comes from the end of *The Structure of Behaviour*, which dates from 1942. Here is a new attempt upon the unsayable from *The Phenomenology of Perception* of 1945:

The communication or comprehension of gestures comes about through the reciprocity of my intentions and the gestures of others, of my gestures and intentions discernible in the conduct of other people. It is as if the other person's intention inhabited my body and mine his.[29]

There is no doubt that empathetic transfer, transferred intuitive understanding, is the most complete and perfect that there is. But it is far from being an everyday occurrence; and it is also very far from being a method of analysis which can be spoken about, deployed, discussed and brought into the light of common day. Here again:

> In the same way, I do not understand the gestures of others by some act of intellectual interpretation; communication between consciousnesses is not based on the common meaning of their respective experiences, for it is equally the basis of that meaning. The act by which I lend myself to the spectacle must be recognized as irreducible to anything else.[30]

One is inclined to shout hurrah and to throw one's cap in the air, for all this is true. But how then *does* one 'understand the gestures of others' if not 'by some act of intellectual interpretation'?

> It is through my body that I understand other people, just as it is through my body that I perceive 'things'. The meaning of a gesture thus 'understood' is not behind it, it is intermingled with the structure of the world outlined by the gesture, and which I take up on my own account. It is arrayed all over the gesture itself . . .[31]

The more one reads, the more worrying becomes this ineffability. There is a dangerous degree of reliance upon the unsayability of gesture in Merleau-Ponty's position. Comprehension, he seems to argue, may be achieved by various empathetic, analogical, transferential means, but they are all ineffable:

> The gesture which I witness outlines an intentional object. This object is genuinely present and fully comprehended when the powers of my body adjust themselves to it and overlap it. The gesture presents itself to me as a question, bringing certain perceptible bits of the world to my notice, and inviting my concurrence in them. Communication is achieved when my conduct identifies this path with its own. There must be mutual confirmation between myself and others.[32]

The trouble with the terms 'adjustment', 'overlapping', 'concurrence', 'identification', 'confirmation' is that none of this is generalizable into a working method that can be manipulated by some other analyst. Like Heidegger and Sartre before him, Merleau-Ponty finally ends up mute before the expressivity of the other. He knows what it's all about, but he can't tell us. He merely says that we, too, know.

We do know. But however long one peruses the pages of this

1. Scene in the market place at Ruhengeri.

2. Mother and newborn: expression of feelings but no attempt to communicate.

3. Mother and young baby: attempting to communicate.

4. Chimpanzee begging for meat.
(Courtesy of D. Bygott)

5. Rhesus monkey and old infant: fear grins.
(Courtesy of L. Barden)

6. and 7. Displaying male chimpanzees.
(Courtesy of D. Bygott)

8. Aggressive displays by male great
and blue tits on a milk bottle.
(After Fisher and Hinde, 1949).

11

9. Detail of the central apse of the cathedral at Cefalù, twelfth century.

10. Detail of St Luke; mosaic in the Basilica di San Vitale, Ravenna.

11. Detail of *The Presentation in the Temple* by Ambrogio Lorenzetti.

12. Detail of *The Virgin and Child* by Masaccio, *c.* 1401–1427/9.

13. Detail of the *Madonna with Sleeping Child* by Giovanni Bellini, *c.* 1430–1516

14. Detail of the *Pietà* by Giovanni Bellini, *c.* 1430–1516.

15

16

17

18

15. Detail of the *Madonna and Child* by Albrecht Dürer.

16. Detail of *Adam and Eve* by Albrecht Dürer.

17. Detail of the *Three Fathers*, Palatine Chapel, Palermo.

18. Detail of the *Universal Judgement* from the twelfth/thirteenth century mosaic in the Basilica at Torcello, Venice.

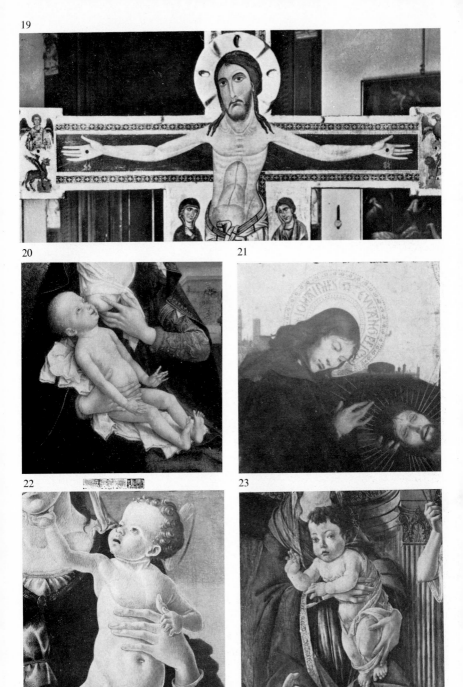

19. Detail of the *Crucifix* by Berlinghiero Berlinghieri, thirteenth century.

20. Detail of *St Luke Painting the Virgin* by Roger van der Weyden.

21. Detail of the Avignon *Pietà*.

22. Detail of the *Madonna and Child* by Marco Zoppo, *c*. 1433–1478.

23. Detail of the *Virgin and Child* by Sandro Botticelli, *c*. 1445–1510.

24. Detail of the *Enthroned Madonna* from San Giobbe by Giovanni Bellini, *c.* 1430–1516.

25. Detail of The Sistine *Madonna* by Raphael.

26. Detail of *Diane de Poitier*, Fontainebleau School.

27. Detail of *La Mezzana* by Niccolò dell'Abbate.

28. Oxford Street dressmaker's shop window model.

29. Detail of a poster advertising *Jesus Christ Superstar*.

श्री विराट स्वामी

Cosmic form of Viṣṇu-Kṛiṣṇa with cakras of the subtle body; from a book.
This illustrates how the divine body of the Universe and the body of the individual
Tantrika may be identified. Gouache on paper, Rajasthan, nineteenth century.

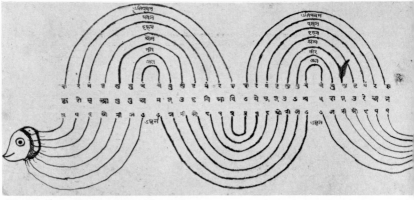

32

31. Jaina diagram illustrating the eternal recurrence of the sevenfold divisions of the Universe as a cosmic river of time and reality. From a manuscript of the Samāraṅganasūtradhāra. Ink on paper, Rajasthan, nineteenth century.

32. One of a set of thirteen leaves from a manuscript illustrating the processes of projective evolution of the Universe. Gouache on paper, Western India, c. 1700.

33. Pair of snakes, symbolizing doubled energy, encircling a yantra of enlaced male and female triangles containing an indwelling goddess; the whole contemplated by a successful saint. Gouache on paper, Rajasthan, eighteenth century.

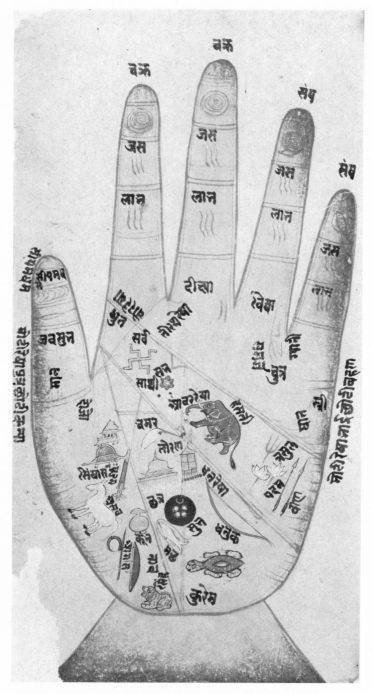

34. Coloured drawing of the palm of the hand with the presiding spiritual
principles marked, and the units of analysis defined for palmistry.
From Rajasthan, eighteenth century.

35. Diagram of the six cakras in the subtle body, Kangra,
Himachal Pradesh. Gouache on paper, eighteenth century.

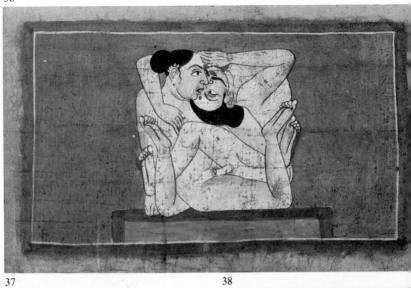

36. The sexual posture Cakra Āsana illustrating how the body may be used to harness
spiritual energies; reverse, representing a diagram of the stimulation points,
with mantras, on the female body. Gouache on paper, Nepal, eighteenth century.

37. The Goddess Kālī, signifying time in its terrible aspect, seated in intercourse
on the corpse Siva – another image for the process presented in the Srī yantra.
Brass, Bengal, eighteenth century.

38. Painting representing the elements penetrating into space beyond the head region.
Gouache on paper, Rajasthan, eighteenth century.

Supreme Buddha with his female wisdom signifying the union of all possible dialectic separations. Gilt bronze, Nepal, sixteenth century.

Srī yantra; a diagram of the functioning of creation, generating time as well as space; used for meditation and worship. The interlaced male and female triangles generate from the seminal dot the realms of the universe signified by the circuits of produced triangles. Gouache on paper, Rajasthan, eighteenth century.

41. Detail of *Nymphs at a fountain* by Sir Peter Lely.
42. Detail of the *Nurture of Jupiter* by Nicholas Poussin.

inspired poet of analogy, it does not seem as if one will ever be able to haul away from the wreckage the essential tools for beginning operations on our own account on the island. Merleau-Ponty can speak for himself, but when finally he turns round to us, he has to remain mute. We know and yet we cannot say.

This language of ineffability comes about because Merleau-Ponty realized so clearly the distinction between physical gesture and intended meaning – the distinction over which we noticed Darwin falling at the beginning of this account. Merleau-Ponty clearly realizes that we are not really, as Husserl and Schutz assume, helpless, isolated monads, gesticulating at each other desperately over an unintelligible medium. There is a common physical world which two counter-subjects inhabit, a world in which one can get cut on sharp edges, fall from heights, climb up inclines, play tennis or tug-of-war and so on. There is a world of space and spatial reality which is a common reference point for us all. Therefore, instead of assuming that space is one of dualistic incomprehension, Merleau-Ponty announces that it is one of inter-pretative potency.

We must therefore recognize as an ultimate fact this open and in-definite power of giving significance – that is, both of apprehending and conveying a meaning – by which man transcends himself towards a new form of behaviour, or towards other people, or towards his own thought, through his body and his speech.[33]

'This open and indefinite power of giving significance' lies behind the message, lies behind even the faculties for emitting messages, the body and speech organs:

It is, however, quite clear that constituted speech, as it operates in daily life, assumes that the decisive step of expression has been taken. Our view of man will remain superficial so long as we fail to go back to that origin, so long as we fail to find, beneath the chatter of words, the primordial silence, and as long as we do not describe the action which breaks this silence. The spoken word is a gesture, and its meaning, a world.[34]

Merleau-Ponty makes, then, a radical distinction between the gesture, the expression and the 'primordial silence' which lies behind it. This means that, for him, the classifying of signs which leaves out of account the principle or ability which produces them, arranges them, counterpoints them or mutates them through grids of intention can never be more than superficial:

> Behaviour creates meanings which are transcendent in relation to the anatomical apparatus, and yet immanent to the behaviour as such, since it communicates itself and is understood. It is impossible to draw up an inventory of this irrational power which creates meanings and conveys them.[35]

The analogy with the central insight of Chomsky is striking. Even as early as his celebrated review of Skinner's *Verbal Behaviour* Chomsky had written: 'The fact that all normal children acquire essentially comparable grammars of great complexity with remarkable rapidity suggests that human beings are somehow specially designed to do this, with data-handling or 'hypothesis-formulating' ability of unknown character and complexity.'[36] In advancing his celebrated hypothesis of linguistic 'creativity' Chomsky has in fact been working at a specific problem within the area sketched out by Merleau-Ponty in 1945. The distinction, vital to Merleau-Ponty, between the innate means we have of creating significance and the actual resultant signs has its counterpart in the distinction, vital to Chomsky, between the processing 'creativity' we are born with, and the actual verbal counters we are given to play with and which we make our conceptual structures process for us. The irreducibility of meaning to sign is common to both thinkers.

The space in which we interpret the bodily expression of the Other then, is, for Merleau-Ponty, not inert but polysemically charged. There is an *ability* to construct and to interpret meaning, and this ability selects *one* contour as significant from an infinity of contours. Just as, for Chomsky, surface structures arrive for our inspection after a vast process of transformational change from deep structures, so the bodily sign arrives, for Merleau-Ponty, as a highly sophisticated product of intentional transformations which emanate, ultimately, from the 'primordial silence'. In this rapid and preliminary shorthand we can relate deep structure to primordial silence, transformations to intentional constructs and surface structures to gestural activity. What both thinkers would no doubt agree on is that the problem, even if more adequately posed in these terms than in previous terms, is still as far from solution as it ever was.

The failure of phenomenology is the failure to examine bodily expressivity in a historical context. It was always the pride of phenomenology that its abstraction guaranteed its purity and, as time went on, this abstraction proved its undoing. Out of a historical context, human expressive use of the body is not capable of analysis. (Once again, we see, from a new angle, why kinesics is also doomed.)

One way round this dilemma of facelessness has been devised by Erving Goffman. In *The Presentation of Self in Everyday Life*, for instance, he draws upon observations made in a specific community (that of the Shetland islanders) in order to build up descriptive categories which are more generally useful in describing the 'theatrical' or 'dramaturgical' uses of the embodied self in everyday life.

But in this early work, and ever more so in his later work, there is a hasty, almost immediate departure from the individual case, in order to arrive at the generally valid descriptive category, and no individual instance is useful for longer than it takes to assign it its job in supporting the larger analytic structure.

Neither are the descriptive categories based on individual examples from any one culture. Goffman illustrates his often racy argument from a variety of observed sources, from different cultures, from literature, contemporary American life, from jokes, in fact from anywhere.

The resulting theoretical assertions are therefore a bit *ad hoc*, a bit ramshackle. Deprived of the intelligence and humour of Goffman himself, they would subside back into the individual elements from which they were constructed. The urgency of extrapolation from individual to category is too great. The individual is simply lost in the category, as Jonah was swallowed by the whale.

The sociology of interpersonal behaviour thus falls into a trap exactly and inversely corresponding to that in which phenomenology was seen to fall. For sociology is committed to classification, to categorization, to generalization. What else could it do? Without transforming individual units of evidence into what are claimed to be generally valid categories, sociology would obviously have lost its *raison d'être*. Goffman's descriptive categories are in fact ideal abstractions which reflect a typical, recurrent or explanatory form of *rationality*.

The great theorist of the sociological study of the rationality of groups is of course Weber. He seems to accept that working at the level of the group is inevitable, and draws out the epistemological consequences explicitly.

Carefully constructed 'ideal types' offer highly *probable* evidence about lived meaning, and this evidence can be sifted by later analysts.* Weber fully accepted the implications, distasteful as they are, of the total relativity of meaning, and set about his work in a flawed and scientifically 'fallen' world.†

He accepts that the intellectual presuppositions of the time, as well as the angle of incidence chosen for the study of the materials, and the principle of selection of evidence (by which principle it is decided *a priori* which phenomena are relevant to the study and which are not) – all these necessarily impose a certain sort of meaning upon the research before it is even begun.[37] The work of

---

*The evidence can of course be denied on empirical grounds. Kurt Samuelsson, in *Religion and Economic Action*, 1957) trans. E. G. French, Stockholm: Scandinavian University Books, 1962) has shown that every intuitive jump that Weber took in writing his celebrated *The Protestant Ethic and the Spirit of Capitalism* was partly or wholly invalid. This would not have dismayed Weber, who could have predicted as much. But there is a pleasant irony in the fact that Samuelsson also shows that all the critics who have pulled Weber's 'ideal types' of the economic and religious individual to pieces have themselves been grossly misled in their use of evidence and in their own conclusions. These critics were not aware that their own work was doomed to the same failure as Weber's, that their own 'ideal types' were just as wrong, as hunches, as Weber's had been. But at least Weber was conscious that his results were only, could only ever be, plausible hypotheses. The Weberian methodological conundrum is Socratic, ineluctable. He who laughs last laughs longest. There is a further irony in considering the critic who will one day, no doubt, show Samuelsson's own theoretical conjectures to be intuitively misled. This is one of the innocent pleasures of relativism.

† On the whole question of the nature and scope of the 'ideal types' see Raymond Aron's essay on Weber in *Main Currents in Sociological Thought 2* (Penguin Books, 1970), pp. 202ff. Aron gives the hierarchy of the 'ideal types' (a matter not easy to clarify) at pp. 208–10. His essay is throughout a model of elegance and precision. Aron himself, probably the leading historian of sociology in the world, writes: 'To me, Max Weber is the greatest of the sociologists; I would even say that he is *the* sociologist' (p. 250). Food for thought for 'objectivity'.

T. S. Kuhn and Michael Polanyi has recently spelled this argument out even more explicitly.

At the level of the group, therefore, just as much as at the level of the individual observed case, interpretation is always hypothetical:

> Every interpretation attempts to attain clarity and certainty, but no matter how clear an interpretation as such appears to be from the point of view of meaning, it cannot on this account alone claim to be the causally valid interpretation. On this level it must remain only a peculiarly plausible hypothesis.[38]

Not only must it remain 'only a peculiarly plausible hypothesis' but it carries with it both a necessary impoverishment and a necessary falsification. Impoverishment:

> As in the case of every generalizing science, the abstract character of the concepts of sociology is responsible for the fact that, compared with actual historical reality, they are relatively lacking in fullness of concrete content.[39]

Again:

> The more sharply and precisely the ideal type has been constructed, thus the more abstract and unrealistic in this sense it is, the better it is able to perform its methodological functions in formulating the clarification of terminology, and in the formulation of classifications, and of hypotheses.[40]

The construction of ideal types carries with it too the partial falsification of any given historical phenomenon:

> For example, the same historical phenomenon may be in one aspect 'feudal', in another 'patrimonial', in another 'bureaucratic' and in still another 'charismatic'. In order to give a precise meaning to these terms, it is necessary for the sociologist to formulate pure ideal types of the corresponding forms of action which in each case involve the highest possible degree of logical integration by virtue of their complete adequacy on the level of meaning. But precisely because this is true, it is probably seldom if ever that a real phenomenon can be found which corresponds exactly to one of these ideally constructed pure types.[41]

Weber is quite conscious about the thorny nature of the dilemma. As soon as one moves from observing the individual case to classing that case in a hierarchy of rational or historical types, the individual expression is suppressed and his intentional meaning lost. But if one stays at the level of describing individual expression, all significant categorization becomes impossible. One is torn between two different sorts of respect – respect for the evidence and respect for ordered and coherent explanation.

It would seem as if we are no nearer a solution. *It is the individual expression, in a given historical place, which creates meaning.* The phenomenology of gesture concentrates on the first and ignores the second, while the sociology of gesture concentrates on the second and ignores the first.

With regard to the meaning of bodily expressivity, both phenomenology and sociology are partially falsifying methods of inquiry, carrying with them specific kinds of distortion. John O'Neill's concept of a 'reflexive sociology', a sociology which pays equal attention to individual expression, historical nexus and cultural–philosophical awareness, seems to indicate a possible new egress from this dilemma. O'Neill's *Sociology as a Skin-Trade* is also dated 1972, and is as much the beginning of a new direction of inquiry as the Hinde collection is the end of an old one. O'Neill is fully aware that the problem of meaning does not lie behind us, or even around us: it still lies well ahead of us. (See his contribution to this volume, p. 291.)

If Merleau-Ponty and Chomsky are right, and there is a divide between expressive ability and any given act of expression, then our problem becomes that of attributing a specific meaning to a moment of passage, of according a certain interpretation to a point on an arc of preliminary and successive movements.

It looks at first rather like Zeno's paradox of Achilles and the Tortoise. But however impossible it may look in theory to catch up with meaning, we do in fact do so. The Pythagorean doctrine of discrete finite units is not unlike Birdwhistell's theory of kines and kinemes. But by following up our first step with others, we do eventually overtake the tortoise.

In our concern for meaning, however, it is of the first importance not to fall into some kind of servitude to the Word, the Logos and all the assumptions which go with classification along purely linguistic lines. Interpretation of the body must be *sui generis*. It is not by a theory of a finite amount of discrete quasi-linguistic basic elements that meaning can be overtaken. We need new principles of interpretation.

First, it is fatal to ignore the fact that each communication is *specific*. I have mentioned, in my recent book, Jan Palach.[42] He carried out an act which had a personal, individual, subjective meaning. But his act was specific – we do not need a class, or an 'ideal type', of Palachs, in order to understand his bodily expression. On the contrary – the signified lies behind Palach – it is the specific event of the Russian invasion of Prague. The specific quality of Palach's act is what is essential to its meaning. Its reference is not to a vast collection of other people who might do the same thing – it is to the political situation which brought it about.

Secondly, we have to study individual expression in the world, not in the bereft sense of Heidegger's *Das Man* or Sartre's and Merleau-Ponty's *Autrui*, but acting in a specific *historical and ethical context*. The concept of context must be radically deepened if we are to escape the Pythagoreans. It is from a specific *historical and ethical* context that the individual derives the expressive possibilities of his body.

Therefore we cannot examine bodily expressivity with our eyes alone. The exact inverse of the Birdwhistell procedure is the right one: erudition, knowledge, historical grasp has to be present.

The eyes see. The brain seizes:

I have seen many curiosities; not the least of them I reckon Coleridge, the Kantian metaphysician and quondam Lake poet . . . Figure a fat, flabby, incurvated personage, at once short, rotund, and relaxed, with a watery mouth, a snuffy nose, a pair of strange brown, timid, yet earnest-looking eyes, a high tapering brow, and a great bush of grey hair; and you have some faint idea of Coleridge. He is a good kind soul, full of religion and affection and poetry and animal magnetism. His cardinal sin is that he wants *will*. He has no resolution. He shrinks from pain or labour in any of its shapes. His very attitude bespeaks this. He never straightens his knee-joints. He stoops with his fat, ill-shapen shoulders, and in walking he does not tread, but shoves and slides.[43]

This description comes from a letter of Thomas Carlyle to his brother John, dated 24 June 1824.

A quarter of a century later, when writing his *Life of John Sterling*, Carlyle gives us a full-length portrait of the man who had so impressed him in youth. Now, his cultural 'placing' of the poet is explicit:

A heavy-laden, high-aspiring and surely much-suffering man. His voice, naturally soft and good, had contracted itself into a plaintive snuffle and sing-song; he spoke as if preaching – you would have said, preaching earnestly and also hopelessly of the weightiest things. I still recollect his 'object' and 'subject', terms of continual recurrence in the Kantean province; and how he sang and snuffled them into 'om-m-mject' and 'sum-m-mject', with a kind of solemn shake or quaver, as he rolled along. No talk, in his century or in any other, could be more surprising . . .

He began anywhere: you put some question to him, made some suggestive observation: instead of answering this, or decidedly setting out towards answer of it, he would accumulate formidable apparatus, logical swim-bladders, transcendental life-preservers and other pre-cautionary and vehiculatory gear, for setting out; perhaps did at last get under way – but was swiftly solicited, turned aside by the glance of some radiant new game on this hand or that, into new courses; and ever into new; and before long into all the Universe, where it was uncertain what game you would catch, or whether any.[44]

It is then, according to Carlyle, the Kantian philosophy which has wreaked this damage. Coleridge's entire physical presence and manner is expressive of inward diremption:

I have heard Coleridge talk, with musical energy, two stricken hours, his face radiant and moist, and communicate no meaning whatsoever to any individual of his hearers – certain of whom, I for one, still kept eagerly listening in hope; the most had long before given up, and formed (if the room were large enough) secondary humming groups of their own . . . Glorious islets, too, I have seen rise out of the haze; but they were few, and soon swallowed in the general element again. Balmy sunny islets, islets of the blest and the intelligible – on which occasions those secondary humming groups would all cease humming, and hang breathless upon the eloquent words; till once your islet got wrapped in the mist again, and they would recommence humming.[45]

While his presence in space, his movement, his speech all contri-bute powerfully to an image of intense inwardness, there is in these, properly speaking, no communicative intent. Coleridge communicates, but not through the endless stream of words he utters. His communication is devastating, worrying, upsetting, even frightening in its unconsciousness of itself:

One right peal of concrete laughter at convicted flesh-and-blood absurdity, one burst of noble indignation at some injustice or depravity, rubbing elbows with us on this solid earth, how strange would it have been in that Kantean haze-world, and how infinitely cheering amid its vacant air-castles and dim-melting ghosts and shadows! None such ever came. His life had been an abstract thinking and dreaming, idealistic, passed amid the ghosts of defunct bodies and of unborn ones. The moaning sing-song of that theosophico-metaphysical monotony left on you, at last, a very dreary feeling.[46]

This mental and moral indecisiveness is given physical expression in Coleridge's walk. Once again, Carlyle returns to his rolling, shambling, bumbling, fumbling manner of walking, and emphasizes a new point, a certain tendency of Coleridge's to corkscrew his way round the garden:

The whole figure and air, good and amiable otherwise, might be called flabby and irresolute; expressive of weakness under possibility of strength. He hung loosely on his limbs, with knees bent, and stooping attitude; in walking, he rather shuffled than decisively stept; and a lady once remarked, he could never fix which side of the garden walk would suit him best, but continually shifted in corkscrew fashion, and kept trying both.[47]

Carlyle has described the garden 'on the brow of Highgate Hill', in some detail, and it is obviously a large one. 'The garden walk' may be taken to mean the path round the lawns and flower-beds. The remarkable thing about Coleridge's gait is that he continually shifts from one side of the walk to the other. Supposing him to be accompanied by a respectful listener, this means that he would continually have shifted from the right to the left of his companion, on the garden walk, and during the progress of the conversation.

There is a thinker, almost an exact contemporary of Coleridge, who shares with Coleridge the same gait, the corkscrew motion. It is worth while inquiring what meaning we can attribute to this case of movement, which we observe in the narrow streets of nineteenth-century Copenhagen:

I once walked through a whole street with him while he explained how one can make psychological studies by so putting oneself *en rapport* to passers-by. As he explained his theory he put it into practice with almost everybody we met. There was no one on whom his glance did not make an obvious impression . . .

The occasion of these experiments was this. I was walking before him deep in thought, and had not heard him call me, nor noticed that he tapped me on the shoulder. When finally I did notice, he said that it was wrong to be so immersed in oneself, and not make the observations one might in so rich a field. To show me his method he dragged me up and down several streets, and surprised me by his talent for psychological experiment. He was always interesting to accompany, but there was one drawback. His movements were so irregular because of his crooked figure that you could never walk straight when he was with you. You were successively pushed in towards the houses and cellar-holes, and out towards the gutter. And when he gesticulated with his arm and his Spanish cane, walking became still more difficult. You had from time to time to get round the other side of him to keep your place![48]

This is Hans Brøchner's account of a walk in the streets of Copenhagen with Søren Kierkegaard. (We can rule out at once the talk about the 'crooked figure' – all Danish contemporaries are obsessed with this.) What is the actual meaning of Kierkegaard's to-ing and fro-ing across the pavement?

Unlike Coleridge's agonized inability to 'fix which side of the garden walk would suit him best' Kierkegaard's corkscrewing is not the result of indecisiveness. It is a ploy, consciously devised, for holding Brøchner's attention and for intercepting, and coming into momentary contact with, every passer-by. The whole object of the exercise being to show that one can come into contact with all and sundry if one does but put one's mind to it, Kierkegaard decisively uses the whole street as his field, in a kind of nineteenth-century 'street-theatre'. He deploys his presence across it in the most striking way possible.

'In towards the houses and cellar-holes, and out towards the gutter.' The corkscrew is a direct indication of decisive, conscious activity. This activity is directed towards a goal, and this goal is actually achieved.

It seems to me that the *inverse* meaning of Coleridge's deportment can be found in Kierkegaard's, since Kierkegaard spent his whole life in opposing the Kantian–Hegelian indecisiveness and in urging that the individual's decision had to be taken, in fear and trembling, in a frightful intersection of time and eternity which he called 'the Instant'.

Since Kierkegaard detests all abstraction, and especially abstraction from ethical decisiveness, it need not surprise us that Kierkegaard's twisting motion in the street should have an active intention behind it, while Coleridge's corkscrewing is an index of inner evasiveness and uncertainty, corresponding to no ethical project whatsoever.

For we have to note that Kierkegaard is trying to *show* Brøchner something, trying to prove what can be *done* by active intervention in the world. Kierkegaard's corkscrewing is an active *praxis* with a certain aim in view. Thus even in their walk, Kantian Coleridge and anti-Kantian Kierkegaard illustrate their relationship to a certain philosophical and cultural context, and illustrate it with their own persons in space.

The body expressivity of Coleridge and Kierkegaard has not got, of course, an explicit *content*. Their bodily expression is *diacritically* significant (i.e. what is asserted stands out against what is not the case, or what is the case throws into relief what is denied). Nevertheless, there is a major distinction to be made. Coleridge's body expression is, in Husserl's terms, an *index*, but Kierkegaard's body-expression is, in Husserl's terms, a *sign*. His activity involves an 'intent to put certain "thoughts" on record expressively'. It belongs to the realm of communication which has an intention behind it, it is quasi-speech. Because it involves an intention to communicate an idea, and because it is an embodied intention to communicate, I call it a *ploy-sign*.

Just because body-expressivity in its use as ploy-sign can have no *specific meaning* attached to it, but receives its entire power from its diacritical relationship to the historical and political conditions prevailing at the time, it might be useful to adduce here a very modern example. Here is Ludwig Wittgenstein using the same ploy-sign as Kierkegaard – but of course, the moment being 1939, the meaning to be ascribed is wholly different:

In 1939 Wittgenstein used to call at my rooms frequently to get me to accompany him on walks. These were usually on Midsummer Common and beyond, along the river. He usually brought bread or sugar to feed the horses on the Common. A walk with Wittgenstein was very exhausting. Whatever we talked about, he turned his mind to it with great seriousness and intensity, and it was a formidable strain on me to keep up with his thoughts. He would walk in spurts, sometimes coming to a stop while he made some emphatic remark and looking into my eyes with his piercing gaze. Then he would walk rapidly for a few yards, then slow down, then speed up or come to a halt, and so on. And this uncertain ambulation was conjoined with the most exacting conversation! The freshness and depth of Wittgenstein's thinking, no matter what the topic, was highly demanding of his companion. His remarks were never *commonplace*.[49]

This is Norman Malcolm's famous account of a walk with Wittgenstein. Malcolm emphasizes the impending political catastrophe again and again – and suggests several times how worried Wittgenstein himself was by the German threat. When Malcolm makes what Wittgenstein considers an inapposite remark, Wittgenstein becomes 'extremely angry'. During 1939, Wittgenstein exploded more and more often, he was tense, and often rude.

But what is the meaning of the walk itself? It is obviously a ploy-sign. Malcolm emphasizes many times how critical, both of himself and of others, Wittgenstein was in matters of applied political and moral discussion. Wittgenstein intended to keep his interlocutor in a state of vigilant and self-critical attentiveness.

And so the comparison with Kierkegaard's ploy-sign makes itself. The gait is uncannily like Kierkegaard's and the intention, obviously, the same: to intersperse and punctuate thought by motion, such that thought does not get lost in the easy successivity of an evening stroll. Regular gait would have allowed thought to be produced at regular intervals, and speech to be uttered at a regular speed. Wittgenstein's abrupt, jerky manner, his slowing-down and speeding-up, was as much of a ploy as Kierkegaard's zigzagging. The interlocutor has to follow, argue, think *and* walk. Decisiveness is the essence of the thing in both cases. And whereas Coleridge was content to be accompanied by a passive disciple, and liked nothing better, as Carlyle puts it, 'than to have an intelligent, or failing that, even a silent and patient human listener', both Kierkegaard and Wittgenstein force the companion of the walk into rapid mental and physical participation in the existential situation. 'A silent or a patient human listener' would have angered both. Thought, for both Kierkegaard and for Wittgenstein, involved activity, involved participation in the world, involved *decision*. The ploy-sign now stands well clear of the index – and Husserl's original warning has been circumvented.

I think it is important to stress this. Husserl was assuming that the expressive action of the body would merely *accompany* or *supplement* speech, words, which themselves were signs in the sense that they corresponded to a mental intention, which in issuing them had been trying to transfer intellection, had been trying 'to put certain "thoughts" on record expressively'. It just never occurred to Husserl that anyone might positively *use* his body in order to express an idea or to cause the re-evaluation of a concept. His mind was literal, his aim exclusive and his concept of meaning restricted.

But Husserl was right when he predicted disaster for the inquiry into the empathetic reconstruction of the *index*, as Coleridge's behaviour clearly shows. An index is indeed only capable of an *ad hoc* interpretation, however culturally expert, the index being unaccompanied by the intention to communicate something.

Where Husserl shows most clearly the logocentric prejudice of his period is in his assumption that body expression would merely accompany, shadow forth, intimate or hint at a process of thought in the Other which was primarily verbal–conceptual. When the body is deployed as a sign, it is as meaningful and as translatable as any correctly formed logocentric proposition whatever.

And it is significant that we have only broken out of Husserl's stranglehold by discovering Kierkegaard's *praxis* of the body. By deploying his body in such a way that a re-orientation of thought was effected, he substituted a Husserlian sign for a Husserlian index, and thus freed us from a conceptual impasse. But this brings up the explicit question of what communication was for Kierkegaard.

Our conclusions then are as follows:

There is no expressive body activity which is not expressed by a body in particular.

But no expressive body activity can be significant without a specific historical and ethical context.

Context gives a specific content (meaning) to the expressive body activity, but this specific meaning is only diacritically significant: in different historical and ethical contexts, the specific content (meaning) will be different.

But similar ploy-signs, even in widely varying contexts, all refer to the Husserlian area of the *sign*: they belong to the area of an 'attempt to put certain "thoughts" on record expressively', their aim is to make aware and they therefore have an equal status with verbal speech.

The meaningfulness of body expressivity is a function of its deliberate intention to force the observer to notice something about the world, or to provoke him to intervene in it in some significant way.

Ploy-signs are therefore not primarily informational, mere units to be classified in order that we may think we know more about signs: their reference is the other way, 180 degrees in the other direction. They demand that the observer observe himself.

The study of the body as medium of expression is therefore adequate only when it studies meaningful historical, political or ethical signs, which are addressed to the observer as either epistemologically or ethically imperative, or both. The sign reaches out towards the observer not content to refer back to the conditions which produced it.

And this opens up the most important, the most vitally necessary subjective research for our time: the vast *terra australis incognita* of indirect communication.

It is the most vitally necessary research because, as we break free from the spell of the time-machine in 1973, the somacentric imperative will make more and more urgent demands upon our rationality every day.

1. Charles Darwin, *The Expression of the Emotions in Man and Animals*, (1872); republished 1965, (ed. Francis Darwin), University of Chicago Press, London and Chicago, pp. 241–2.
2. ibid., p. 186.
3. ibid., pp. 186 and 190.
4. ibid., p. 194.
5. ibid., p. 195.
6. *Encyclopedia Britannica* (1964), Article: 'Behaviourism'.
7. R. A. Hinde, ed., *Non-Verbal Communication*, Cambridge University Press, 1972, p. 233.
8. Ray L. Birdwhistell, *Kinesics and Context: Essays on Body-Motion Communication*, Allen Lane The Penguin Press, 1971; University of Pennsylvania Press, Philadelphia, 1971, p. 235.
9. Julia Kristeva, 'Le Geste: pratique ou communication?', *Semiotike: Recherches pour une Sémanalyse*, Editions du Seuil, Paris, 1969, Section 2, pp. 100ff, especially pp. 103 and 106.
10. Birdwhistell, op. cit., p. 224.

11. ibid., p. 227.
12. Søren Kierkegaard, *Concluding Unscientific Postscript*, trans. D. Swenson and W. Lowrie, Princeton University Press, Princeton, N.J., 1941, pp. 291–2.
13. Edmund Husserl, *Logical Investigations: Investigation 1*, trans. J. N. Findlay, Routledge & Kegan Paul, 1970, p. 275.
14. Edmund Husserl, *Cartesian Meditations*, trans. Dorion Cairns, Nijhoff, The Hague, 1969, Fifth Meditation, Para. 50–end. See on this Paul Ricoeur, *Husserl: An Analysis of his Phenomenology*, Northwestern University Press, Evanston, Ill., 1967, Ch. 5 passim.
15. Martin Heidegger, *Being and Time*, trans. J. Macquarrie and E. Robinson, Student Christian Movement Press, 1962, p. 164.
16. Alfred Schutz, *The Phenomenology of the Social World*, Heinemann, 1972, p. 106.
17. ibid., p. 165.
18. ibid., p. 165. At pp. 239–42 Schutz has to agree finally to the hard conditions of the 'ideal types'.
19. ibid., p. 103.
20. Jean-Paul Sartre, *Being and Nothingness*, trans. H. Barnes, Methuen 1957, p. 308.
21. ibid., p. 255.
22. ibid., p. 256
23. ibid., p. 257.
24. ibid., p. 364.
25. ibid., p. 429.
26. ibid., Part 3, Ch. 3.
27. Jean-Paul Sartre, *Critique de la raison dialectique*, Gallimard, Paris, 1960, pp. 450–51, 455 are examples.
28. Maurice Merleau-Ponty, *The Structure of Behaviour*, trans. A. L. Fisher, Methuen, 1965, p. 222.
29. Maurice Merleau-Ponty, *Phenomenology of Perception*, trans. Colin Smith, Routledge & Kegan Paul, 1962, p. 185.
30. ibid., p. 185.
31. ibid., p. 186.
32. ibid., p. 185.
33. ibid., p. 194.
34. ibid., p. 184.
35. ibid., p. 189.
36. Noam Chomsky, 'A Review of B. F. Skinner's *Verbal Behaviour*', reprinted in *The Structure of Language*, ed. J. A. Fodor and J. J. Katz, Prentice-Hall, Englewood Cliffs, N.J., 1964, p. 577. See also Chomsky, *Cartesian Linguistics*, passim.
37. See '"Objectivity" in Social Science and Social Policy', in *The Methodology of the Social Sciences*, trans. and ed. E. A. Shils and H. A. Finch, Free Press, Glencoe, Ill., 1949, pp. 80–82, 90, 92–4, 97, 110
38. Max Weber, *The Theory of Social and Economic Organization*, trans. A. R. Henderson and Talcott Parsons, William Hodge, Edinburgh, 1947, p. 87.

39. ibid., p. 99.
40. ibid., p. 101.
41. ibid., p. 100.
42. *Towards Deep Subjectivity*, Allen Lane The Penguin Press, 1972 and Harper & Row, New York, 1973.
43. Thomas Carlyle, letter to his brother John dated 24 June 1824, in *Carlyle: Selected Works*, ed. J. Symons, Reynard Library, Hart-Davis, 1955, p. 712.
44. Carlyle, 'The Life of John Sterling', in Symons, ed., op. cit., pp. 453 and 454.
45. ibid., p. 454 and p. 455.
46. ibid., p. 455.
47. ibid., pp. 452–3.
48. 'Hans Brøchner's recollections of Kierkegaard', in *Glimpses and Impressions of Kierkegaard*, selected and trans. T. H. Croxall, James Nisbet, Welwyn, 1959, pp. 12–13.
49. Norman Malcolm, *Ludwig Wittgenstein: A Memoir*, Oxford University Press, 1958, p. 31.

A Comment by Professor R. A. Hinde (editor of *Non-Verbal Communication*), **and a short reply by Dr Poole**

In his essay Dr Poole makes a number of remarks about *Non-Verbal Communication* (*N-V.C.*), a collection of essays that I was recently privileged to edit. I am grateful to the Editors of the present volume for inviting me, and Dr Poole for permitting me, to make some comments.

Those involved in the production of *N-V.C.* held the view that, in the study of non-verbal communication, there are a variety of questions to be asked and this makes a diversity of approaches essential. The biologists were concerned with the questions of the ontogenetic development and immediate causation of expressive movements and of responsiveness to them, and where relevant with related evolutionary and functional questions. Those interested in principles of communication *per se* or language were concerned with the relation of non-verbal communication to their own areas of interest. Anthropologists emphasized the diversity, richness, subtlety and especially the culture-dependence of non-verbal communication in human societies. Chapters on non-verbal communication in Western art and in the theatre were included. None of the authors thought of his contribution as the only way to ultimate understanding: each believed in the importance of groping towards a synthesis. For this reason they met many times, attempting so far as possible to understand each other's approaches. No small part of their endeavours was directed towards understanding the questions others were asking, and to defining the interrelations between those questions.

In these respects they differed from Dr Poole. He is interested in only one question, the problem of 'meaning', and regards everything else as irrelevant. Furthermore what he means by 'meaning', individualistic and intersubjective, is not necessarily the same as other people mean. His view of 'meaning' may be a proper one, and the questions he is asking may be important, but he does not help his enterprise by dismissing all other questions as trivial. He criticizes *N-V.C.* because, he alleges, on nearly every page it is implicitly assumed that human 'expressivity' is 'meaningful' in so far as it is related to the expressive gestures of lower forms, or to cultural structures, or in so far as it can be formalized in terms of information theory. Each of these areas are foci of interest in some parts of *N-V.C.*, but none of the contributors would consider human 'expressivity' meaningful *only* in so far as it relates to one or all of them.

It is perhaps because of his singlemindedness that Dr Poole's critique of *N-V.C.* so often gives the impression that he has not read it. In emphasizing his view that *N-V.C.* represents little advance over Darwin's book published a century earlier, he omitted to notice that the contributors came together in part just because the study of expressive movements was neglected for so long after 1872 and only recently became a matter of interest for workers with diverse backgrounds. In writing 'There is no suggestion anywhere in the book that human expressivity might be important as a subject of inquiry in its own right' he cannot have noticed that over half the book is concerned with our own species. He must have skipped over the chapters by Lyons and MacKay, not to mention the other references to the problem, to be able to write 'the problem of meaning seems to have been abrogated altogether' – though admittedly none of the authors in *N-V.C.* saw the problem in quite the same way as he does. His complaint that ethical and political contexts are not considered could suggest that he did not read the chapters by Leach and Gombrich, and he seems to have missed MacKay's discussion of intentionality. Of course I am not suggesting that *N-V.C.* came anywhere near the last word on any of these matters, but it contains serious discussion which it would behove one genuinely seeking understanding to attempt to relate to his own views rather than to subject it to dismissal.

Again, it is difficult to see why Dr Poole complains so much that differences between animal and man are neglected, when they are discussed in some detail by MacKay, Lyons and Leach as well as in editorial contributions, and are assumed by other contributors. Perhaps a clue to Poole's critique here comes from a few words suggesting that he has been reading Desmond Morris. He should be assured that, for most biologists, the most important result of their training is an awareness of species differences, a sense of humility in the face of the diversity of nature, and a consciousness that generalizations must be coupled with reservations. *Of course* there are many ways in which human behaviour and experience is unique: attempts to specify in precisely what respects they differ from those of animals are more likely to lead to increased understanding of both animal and man than are Dr Poole's *ex cathedra* statements on this issue.

But in his generalizations about a book whose authors come from such diverse disciplines perhaps Dr Poole is unwittingly paying it a compliment: I would like to think that he lumps the authors together not merely because he disagrees with all of them, but because the volume did achieve some degree of synthesis.

Roger Poole has contributed the following reply:

Dialogue de sourds.

R. A. Hinde

The Comparative Study of Non-Verbal Communication

This volume is concerned primarily with the human body as a medium of expression. My role is to introduce a comparative element – to discuss some of the material now available concerning expressive movements in animals. In attempting to understand our own behaviour it is often profitable to look also at that of sub-human forms, since we can study issues unclouded by the complexity of the human case. This is perhaps especially the case in the study of expressive movements: in man, as Dr Crystal shows in this volume (p. 162), non-verbal communication and verbal communication are closely intertwined, and lower forms provide us with an opportunity to study the former without the latter. Of course this does not mean that slick and superficial parallels between animal and man, of the type generated by a number of popular writers in recent years, are in order. The study of animal behaviour can help the understanding of our own only in certain limited ways, but used appropriately and with discipline it can be a powerful tool. In this lecture I shall not attempt a review of animal expressive movements, but shall take up a few issues which bear particularly on the human case. In doing so, it will be apparent that I am indebted in many ways to the contributors to a recent volume (1972) which I had the privilege to edit, the product of a study group sponsored by the Royal Society. I am also grateful for Jonathan Benthall's (1972) provocative article in *Studio International*, which announced this programme at the I.C.A. (see above, p. 5), since over some issues it has provided me with something to tilt at.

Perhaps I should start with a few facts. In practically every animal species it is necessary for the behaviour of each individual to influence and be influenced by the behaviour of others. The signals involved are diverse. The behaviour of one individual may be affected by the mere presence of another. Or he may come to respond to movements that the former makes in the course of his day-to-day business as indicators of what he is likely to do next. As a young research worker I learned that when the little finger of my head of department started to tap on his desk, the movement

Figure 1. Display of an adult male robin in a territorial encounter.

would soon spread through his other fingers to his hand and whole arm, and that it was better for me to leave the room before the pounding on the desk stage was reached. But of special interest in the present context are the signals which have been evolved specifically because of their effectiveness in influencing the behaviour of others. These signals may be visual, auditory, tactile or olfactory, or they may involve sensory modalities that we humans do not possess.

Let me give just three examples. The robin (*Erithacus rubecula*), when it encounters an intruder on its territory, approaches and displays its red breast (Figure 1). It turns its body so that its breast is orientated towards its rival. The red breast is a signal, adapted in evolution as a threat (Lack, 1939). It is conspicuous and distinctive, and is responded to appropriately by other members of the species.

Many male birds, when on their territories, sing a characteristic song which has the effects of warning off other males which approach and of attracting unmated females. That of the chaffinch is shown in Figure 2: this is a sound spectrogram, which shows how the frequencies of the notes in the song change with time (Thorpe, 1961).

When a female rhesus monkey becomes sexually receptive, her vagina produces a secretion whose smell greatly enhances her attractiveness to males. The secretion consists of a simple mixture of fatty acids, and seems to be similar in a number of other primates (Michael and Saayman, 1968; Michael and Keverne, 1968; Herbert and Trimble, 1967).

These are the sort of facts, and I shall present more later, which form the background to what I am going to say. Now let us turn to some specific issues, in each of which I shall try to show how data from lower forms aid our understanding of expressive movements in man. The first of these concerns the continuum of meaning between the terms 'expression' and 'communication'. Jonathan Benthall's article in *Studio International* seemed to me to slide from one to the other, thereby fudging some important issues. These concern three distinctions, none absolute but each marking the extremes of continua important in the present context.

The first distinction is the obvious one between behaviour that does and does not affect the internal state or behaviour of another individual. Behaviour may be expressive but yet not communicative in the sense that it does not affect the behaviour of others. Of course an individual may learn to interpret or respond to behaviour which previously had been merely expressive, as I learned to respond to my professor's fingers. But while all expressive behaviour is perhaps *potentially* communicative in this broad sense, it need not be actually so. Conversely behaviour that is communicative need not be expressive in any important sense. The explorer, alone in his tent, may become anxious when he ceases to hear his companion outside: his companion's movements, though trivial, had thus previously been affecting his behaviour. And as Benthall points out, words can too easily be communicative with a minimum of expressive content.

The second distinction is between movements *intended* to affect the behaviour of others and movements *not* so intended. Up to the

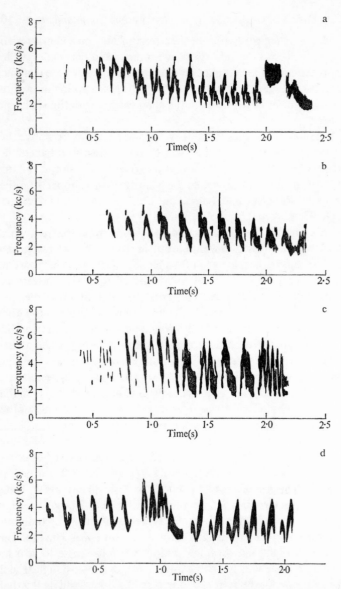

Figure 2. Chaffinch song. (a) Characteristic normal song; (b) song of an individual reared in isolation; (c) song of an individual from a group reared in isolation; (d) song produced by a bird reared in isolation, after tutoring with a rearticulated chaffinch song with the ending in the middle (after Thorpe, 1961).

1950s the problem of intentionality was sidestepped by students of animal behaviour: while they did not underestimate its importance, the problem of inferring intentionality (or for that matter any other subjective state) from behaviour seemed too daunting. However the sort of criterion that can be used is whether the effect of the sender's behaviour on the receiver is monitored by the sender, who may take additional or corrective action if the signal appears to be ineffective. This makes 'intended' equivalent to 'goal-directed', and need carry no implication one way or the other about consciousness. Thus the old man in Plate 1 may call forth feelings of humility, pity or what have you in us, but neither posture nor gestures were intended to call forth either such emotions or any behaviour that might accompany them. Similarly the mother in Plate 2 is expressing her pride and delight in her sleeping newborn baby, but is not intending to influence the behaviour of either baby or onlooker. In Plate 3, taken a few weeks later, she is using almost the same expression in an attempt to obtain a response: although they are not apparent in the still photograph, the expression was accompanied by vocalizations and movements directed towards catching the baby's attention. The chimpanzee begging in Plate 4 is attempting to influence the behaviour of the individual holding the meat: changes in the latter's behaviour will influence the form of her begging. And the rhesus monkey's grin in Plate 5 is not merely expressive of fear, but will vary in intensity and orientation with the behaviour of the potential attacker. It has been suggested (MacKay, 1972) that the term 'communication' should be limited to cases in which the behaviour of one individual is goal-directed towards influencing the behaviour of another. Whether or not one accepts the terminology, the distinction between an animal which acts merely *in such a way as* to bring about a particular event and an animal which acts *in order to* is clearly an important one; and the facts that there are intermediate cases, and that the distinction is not always easy to make (Hinde, 1972), in no way detracts from it.

The third distinction, to which I have already alluded, concerns whether or not there is evidence that the movement has been affected in evolution by selection for effectiveness as a signal. The nature of this evidence, which is often circumstantial, is referred to briefly later: it comes in part from the nature of the movement itself, in part from the context in which it appears, and in part from the study of closely related species (Cullen, 1972). But the bizarre posture used by the great tit to threaten rivals (Figure 3), accentuated by a conspicuous black ventral stripe, and represent-

Figure 3. (a) Head up threat display of great tit; (b) Head forward threat display of blue tit (from drawings by Yvette Spencer-Booth).

ing an accentuation of postures seen in related forms, is clearly an example. So too is the robin's threat posture (Figure 1) and the monkey's fear grin (Plate 5). Some biologists have limited the use of the term 'communication' to signals that appear to be adapted in this way.

Thus we have three independent distinctions – does the movement influence the behaviour of others? Is it intended to do so? Has it been adapted in evolution to that end? While behaviour that is intended or adapted to affect others is likely to do so if given appropriately, behaviour may be adapted for communication but used without intention (like the mother's smile in Plate 2) or intended but not adapted in an evolutionary sense (like a soldier's salute). Whether we limit the term 'communication' to one or more of these is perhaps not important, but the distinctions are. Before one can start to erect hypotheses about whether or not verbal language should have priority in the expression of 'meaning', and I refer here again to Benthall's article, it is clearly essential to agree first as to whether the 'meaning' is intended to be communicated, and whether the means employed are or are not common to all members of the species because they have been adapted to that end by natural selection. I might also add that a discussion of the meaning of 'meaning' could fill many pages (see e.g. Lyons, 1972).

From here on I shall be concerned with movements which do influence the behaviour of others – with communication (in a broad sense) between individuals. The next issue to be discussed concerns the role of experience in the development of signal systems. This has already been raised in this series in terms of the hoary old nature–nurture dichotomies: for example the announcement of Ted Polhemus's lecture referred to 'learned' versus 'genetically transmitted' types of bodily expression. It cannot be too strongly stated that such dichotomies are not only false but sterile (Hinde, 1968; Lehrman, 1970). In the first place all expressive movements, indeed all characters of the body itself, depend on both nature and nurture. Genes create a living being only through interaction with an environment. Indeed many genes affect development if the organism grows up in one environment but not in another, and some effects of nurture may occur if certain genes are present but not others. Nature alone or nurture alone is without issue. Thus the impossibility of separating aspects of behaviour that are genetically determined from those that are culturally determined (emphasized by Benthall, and we agree on this issue), stems not merely from the complexity of behaviour, but is basic. Patterns of behaviour are a consequence of interactions between organism and environment that start before parturition.

If we cannot divide behaviour into that which is innate or genetically determined and that which is learned, what questions can we usefully ask? The useful questions concern differences – is the difference between this pattern of behaviour and that due to a difference in genetic constitution or to a difference in experience? Does this difference in experience (or in genetic constitution) affect that pattern of behaviour?

Consider as an example the development of an expressive movement that we have already mentioned – the song of the chaffinch. The normal song is shown in Figure 2a. This song develops from a rather amorphous rambling sub-song during the bird's first spring: the sub-song becomes gradually abbreviated and the full song as it were 'crystallizes out' from it (Figure 4). If chaffinches are reared in auditory isolation from a few days of age they sing only a simple song, as shown in Figure 2b. The difference between the normal song and that of the isolates must be a conse-quence of experience. If the isolates are played recordings of chaffinch song in the autumn, the songs they produce when they come into breeding condition some months later bear a much closer resemblance to normal chaffinch song. Evidently hearing normal song is at least part of the experience necessary for the development of normal song. Since the experience occurs some months before the bird itself starts to sing, it must be stored in some way. Indeed it seems that learning must occur in two stages, the bird learning first what the song should be like and then, in its first spring, how to sing it: it is the latter which is occurring when the full song 'crystallizes out' from the sub-song. That further learning does occur during the period of song development is shown by the behaviour of birds isolated from hearing normal song since birth but kept in groups. Each such group works out a group song-pattern (Figure 2c), usually considerably more elabor-ate than that of individually isolated birds, but often quite differ-ent from normal song. The songs of all birds in a group are usually closely similar, but they differ between groups. Some of the experi-ments to which I have referred are summarized in Figure 5. Further experimental evidence is in harmony with the view that song-learning involves two stages (Stevenson, 1969; Nottebohm, 1967).

But chaffinches will not learn any song that they hear: apparently

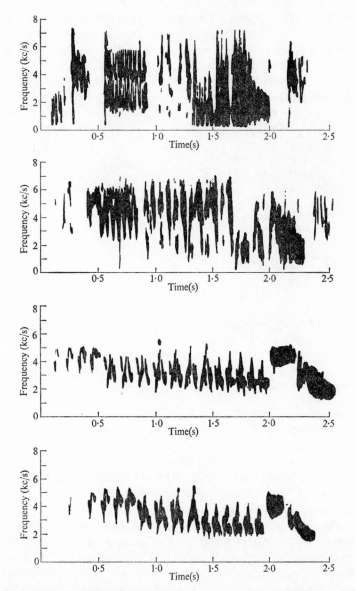

Figure 4. Stages in the development of the full song of the chaffinch (bottom) from subsong (after Thorpe, 1961).

the limitation operates through the note-structure. Thus they will learn a chaffinch song with the ending displaced to the middle (Figure 2d), which thus retains the note-structure but lacks the overall pattern of the normal song. But they will not learn the best possible representation of a chaffinch song on a chapel organ, or the song of an alien species. The difference between what a

Reared	Cage Conditions	Exposure to Normal Song	Song
Wild		———— ————	Normal
Hand reared from eight days	Isolation	–	Isolate
Hand reared from eight days	Group	– Group ————	Group isolate
Hand reared from eight days	Isolation	– Tutor ————	Nearly normal
Wild	Isolation	————	Nearly normal
Wild	Group	———— Group ————	Normal

| | | 0   Age (months)   10 | |

Figure 5. Summary of experiments on the development of song in the chaffinch (from data in Thorpe, 1961).

chaffinch will learn and what an individual of another species will learn is in part genetically determined. This brief survey indicates only some of the complexity inherent in the development of chaffinch song (see e.g. Nottebohm, 1970), but is sufficient to show that song development depends on a rather complicated interaction between the organism and its environment over a considerable span of time.

The second point about the 'learned' versus 'genetically trans-mitted' dichotomy concerns the implication that all experience acts through processes suitably described as 'learning'. This is far from the case. Experience affects development in many subtle ways, and to describe them all as learning would be to destroy the usefulness of that term. To give but one example: if rat pups are handled for a minute or two a day for a week or two in early life, the extent to which they exhibit fear when placed in a strange situation in adulthood is profoundly affected: but although their behaviour is changed the process can hardly be called learning. At any rate its characteristics are quite different from those of any of the processes normally labelled as learning, and there is evidence that its physiological basis is quite different (Levine, 1962). There is, incidentally, evidence that stimulation in infancy has similar effects in our own species.

The third point about this dichotomy concerns the implication that 'learning' is independent of the genes. Organisms do not come into the world as *tabulae rasae*, but with proclivities for learning some things but not others (Hinde and Stevenson-Hinde, 1973). This is already apparent from the chaffinch example: chaffinches might soon get into difficulties if they imitated every sound that they heard, so it is predetermined that they learn only songs with a note-structure resembling that of normal chaffinch song. In other species the restriction is imposed in a different way, the young learning only the song that the male that reared them sings.

Where does this leave us with the expressive movements used by man? To what extent are they affected by cultural differences in the environment during development? The position can be summarized thus:

1. Certain movement-patterns used as signals, while intrinsically improbable, are common to all cultures so far investigated. What Ekman (Ekman and Friesen, 1971) calls the 'primary affects' (happiness, sadness, anger, surprise, disgust and fear) are associated with similar facial expressions in various literate and preliterate cultures (see also Eibl-Eibesfeldt, 1972). Thus cultural differences in the experience of developing individuals do not affect the development of these patterns. Since many of these movement-patterns occur also in those born blind and deaf, it is also improbable that social learning plays a part in their development. Of course this does not mean that experience of the environment does not affect their development, but only that their development is so stable that it follows the same course despite wide differences in experience.

2. Similar conclusions apply at least qualitatively to certain syndromes of behaviour: for instance anger is expressed by a

particular facial expression, clenching of the fists, and stamping of the feet in at least many cultures.

3. In many of these cases not only the motor patterns themselves but the contexts in which they are used and their interpretation by others are similar between cultures, and presumably independent of social learning – for instance strange tastes elicit disgust even from very young babies. The fearful expression shown by a young child confronted by a stranger is of course in part a consequence of previous experience with familiar persons, but the fact that strangers evoke fear and its associated expressive movements, and not some other state, is not a consequence of social training. However even with basic expressive movements of this sort there may be differences between cultures in that a pattern may be used in a wider range of emotional states in some cultures than others, or it may be suppressed, or have special uses. For example, the contexts in which laughter occurs vary widely between cultures: in some it is used in mourning.

4. Similarities between cultures do not necessarily imply that movements are genetically determined independently of experience. The course of development could be due to elements of experience common to all human beings or to properties of all human beings which are themselves unrelated to communication but affect its development. To take a simple example, rapidly enlarging objects are potentially frightening to most animals as well as to man, and this could affect, in opposite ways, the development of both threat and submissive movements. Hand-clapping is widely used as an expressive movement, perhaps because the mere noise provides a reinforcement which facilitates its acquisition by the young. Miss Dian Fossey recently showed me a young wild gorilla which had learned to clap its hands – though hand-clapping is not a usual gorilla expressive movement.

5. In many cases there are marked differences between cultures in the form even of relatively simple expressive movements, and in the contexts and manner in which they are used. The diversity to be found in kissing, greeting and other ceremonies between cultures is considerable, and indicate a predominant role of cultural differences in producing the differences observed. Differences between cultures are especially likely in movements that take the place of words (e.g. yes, no), or symbolize aspects of the culture

that depend on verbal language. But even where differences appear to be marked, they may conceal similarities at a deeper level of analysis (Lévi-Strauss, 1964), or depend on common tendencies to learn in a particular context although the learning happens to have taken different courses.

What is apparently the same emotional state may be expressed in different ways in different cultures. Furthermore cultural factors may affect the extent to which emotional states elicit further emotional states – for example the extent to which we are angered by our own fear or frightened by our own anger. And to the extent that we are aware of our expressive movements, we may inhibit or dissimulate them because of their known social consequences.

We see, then, that the movements used by man for expression and communication cover the whole spectrum from those whose development in the individual is affected hardly at all by cultural differences in early experience to those whose development is closely influenced by social factors during rearing. Responsiveness to these expressive movements is likely to be more influenced by cultural factors than are the movements themselves, but has been much less studied. By analogy with subhuman forms, however, it seems likely that social experience is not necessary for appropriate responsiveness to expressions of the 'primary affects' (see above), but that social learning does play an essential role in responsiveness to their subtle nuances. Social learning is of course crucial for responsiveness to movements that are specific to particular cultures.

Returning to those movements that appear to be part of the phylogenetic heritage of the species, and develop similarly in the individual despite wide variations in experience, we may now ask whether we can say anything about their evolution. We may consider first some examples from animals.

Some movements which act as signals are in fact movements which function also in another context. For instance the normal wing-beat of the female *Aedes* mosquito attracts the male. More usually the signal movements differ from comparable movements with a secular function. Thus in certain Braconid wasps the wing-beat frequency alters when the animal is ready to mate (cited by Cullen, 1972). By comparing the display movements with other movements of the same species that have no signal function, and by comparing also the display movements of closely related species, it is possible to form hypotheses both about the evolutionary origin of many signal movements and about the changes they have undergone in evolution. In studies of fish, birds and mammals, three main sources of signal movements have been recognized.

1. Preparatory movements. These are the incomplete movements which often appear at the beginning of an activity or sequence. I have already given one example in the little finger of my professor. In animals such movements have sometimes become

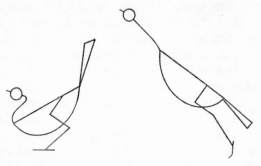

Figure 6. Two stages in the take-off leap of a bird (after Daanje, 1915).

stereotyped to serve as signals, and a responsiveness to such movements has evolved in parallel. For instance the take-off leap of a bird before flying consists of two phases: first it crouches, withdraws its head and raises its tail, and then reverses these movements as it springs off (Figure 6). Many avian displays are derived from these movements, though the relative extent and co-ordination of the various elements may have been altered considerably in the course of evolution. Preparatory movements of biting and striking are a common source of the components of threat postures: the upright threat posture of the herring gull (*Larus argentatus*), shown in Figure 7, includes a raising of the wings preparatory to beating, and a downward-pointing bill, preparatory to striking.

2. Displacement activities. Animals which have tendencies to behave in more than one way at the same time sometimes show behaviour which is related to neither of them and appears, to the

Figure 7. Upright threat display of the herring gull; (a) Aggressive upright; (b) Intimidated upright; (c) Anxiety upright (after Tinbergen, 1959).

human observer at least, to be functionally irrelevant in the context. For instance in many aggressive and sexual situations, where there are factors making for an approach towards the other individual as well as factors for a retreat, birds may wipe their beaks, preen their feathers or engage in some other activity that appears to be unrelated to the context. Such apparently irrelevant activities, although their causal bases are undoubtedly hetero-geneous, are referred to as 'displacement activities'. Some of these have been elaborated in evolution as signal movements (Tin-bergen, 1952).

3. Many signal movements are derived not from movements of the skeletal musculature, but directly or indirectly from responses controlled by the autonomic nervous system. This includes move-ments of the hair or feathers, movements of urination and de-faecation, and changes in skin coloration due to changes in the surface vessels. In addition, many movements of the limbs or head, such as those involved in grooming or preening, are re-sponses to stimuli resulting from activity of the autonomic ner-vous system. For instance movement of the hair may produce irritation, which leads to grooming (Morris, 1956; Andrew, 1956).

When the evolutionary source of a signal movement has been identified, the changes which it has undergone in the course of evolution can be described. The changes involved are usually collectively termed 'ritualization'. They include

(a) Changes in the frequency of occurrence, intensity, and speed of performance.
(b) Changes in rhythmicity.
(c) Changes in the coordination and/or relative intensity of the components.
(d) Changes in orientation of the whole or its parts.
(e) The evolution of structures by which the conspicuousness of the movement is enhanced.

Some examples will be evident in Figure 7. Let us consider one more. The 'head-up' posture of the great tit shown in Figure 3 is more elaborate than that of many related species, which show only a brief upright movement. These in turn resemble an in-complete movement of flying up and away. It is a reasonable supposition that the elaborate posture of the great tit evolved from the incomplete flight movement, and that it has been elaborated in evolution in connection with its function as a social signal. This has been accompanied by the development of conspi-cuous structures, such as the black ventral stripe, which also con-tribute to its effectiveness. These are less conspicuous in related species in which the posture is less developed. There is a correlation between the elaboration of the movement and the evolution of conspicuous structures which accentuate it. Furthermore in the blue tit, where the head-up posture is almost absent, a head-forward posture is used in similar contexts. The blue tit has an ability, lacking in the great tit, to raise the feathers of its white cheek-patches, and thereby to make the head forward posture more conspicuous. In each case evolution of movement and structure must have gone hand in hand. In both cases the movements have often become altered, elaborated and made more suitable for a signal function through the operation of natural selection.

A moment's thought will show that the preceding discussion could refer to only some of the signals used by animals: there is still much that is not known about the evolution of communication in animals. But the point is that there are some signal movements whose evolution can be traced with fair certainty. And I think it would be superfluous for me to point out how many of the evolutionary changes which have led to the greater effectiveness of signal movements could be paralleled by the stylization of movements and the use of make-up and costume in the theatre.

Is there any evidence that any of man's expressive movements are related to those of his animal ancestors? Comparisons are of course possible only with present-day forms, but there are many similarities. At a general level, a human observer has no difficulty in knowing which of the monkeys in Figure 8 is dominant and which subordinate. At a slightly more specific level, there are many similarities between the behaviour of a displaying male chimpanzee, which involves waving of the arms, stamping of the feet and the use of objects to make a noise (Plates 6 and 7), and anger in man. But in the absence of further study it is difficult to interpret the significance of such cross-species similarities.

Of more interest is the hypothesis, recently advanced by Van Hooff (1972), for the origin of human smiling and laughter. He was concerned first with the relationship between laughter and smiling in our own species. Now, as will be mentioned shortly, the variation in many signal movements of animals can be described in terms of variations in tendencies to perform two incompatible types of behaviour, such as to attack and flee from a rival. Thus Figure 9 shows how some threat postures of a cat change as its

Figure 8. Submissive female rhesus monkey and dominant male rhesus monkey (from drawings by Yvette Spencer-Booth).

internal state changes in a way producing an increased tendency to attack, to flee, or both. On the basis of considerable comparative, observational and experimental evidence Van Hooff has concluded that laughter and smiling similarly involve a continuum of intergrading signals, the variation in which can be indicated in at least two dimensions (Figure 10): these dimensions can be roughly described as 'friendliness' and 'playfulness'. The two extreme

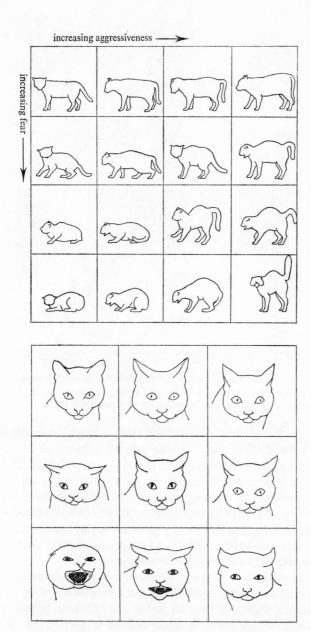

Figure 9. Threat and fear expressions in cats. In each section fear increases from above downwards, and aggressiveness from left to right (from Leyhausen, 1956).

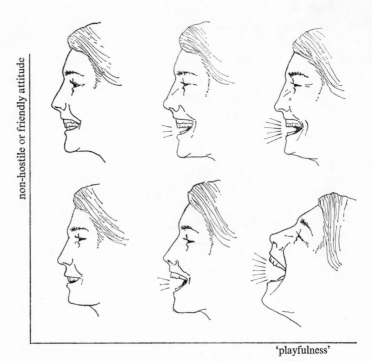

Figure 10. Two dimensions of variation of the smile–laughter continuum. From bottom to top there is increased baring of the teeth. From left to right: increased mouth-opening and vocalization (from Van Hooff, 1972).

forms, the 'broad smile' and the 'wide-mouth laugh', resemble the 'silent bared-teeth display' and the 'relaxed open-mouth display' of lower primates. The former is an expressive movement originally indicative of fear, which has come to express non-aggression and thus friendliness in greeting-situations; while the latter is used during play. Figure 11 indicates the sort of way in which evolution could have occurred, though of course it must not be interpreted too literally: for instance there is no suggestion that the chimpanzee is descended from present-day monkeys.

Just because the precise role of experience in the development, use and interpretation of human signal movements is so difficult to unravel, the nature of changes in the use of signal movements between human cultures is often difficult to specify. But it is worthwhile considering one case, which has been studied in some detail by Eibl-Eibesfeldt (e.g. 1972) – though his conclusions are admittedly speculative.

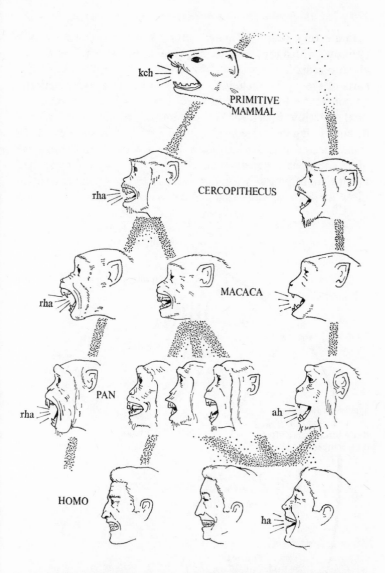

Figure 11. The phylogenetic development of laughter and smiling as suggested by homologues in existing members of the phyletic scale leading to *Homo*. On the left is the speciation of the *silent bared-teeth* display and the *bared-teeth scream* display. The *sbt*-display, initially a submissive, later also a friendly response, seems to converge with the *relaxed open-mouth* display (on the right), a signal of play (from Van Hooff, 1972).

In greeting, people of many cultures smile, nod and raise their eyebrows with a rapid movement, keeping the eyebrows raised for about one sixth of a second. This eyebrow-flash is found in many parts of the world, including cultures which have had practically no contact with the Western world. There is however some cultural variation: in central Europe reserved individuals do not use it, and in Japan it is considered indecent and is suppressed. In some cultures it is used also in other contexts – for instance we often use it as a general sign of approval or agreement, when making confirmation, when flirting, strongly approving and so on. Eibl-Eibesfeldt suggests that the common denominator in these

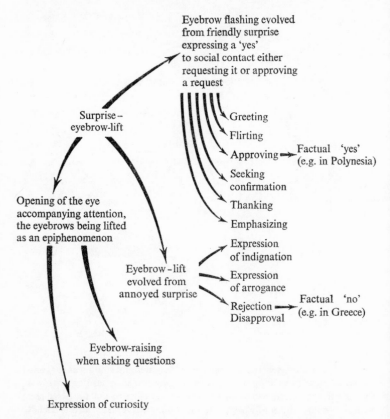

Figure 12. Hypothetical evolution of eyebrow movements into signals in man (from Eibl-Eibesfeldt, 1972).

situations is a 'yes' to social contact, the eyebrow-flash being used either for requesting or for approving a request for contact. It is in fact used for 'yes' in Polynesia.

By looking at other contexts in which it is used, Eibl-Eibesfeldt was able to make a suggestion as to its 'evolutionary' origin. It occurs in surprise, and in other situations associated with attention including those involving disapproval and indignation. Eibl-Eibesfeldt thus suggested that the eyebrow-lift of surprise was the starting-point for the ritualization of several attention signals, as shown in Figure 12. This scheme is of course very speculative. Furthermore it is not clear which (if any) of the changes are supposed to be evolutionary changes now common to all cultures, and which are culture specific. But it does provide a reasonable framework for synthesizing diverse observations, and demonstrates how the comparative method, developed in studies of lower species, could be applied to our own.

Now let us consider how the signal movements are used in communication. First we must note that signal movements may be rigid and stereotyped, or graded. If they are stereotyped – like, for instance, the song of the chaffinch – they are presumably simple to receive and interpret. Often however the signals are graded, each point on a continuum corresponding to a particular motivational state. For example the vocalizations used by rhesus monkeys in situations of aggression or fear form an intergrading series, as shown in Figure 13 (Rowell, 1962). Such signals are able to carry much more information than stereotyped ones – for

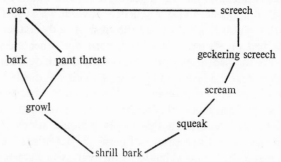

Figure 13. Relations of certain noises made in agonistic situations by rhesus monkeys. The lines indicate named noises between which intermediates have been recorded (after Rowell, 1962).

instance about the intensity as well as the nature of the internal state of the signalling individual – but are correspondingly difficult to interpet. Additional complexity in the information that can be carried arises from the fact that many signal movements are given when an animal is subject to conflicting tendencies – for instance threat movements occur when an animal has simultaneous but conflicting tendencies to attack and to flee from a rival, many courtship postures when a bird has tendencies to mate with, attack and flee from its partner. In such cases each of the more elemental components of the posture may be associated primarily with one or other of the conflicting tendencies. For instance in the upright threat-posture of the herring gull, raising of the wings out of the supporting body feathers and a downward-pointing beak are associated with a high probability of attack on a rival – they are in fact intention-movements of striking with the wings and beak. By contrast an upward-pointing beak and a more vertical position of the neck are associated with withdrawal (Figure 7). The precise form of the posture thus indicates the balance between the probabilities of attack and withdrawal.

The relationships between the components of a posture may, however, be subtler than this. In disputes over food in winter blue tits use a threat posture (Plate 8) which has a variety of components – e.g. crest up or down, wings raised or not, and so on. In a detailed study at a winter feeding station Stokes (1962) recorded the presence or absence of nine of these behavioural components, and the subsequent action of the displaying bird: the latter was classified as attacking, staying or fleeing. The associations between individual components and subsequent behaviour were usually not large: although birds which raised the crest or body feathers subsequently fled on 90 per cent of occasions, for other individual components the probability of subsequently attacking, fleeing or staying was at most 52 per cent (Figure 14). This was due in part to interactions between the components. For example, when the nape feathers were raised in an otherwise non-aggressive posture, there was an increased probability that the bird would attack. This is shown in the lower three cases in Figure 15. But when the nape feathers were raised in combination with aggressive elements, this was associated with little change in the probability of subsequent aggression, but an increase in the probability of staying.

Although single components seldom provided a reliable indication of subsequent action, combinations of components were better. Figure 16 shows that one combination was followed by escape on 94 per cent of the occasions on which it occurred,

Best single indicator of outcome	Subsequent action (percentage of total occurrences)		
	Attack	Escape	Stay
Body horizontal	40		
Crest erect		90	
Crest normal			52

Figure 14. The use of single behaviour elements to predict outcomes of encounters between blue tits at feeding station (data from Stokes, 1962).

First element Nape erect	Second element	Resultant behaviour (percentage of total occurrences)			
		Attack	Escape	Stay	Probability
+	Body horizontal	39	15	46	ns
–	(aggressive)	39	26	35	
+	Wings raised	27	13	60	ns
–	(aggressive)	35	21	44	
+	Body normal	32	16	52	*
–	(non-aggressive)	6	47	47	
+	Wings normal	43	15	42	*
–	(non-aggressive)	12	45	43	
+	Body feathers normal	41	12	47	*
–	(non-aggressive)	17	34	49	

ns —not significant at ·05 level
* – $P < ·01$

Figure 15. The effect of nape position combined with other behaviour upon subsequent action in encounters between blue tits (from Stokes, 1962).

another by staying on 79 per cent, and another by attack on 48 per cent – figures considerably higher than the best relationships with single components shown in Figure 14. Similar interactions between the components of expressive movements undoubtedly occur in our own species, and account for some of the difficulties experienced in earlier attempts to interpret them as merely the sums of their components.

The fact that no combination of components gave a precise indication of what the blue tit would do next could of course be due to insensitivity of the observer to subtle aspects of the bird's behaviour. But we must remember that we are concerned here

Initial behaviour elements					Subsequent action (percentage of total occurrences)		
Crest erect	Nape erect	Facing rival	Body horizontal	Wings raised	Attack	Escape	Stay
+	–	+	–	–	0	94	6
+	–	–	–	–	0	89	11
–	–	–	–	+	7	14	79
–	–	–	–	–	0	35	66
–	+	+	+	+	28	16	56
–	+	+	+	–	48	10	42
–	–	+	+	+	44	20	37
–	–	+	+	–	43	21	36
Best single indicator of outcome							
Body horizontal					40		
Crest erect						90	
Crest normal							52

Figure 16. The use of five behaviour elements to predict outcome of encounters between two blue tits at a feeding station (from Stokes, 1962).

with an interaction between two individuals, so that the behaviour of each depends on that of the other, as well as on its own internal state. If an animal is going to attack or going to flee, its behaviour is most likely to be effective if it does so directly, without signalling its intention. Signalling is necessary if it may do either one or the other, and which it does depends on the behaviour of the other.

This point is illustrated by Simpson's (1968) study of the threat display of the Siamese fighting fish (*Betta splendens*). In this species two rivals may display for many minutes before any actual biting occurs (Figure 17). Various measures of the display behaviour of both individuals increase in parallel, so that it is not at all apparent to an observer which will win, until finally one of them gives up. Simpson's elegant analysis shows that an encounter is much more than a show of strength, for each fish varies its behaviour in

Figure 17. Siamese fighting fish. The fish in (a) and (b) are not displaying, whilst the fish in (c) and (d) are.
o – the operculum   bs – the black branchiostegal membrane (from Simpson, 1968).

response to the timing of its rival's display relative to its own. Thus displaying between two individuals, although non-verbal, can have many of the properties of a dialogue, with each response of each individual depending on previous responses of the other until a climax is reached. This adds a new dimension to the study of animal communication, lifting it from the stimulus–response framework in which it has been constrained for too long. Human parallels in the use of non-verbal communication to make love or war are obvious.

In considering the information available to the recipient of a display, we must remember that in discussing a signal movement on its own we are artificially isolating it from the context in which it occurs. Every signal is made in a context, and that context provides information which assists the recipient to interpret the meaning of the message (Smith, 1969). I will mention one case from Smith's (1966) studies of Tyrannid flycatchers. These birds give a particular vocalization, termed the 'Locomotory Hesitance Vocalization', in a wide variety of situations, the common factor in which seems to be a conflict between some form of locomotion and either locomotion in a different direction or some other form of behaviour. For instance a male, patrolling his territory, gives the call every time he ceases flying, and even when he approaches a perch but veers off without landing; and a young bird gives it when approaching for food a parent who may respond aggressively. The response to the call varies with the recipient and with the context. For example, if the caller is a patrolling male, an unpaired female is likely to approach; another territorially inclined male may approach aggressively or withdraw; a migrating individual may avoid displaying, and so on. A caller's mate may simply repeat the call. Thus a single call which occurs in a wide variety of situations can evoke diverse responses, depending on the respondent and the context. The importance of context in giving meaning is of course not peculiar to non-verbal signalling.

It will be apparent that, with graded and composite signals, with the addition of contextual information, and especially in its use in interactional dialogues, the signalling systems of animals may achieve considerable complexity. Attempts have been made to assess the extent to which they approach the effectiveness of human speech, but none of these is especially successful. One of the most elaborate is that of Hockett and Altmann (e.g. 1968; Altmann, 1967), and is worth mentioning here since it is equally applicable to comparisons between human verbal and non-verbal communication – and there may be others in addition to Benthall who are interested in making value-judgements between them. The

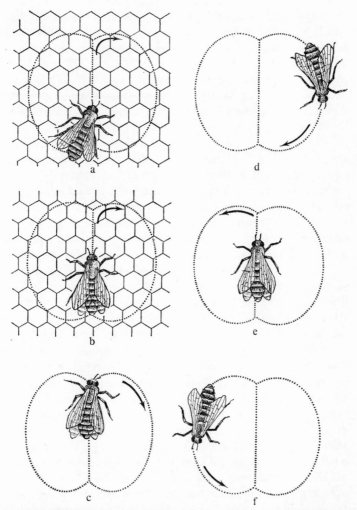

Figure 18. Communication of the distance and direction of a food source by the honey bee. The waggle dance (from von Frisch, 1954).

system depends on the isolation of sixteen 'design features' of human verbal communication, and the assessment of whether or not they are present in the system under study. For instance, human language uses symbols which are arbitrary in that they do not physically resemble that which they represent; it is based on discrete signals; it can refer to events remote in space and time; and it is 'open' in the sense that new messages can be carried easily. One may ask whether these properties are shared by the dance of the honey-bee (von Frisch, 1954). It is now well known that the worker bee can convey the distance and direction of a new source of nectar by signals related to the pattern of movement it performs in a dance in or near the hive. Direction is related to the direction of a certain phase of the dance, distance to the rapidity of certain movements within it (Figures 18 and 19). Since the symbols (e.g. the direction of the dance) are physically related to the direction of the food source, and vary continuously, they are neither arbitrary nor discrete. The dance can be said to permit the coining of new messages in only a very limited sense, but it does refer to a food source remote in space. To take another case, the vocal signals of doves are arbitrary and discrete, but are not open and cannot refer to things remote in time and space (Figure 20).

These 'design features' are concerned with capabilities and properties of communication systems, and not with their mechanisms. They may be fertile in posing new questions but, as Hockett and Altmann recognize, their value for comparing systems is limited by the flexibility with which they can be interpreted. For instance some have argued that the bee dance is open because it can refer to a new food location which has never been referred to before, but this is a very limited sort of openness, not to be compared with that of human language. Indeed these distinctions are hard to make even with verbal language. It is not easy, for instance, to say precisely which of the following statements describe the internal state of the speaker, and which an event remote in space: 'There is a lion behind that tree'; 'I know there is a lion behind that tree'; 'I am afraid because there is a lion behind that tree'; 'I am afraid'. Which, if any, of these statements conveys information only about the speaker and which, if any, only about the environment?

Finally, I must return briefly to the value-judgements between verbal and non-verbal communication which Benthall hankers after in his article. While acknowledging that words were put to good purpose by Homer and Shakespeare, he reminds us of 'how verbal language enacts the stratification of social classes, the repression of deviant minorities' and of how it is responsible for other social evils, and advances the hypothesis that 'since our

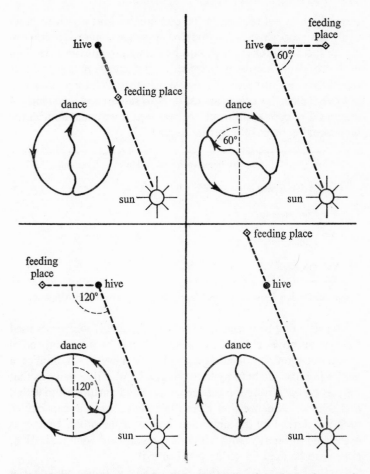

Figure 19. Communication of the distance and direction of a food source by the honey bee. Indication of sun's bearing on a vertical comb surface (from von Frisch, 1954).

society uses words as its primary means of social control, all repressed groups will tend to find their most effective and confident expression through the body's wider resources rather than within the enclosure of verbal language'. This, of course, is a *non sequitur* on a number of counts. But in any case this attempt to link social issues with the importance of the body as a medium of expression is, to say the least, ill-considered. First, repression certainly does not require verbal communication: a visit to practically any zoo which has a group of monkeys confined together in a cage too small for them should be enough to convince Benthall of that. Second, non-verbal expressive movements play a vital role in nearly every instance of repression: what dictator's cause has not been helped by a clenched fist or Nazi salute; and how much of the power of capitalism would be removed if we could abolish the non-verbal content of advertisements?

	Human speech	Bee dance	Dove calls
Arbitrariness	✓	X	✓
Discreteness	✓	X	✓
Remoteness	✓	✓	X
Openness	✓	X	X

Figure 20. Design features selected from those of Hockett and Altmann.

The view that because verbal communication is sometimes used for evil purposes it is always evil, and that because non-verbal communication is sometimes good it is always so, implies a hankering for a dichotomy between good and evil as naïve as that implied by the distinction between nature and nurture. Both verbal and non-verbal expression have their place, and the capacity of each is enlarged by the simultaneous use of the other. Neither is associated primarily with either expression or communication, either can be used for either good or evil.

Benthall believes both that our society is unjust and that it undervalues the body, and most of us agree, but these issues are not related. Both the socio-political question that Benthall raises, and the use of the body as a medium of expression, are important issues for all of us here; but no good is done to either by stirring them up together.

Altmann, S. A., 'The structure of primate social communication' in S. A. Altmann, ed., *Social Communication among Primates*, University of Chicago Press, London and Chicago, 1967.

Andrew, R. J., 'Some remarks on behaviour in conflict situations, with special reference to *Emberiza* spp.', *British Journal of Animal Behaviour*, 4, 1956, pp. 41–5.

Cullen, J. M., 'Some principles of animal communication' in R. A. Hinde, ed., *Non-Verbal Communication*, Cambridge University Press, 1972.

Daanje, A., 'On locomotory movements in birds', *Behaviour*, 3, E. J. Brill, Leiden, 1951, pp. 48–98.

Eibl-Eibesfeldt, I., 'Similarities and differences between cultures in expressive movements' in R. A. Hinde, ed., *Non-Verbal Communication*, Cambridge University Press, 1972.

Ekman, P., and Friesen, W. V. 'Constants across cultures in the face and emotion', *Journal of pers. soc. Psychol.*, 17, 1971, pp. 124–9.

Fisher, J., and Hinde, R. A., 'The opening of milk bottles by birds', *British Birds*, 42, Macmillan, 1949, pp. 347–57.

Frisch, K. von, *The Dancing Bees*, Springer und Verlag, Heidelberg, 1954.

Herbert, J., and Trimble, M. R., 'Effect of oestradiol and testosterone on the sexual receptivity and attractiveness of the female rhesus monkey', *Nature*, 216, 1967, pp. 165–6.

Hinde, R. A., 'Dichotomies in the study of development' in J. M. Thoday and A. S. Parkes, eds., *Genetic and Environmental Influences on Behaviour*, Oliver & Boyd, Edinburgh, 1968.

Hinde, R. A., ed., *Non-Verbal Communication*, Cambridge University Press, 1972.

Hinde, R. A., and Stevenson-Hinde, J. S., eds., *Constraints on Learning: Limitations and Predispositions*, Academic Press, London, 1973.

Hockett, C. F., and Altmann, S. A., 'A note on design features' in T. A. Sebeok, ed., *Animal Communication*, Indiana University Press, London and Bloomington, Indiana, 1968.

Lack, D., 'The behaviour of the robin: I and II', *Proc. Zool. Soc. Lond. A*, 109, 1939, pp. 169–178.

Lehrman, D. S., 'Semantic and conceptual issues in the nature–nurture problem' in L. R. Aronson, *et al.*, eds., *Development and Evolution of Behavior: Essays in memory of T. C. Schneirla*, Freeman, San Francisco, 1970.

Levine, S., 'The psychophysiological effect of early stimulation' in E. L. Bliss, ed., *Roots of Behaviour*, Hafner, New York, 1962.

Lévi-Strauss, C., *Mythologiques: I: Le Cru et le cuit*, Plon, Paris, 1964; English edn, Cape, 1970.

Leyhausen, P., 'Verhaltensstudien an Katzen', *Tierpsychologie.*, *Beiheft*, 2, Paul Parey Verlag, Berlin, 1956.

Lyons, F., 'Human language' in R. A. Hinde, ed., *Non-Verbal Communication*, Cambridge University Press, 1972.

MacKay, D. M., 'Formal analysis of communicative processes' in R. A. Hinde, ed., *Non-Verbal Communication*, Cambridge University Press, 1972.

Michael, R. P., and Keverne, E. B. 'Pheromones in the communication of sexual status in primates', *Nature*, **218**, pp. 746–9.

Michael, R. P., and Saayman, G. S. 'Differential effects on behaviour of the subcutaneous and intravaginal administration of oestrogen in the rhesus monkey (*Macaca mulatta*)', *J. Endocrin.*, **41**, (1968), pp. 231–46.

Morris, D., 'The feather postures of birds and the problem of the origin of social signals', *Behaviour*, **9**, 1956, pp. 75–113.

Nottebohm, F., 'The role of sensory feedback in the development of avian vocalizations', *Proc. 14th Int. Ornith. Cong. Oxford*, Blackwell, Oxford, 1967, pp. 265–80.

Nottebohm, F., 'Ontogeny of bird song', *Science*, **167**, 1970, pp. 950–56.

Rowell, T. E. 'Agonistic noises of the rhesus monkey (*Macaca mulatta*)', *Symp. Zool. Soc. Lond.*, **8**, 1962, pp. 91–6.

Simpson, N. J. A., 'The display of the Siamese fighting fish, (*Betta splendens*)', *Anim. Behav., Monogr. 1*, no. 1, Baillière Tindall, London, 1968.

Smith, W. J., 'Communication and relationships in the genus *Tyrannus*', publication no. 6, Nuttall Ornithological Club, Cambridge, Mass., 1966.

Smith, W. J., 'Messages of vertebrate communication', *Science*, **165**, 1969, pp. 145–50.

Stevenson, J. G., 'Song as a reinforcer' in R. A. Hinde, ed., *Bird Vocalizations in Relation to Current Problems in Biology and Psychology*, Cambridge University Press, 1969.

Stokes, A. W., 'Agonistic behaviour among blue tits at a winter feeding station', *Behaviour*, **19**, E. J. Brill, Leiden, 1962, pp. 118–38.

Thorpe, W. H., *Bird-Song*, Cambridge University Press, 1961.

Tinbergen, N., 'Derived activities: their causation, biological significance, origin and emancipation during evolution', *Quart. Rev. Biol.*, **27**, 1952, pp. 1–32.

Tinbergen, N., 'Comparative studies of the behaviour of gulls (*Laridae*): a progress report', *Behaviour*, **15**, E. J. Brill, Leiden, 1959, pp. 1–70.

Van Hooff, J., 'A comparative approach to the phylogeny of laughter and smiling' in R. A. Hinde, ed., *Non-Verbal Communication*, Cambridge University Press, 1972.

A comment by Jonathan Benthall

Professor Hinde criticizes my 'Prospectus' in two passages of his essay, and I shall reply to each passage in turn.

First, the distinction between 'communication' and 'expression'. It is true that my article 'slides' between one term and the other. This is because both terms raise profound philosophical questions that I chose to skirt round, rather than address head-on. The term 'communication' has been well criticized by Julia Kristeva, as I mention in a footnote (p. 7); the term 'expression' is equally laden with philosophical assumptions, since it normally implies that meaning can exist independently of its material form. As for 'intention', I am glad that the problem of how to 'get into people's heads' (or animals' heads) has been aired by both Dr Poole and Professor Hinde in this volume (though neither deals with the further difficulties introduced by the psychoanalytic theory of the unconscious); but I cannot see how my article's arguments are in any way invalidated just because the problem of intentionality was not covered there. As for the question of evolutionary adaptation, my article was almost exclusively concerned with human societies, and I don't see why any allusion to the theory of evolution was obligatory.

The fact is that my article and Hinde's essay belong to different fields of discourse. I admire the method and lucidity which Hinde brings to bear on his fascinating subject. But the cybernetic, 'black box' model of behaviour which Hinde relies on is not a specially useful tool for investigating the social and personal issues which my article attempted to explore.

Secondly, Hinde accuses me of making 'value-judgements' between verbal and non-verbal communication, identifying the former with evil and the latter with good. This seems to me a travesty of my argument. I cannot accept that my admittedly sketchy and speculative arguments are seriously challenged by the counter-examples offered by Hinde on pp. 137-8. After all, the monkeys in the zoo that he mentions must have been put in their cage either by taxonomic scientists or by commercial entrepreneurs. Again, it is true that the exploitation of the body by Nazism and by modern advertising are examples of the repressive or manipulative use of 'non-verbal communication'; but they are surely *ancillary* techniques of manipulation. The real power of both the Nazi state and present-day merchandising economies must be seen as technocratic and thus inheriting a whole long tradition of Western 'logocentricity'. I certainly did not mean to imply that non-verbal communication is not used repressively, nor that opposition to social and political repression must necessarily take non-verbal forms. I saw repressed groups as caught in a painful dilemma, between 'self-assertion' and 'integrating with the norms of the majority'. Their self-assertion – which may at any given time be politically unfashionable – will often (if my argument is right) choose a less narrow medium of expression than that of verbal language only.

Paul Willis's essay in this volume (p. 233) on motor-bike culture provides some unforeseen ethnographic support for these speculations. However, I now see that any adequate account of the repression of the body in Western culture would have to take account not only of minority groups but also of the oppressed proletarian majority, drawing on Marx's theory of labour and the writings of Adorno and Marcuse, among others. Sartre sums up the matter neatly when he describes the body as the 'presence within the oppressor of the oppressed in person'.

I am grateful to Professor Hinde for forcing me to clarify what I meant.

Michael Argyle

The Syntaxes of Bodily Communication

Introduction

In this essay I shall give some account of experimental work on
bodily expression, or 'non-verbal communication' as psychologists call it. I shall also try to say something new, and this will be an
attempt to describe and disentangle the different communicative
systems in which the body is involved.

There is an extensive body of experimental work in this area –
several thousand experiments. We think experiments are necessary
for a number of reasons:

1. Some kinds of bodily communication need special equipment
or special statistical treatment, for example very rapid facial expressions, or dilation of the pupils of the eye.

2. Special experimental techniques are need to study, for example, the separate effects of gaze, facial expression, posture and
distance, in communicating interpersonal attitudes.

3. New data have to be collected to find out, for example,
whether forms of bodily expression are innate, by the study of
infants and cross-cultural research.

However, experimental research in this area has been criticized
from several points of view, and I think it is important to consider
these criticisms and see how far our research methods can be
modified to answer them.

1. A certain amount of research in social psychology is very
artificial, and hence in danger of producing results which do not
apply in real-life situations. I did an experiment, with Robert

McHenry, which showed that this can happen. There are experiments which show that the same person when wearing spectacles is seen as more intelligent than he is without them. We made video-tapes of people with and without spectacles, but also varied how much was seen of the target person. When they were seen briefly, doing nothing, spectacles added fourteen points to their rated I.Q.; when they were seen in conversation for four minutes spectacles made no difference at all. We have been trying to make our experimental work more realistic – for instance by field experiments, and by the 'waiting room' technique – where subjects think they are talking to other subjects in a waiting room.

2. Sociologists criticize what they see as an unduly behaviouristic approach on the part of social psychologists. They point out that much social behaviour, many bodily movements, consist of meaningful 'social acts'. For example a person raises his finger; the significance of this depends on whether he is a cricket umpire or a person at an auction sale. Measuring the physical movement is not enough. On the other hand social psychologists find that communication goes on at a more microscopic level than the social act, for example the small eyebrow-movements and gaze-shifts during conversation.

3. Students of semiotics object that psychologists fail to treat behaviour as part of a communication system. Non-verbal signals, as well as being intended to communicate, combine together to form larger meaningful units, and there may be syntactical rules of sequence.

My view is that in order to study the phenomena of bodily communication we need to keep to a rigorous scientific approach, but that traditional methods in psychology need to be broadened to take account of the criticisms which have been summarized above.

The biological and cultural background

Rather similar research was conducted on non-verbal communication in animals and humans during the early 1960s – studying the roles of gaze, posture, etc. We know that animals establish a range of interpersonal relationships which are rather similar to those of humans – they find mates, rear children, make friends and co-operate in groups under leaders. In order to do this they make use of a standardized set of facial expressions and other signals, using parts of the anatomy designed for the purpose. Some animal signals are fairly complex. For example, a bird which is frightened by a predator makes a warning call, which is short and low to conceal its position. This may imitate the call of the predator; it signals the degree of danger by its speed or loudness, and may indicate the identity of the bird giving the call. Human beings establish a similar set of social relationships, and use very similar non-verbal signals for expressing interpersonal attitudes and emotions. For example, the facial expressions for emotion are largely innate. However, we exercise more cognitive control over these signals, they are affected by linguistic categorization of situations and emotions, and there are systematic cultural variations in the signals we use. In addition we make use of speech, which is supported by a number of language-dependent signals that sustain and support it in various ways. We also use various kinds of symbolic bodily behaviour in connection with rituals. Human social behaviour is characteristically a combination of verbal and non-verbal, and uses both the vocal and visual channels, in close combination. For example, a person speaking makes simultaneous use of visual feedback.

Cultures work out distinctive patterns of bodily expression. For example in Arab cultures people stand closer, thus making more use of touch and smell, but less use of vision. The meaning of some non-verbal signals depends on idea structures, as with the umpire raising his finger at a cricket match.

The meaning of non-verbal signals

We generally assume that some state of the sender is encoded into a message which is then decoded by the receiver. Experiments on encoding can be done by putting the sender into some state, for example arranging conditions so that he will like a second person, or by asking him to enact this condition. We can then study his posture, tone of voice, etc. Experiments on decoding are done by preparing signals, for example on videotapes, and asking subjects to estimate how friendly or hostile, etc., the sender appears to be. An example of an encoding experiment is one by Mehrabian in which he asked subjects to approach a hat-rack said to be a person of certain age and sex, who was either liked or disliked, and of higher or lower status. The way in which the subjects expressed these attitudes are shown in the following regression equations.

Positive attitude (*males*) (i.e. liking as opposed to disliking)	= 2.90 (gaze) − 1.35 (arms akimbo) − 1.34 (distance)
Positive attitude (*females*)	= −5.89 (arms akimbo) − 1.07 (distance) + 0.40 (arm openness)
High Addressee status (*males*)	= 6.00 (head tilt) + 3.25 (leg openness) + 2.50 (gaze) − 2.45 (arms akimbo) − 1.16 (leg relaxation) − 0.89 (hand relaxation)
High addressee status (*females*)	= 2.13 (head tilt) + 2.02 (gaze) − 3.69 (arms akimbo) − 2.74 (leg relaxation) − 4.64 (hand relaxation) + 1.43 (arm openness)

Table 1 Encoding interpersonal attitudes
(from Mehrabian, *J. Consult. clin. Psychol.* **32**, 1968, pp. 296–308)

Messages are coded in three main ways. (1) *Intrinsic.* Here the signal is the social act, for example hitting someone *is* aggression, not a signal for it. (2) *Iconic, or analogical.* Here the signal resembles or is part of what it refers to, for example animal intention movements for aggression consisting of showing the teeth, or in humans of clenching the fists. (3) *Metonymic or arbitrary.* Here the signal is associated with the referent, for example sign languages using the fingers.

However there are a number of further problems about the meaning of bodily signals. (1) Some signals have meanings which cannot readily be expressed in words, as is the case with art or music. It is possible to extract non-verbal dimensions of meaning by asking subjects to rate the similarities between pairs of signals and to carry out a statistical analysis. (2) Some signals have no phenomenological meaning, but only a behavioural one. Examples are the head-nods and other signals used for synchronizing speech, and the gestures and bodily contact used in rituals. (3) The meaning of a signal depends on the antecedents and the alternatives, and the probabilities of these. Melbin recently analysed the meaning of social acts in a mental hospital: for example 'banters' on the part of a nurse occurred when patients were difficult, and the main alternative was to stop them doing something. He concluded that the meaning of banters is somewhere between forbearance and direct management. (4) Some signals have connotations, that is, meanings in terms of a whole structure of ideas, as in a case of signals used in games, rituals and other complex settings. (5) Birdwhistell maintains that signals have no meaning apart from the situation they are in. However, facial expressions for emotions and hand gestures for illustrations have fairly constant meanings, though a number of signals do depend very much on the situation, for example raising a finger and waving. (6) Some signals can only be decoded by experts, for example autistic gestures and primitive rituals which can apparently be decoded only by psychoanalysts and anthropologists respectively.

Syntaxes

There are a number of different systems of bodily communication, and each has quite distinctive properties as a communication system, for example in terms of Hockett's criteria of linguicity. Table 2 sets out the different communication systems and the signals which are used in each.

Let us consider briefly four aspects of communication systems.

1. *Intention to communicate* can be established by whether a signal is used more or less when others are present. Hand illustrations accompanying speech clearly are intended to communicate, while autistic gestures are not, since they are used more in the absence of other people. The facial expressions for emotion may not be intended to communicate by the individual, though it has been suggested that there is a general biological purpose that they should do so.

2. *Two-tier structure.* Language consists of meaningless sounds or phonemes, which are combined into larger meaningful units, or words. Bodily signals also have a hierarchical structure, though they do not have two clear levels in this way. Meaningful social acts, such as shaking hands, consist of a series of smaller and quite meaningless elements.

	Illustrations, sign language	Accompaniments of speech	I—P attitudes	Emotions	Social acts	Personality and role	Ritual
Appearance			(×)			×	(×)
Head-nods		×					
Face		×	×	×	×	×	
Gaze		×	×				
Spatial behaviour			×		×	×	
Touch			×		×		×
Posture			×	×		×	×
Gestures	×	×	×	×	×	×	×

Table 2 Areas of body × type of communication

(×) = weaker or less definite relationship

3. *External reference*. Hand illustrations often refer to absent and distant objects or events, while facial expressions usually do not.

4. *Rules of sequence*. Several kinds of bodily signal follow rules of sequence, for example greetings, rituals and the language-dependent signals. These rules can be studied by experiments on rule-breaking, for example by preparing a number of sequences experimentally varied in different ways, and asking observers to judge which ones are acceptable and appropriate. I have used this method to find the rules governing interruptions: it was found that interruptions are acceptable if they come at the end of a sentence, and it is irrelevant how long the person interrupted has been speaking. It is intended to study the rules governing gaze, by preparing videotapes of people with gaze patterns which are systematically varied along different dimensions.

The different non-verbal codes

1. *Sign Languages*

Deaf and dumb languages based on finger movements for letters of the alphabet are essentially a case of verbal communication. Deaf people also use manual shorthand in which gestures stand for words or phrases, for example a finger to the brow stands for thinking. This is a simple iconic signalling system, which is acquired with little instruction, is much the same in different countries, and is very similar to the sign languages used by American Indians. It has a simplified syntax with no articles or tenses.

2. *Illustrations used during speech*

This is a language-dependent system, where illustrations are used to amplify speech. Hand movements are used to illustrate actions, objects, movements, or to point to people or things. Illustrations are used when it is easier to express an idea by a movement than by a word for some reason.

3. *Synchronizing signals and feedback used during speech*

(a) Synchronizing signals

Speakers need to indicate when they are about to start and stop speaking. This is done by means of head-nods, gaze-shifts, gestures and changes in volume. For example keeping a hand in mid-gesture at the end of a sentence holds the floor, giving a head-nod at the end of another's utterance declines it, and a prolonged gaze at the end of a sentence yields the floor.

(b) Prosodic signals

The meanings of utterances are completed by the pattern of stress, timing and pitch. Utterances are also accompanied by fine movements of hands, face and head, perhaps down to the level of the syllable. As well as providing illustrations, these movements display the structure of sentences, provide emphasis and give a gestural commentary on what is being said.

(c) Feedback

While one person is speaking, others respond continuously, by movements of head and face. For example they indicate by the position of their eyebrows whether they are puzzled, surprised, cross or disbelieving of what has been said.

4. *Emotions and interpersonal attitudes*

Most animal communication is in this area. They signal clearly by facial expression and posture whether their intentions are aggressive, sexual, appeasing, affiliative or fearful. In many cases the evolutionary origins of these signals have been traced in terms of intention movements, displacement and ritualization. The human face displays seven emotions fairly clearly – happiness, surprise, fear, anger, sadness, disgust/contempt and interest. In addition there are several basic attitudes to others: friendly/hostile and dominant/submissive (see Figure 1).

As Paul Ekman and others have shown, there are strong cultural similarities in the way emotions are expressed; the main difference appears to be in how far they are inhibited. The Japanese for example restrain their facial expressions when in the presence of other people. There may be further differences: we have found that videotapes of two expressive Japanese portraying different emotions were very difficult to judge by English and Italian subjects.

Interpersonal attitudes can be expressed by verbal and non-verbal signals. We carried out some experiments (see Figure 2) to

Figure 1

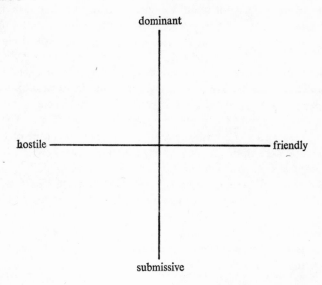

Figure 2. Effects of inferior, neutral and superior verbal and non-verbal signals on semantic rating.

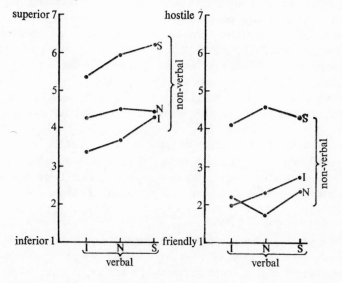

compare the effects of these two sorts of communication, making videotapes on which performers spoke friendly, hostile, inferior or superior messages, and also varied their non-verbal style along the same dimensions. We found that with initially equated signals the non-verbal messages outweighed the verbal ones by at least 5 to 1, and where they were in conflict the verbal messages were virtually disregarded. Such inconsistent messages are usually sent where the cognitive control of expression is only partly successful, for example where a girl says to a boy 'no, don't', but in a tone of voice suggesting the opposite. As our experiments have shown, it is the tone of voice to which the boy is likely to respond. Cognitive control of bodily messages may extend only to certain parts of the body; a person may succeed in controlling facial expression, but not his hands or feet for example. While the face is the most expressive area for emotions, it is often controlled so well that it does not communicate very usefully, and more can be learnt by studying other parts of the body.

5. *Rituals and ceremonies*

Bodily signals are used in rites of passage such as weddings and graduations, and in religious ceremonies, primitive healing and so on. The acts in question include laying-on of hands, drinking wine, adopting various postures, wearing certain clothes or decorating the body. These acts often have no clear phenomenological meaning, in that if the participants are asked for the meaning of a particular act they give varied and unsatisfactory replies. It may be suggested that the meanings are non-verbal and also behavioural, in that these rituals have definite consequences in terms of changes of state of individuals or changes in social relationships. Ceremonies also have a clear sequential structure. Van Gennep suggested that rites of passage always have a three-step structure of separation, transition and incorporation, though there may be further sequences such as re-enacting historical events.

6. *Sequences of social acts*

In many situations in everyday life there are repeated sequences of social acts. In games it is required that these sequences shall be followed for the game to be possible; here there is a clear distinction between rules, such as the number of balls to an over in cricket, and conventions, for example about what kind of trousers players should wear. The rules of a game give meaning to many of the acts which take place, and the game can only be understood in terms of the goals and concepts involved in the game. Barker and Wright found that in a town in Kansas there were over 800 standard 'behaviour settings' – going to church, going to the drug store, etc.; each of these situations had its own rules. We can discover which rules are essential by breaking them to see what happens. Garfinkel used the game of noughts and crosses, and in the middle of a game the experimenter would make a move as follows:

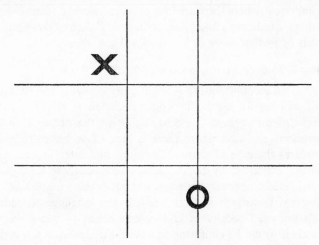

Figure 3

In my own studies of social rule-breaking I have found that there is a difference between rules and conventions, as in the case of cricket. There are certain rules which seem to be basic to each situation; for example at an interview it doesn't really matter if the candidate wears the wrong clothes, but it does matter if he doesn't tell the truth or refuses to speak at all. Similarly if a guest at a meal uses the wrong implements it doesn't matter very much, but if he refuses to eat or is rude to the other guests it does matter.

There are some sequences of social acts which occur in many situations. Greetings and farewells are an example; here there is a standard pattern, with a three-step sequence, where the second step is the 'close phase', usually involving some kind of bodily contact. As Goffman has pointed out, a greeting may itself have a greeting, so that there is a process of 'embedding'. Another common sequence is what Goffman has called the 'remedial sequence': this happens when someone has offended in some way. There are five steps: the offence, the apology or explanation, acceptance of this, thanks and minimization of what was done. Here there is a possibility of recycling if the first apology is not accepted, so that further apologies or explanations have to be given until the offended party is satisfied. There are also culturally defined sequences of social behaviour, as for example in a selection interview, where there are four phases: welcome, interviewer's questions, candidate's questions, ending. And each of these phases consists of further more or less standard sequences.

7. *Why is bodily communication used at all?*

Since verbal communication is much more complex and sophisticated, why do we use bodily communication at all? There are several different reasons, corresponding to the different codes. Illustrations are used where there is lack of verbal coding, for example in the case of shapes. Emotions and interpersonal attitudes are expressed by bodily signals because these have more powerful effects; perhaps language did not develop particularly in these areas because it was not needed. The language-dependent signals are used because it is very convenient to use a second channel; it would be confusing to have these signals in the verbal channel. The reason why non-verbal communication is used in ritual is probably that it would be disturbing to make these messages too conscious, and probably also that they have a more powerful effect than verbal ones would have.

The properties of different parts of the body as communication channels

1. *Appearance.* As Table 1 shows, appearance sends only one main kind of signal – information about the person. Most aspects of appearance are under voluntary control – clothes, hair, badges, decoration and many aspects of face, skin and physique. Appearance is used to send messages about the status, occupation and

personality of the sender. Gibbins showed photographs of different outfits of clothes to teenage girls in Newcastle. He found that they had a high degree of agreement as to whether girls who wore such clothes were fun-loving, rebellious, snobbish, smoked, drank or had a lot of boyfriends. When asked which outfit they would prefer to wear themselves they chose one which was closest to their own self-images. Appearance also signals to some extent a person's general attitude to other people, such as sexual availability, rebelliousness and (in primitive societies) threat. A curious feature of this code is that the meaning of the signals changes very rapidly, more so than those in other non-verbal areas.

2. *Face*. The face sends signals at three different time-scales. (a) Permanent features are interpreted in terms of personality traits, via stereotypes of class, race, and age; through analogy, e.g. thick lips are used for kissing; habitual expression, e.g. sneer or smile; and grooming. However most of these inferences are highly invalid. (b) Slow changes of facial expression indicate emotions and interpersonal attitudes. Here the basic encoding and decoding systems are innate, but there is considerable cognitive control over many aspects of expression. Minor cues such as perspiration and pupil expansion cannot be controlled in this way. (c) Rapid changes of facial expression are used to accompany speech. The speaker completes his message and the listener provides immediate feedback in this way.

3. *Gestures*. Gestures are particularly complicated, since they are used in all the different bodily codes, as Table 1 shows. Biologically the hands are made for grasping and manipulating, but they are also very expressive. They can represent interpersonal attitudes by truncated acts of touching and hitting, they can illustrate objects and movements as in manual shorthand, and they can be used for arbitrary signals as in deaf-and-dumb language and the symbolic movements used in rituals.

There is a particular problem about autistic gestures, which are made more when a person is alone. Psychoanalysts claim to interpret these gestures: for example playing with a wedding ring is thought to stand for marital conflict, covering the eyes for shame, and so on. George Mahl thinks that they stand for thoughts which have not yet been verbalized, but which may be expressed, for example during psychotherapy, a few minutes later. Krout carried out an experiment in which such gestures were elicited: he aroused various feelings in an interview, but asked respondents to delay their verbal reply until a sign was given, and the sign was given after a gesture had appeared. There was a strong tendency for anger to produce fist-formation, fear produced a hand-to-nose signal, and frustration produced an open hand dangling between the legs. It is not clear why these signals are made, or to whom they are addressed, if anyone.

4. *Spatial behaviour.* People signal their attitudes to one another by their spatial position. For example experiments have shown that if a person likes another he will stand much closer, 57 inches versus 98 inches in one experiment. Studies by Sommer and Cook found that people would sit at different positions round a table, depending on the social relationship with a second person.

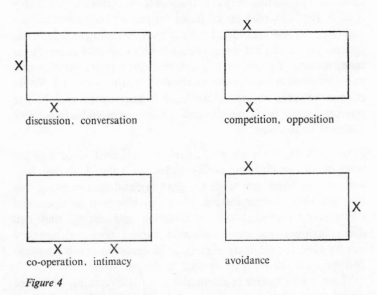

Figure 4

This study illustrates two important points about bodily expression. Firstly, one can become more aware of what is going on by becoming sensitive to these signals. Secondly one can, if one wishes, deliberately manipulate the signals one sends to others; for example if you want to co-operate with someone you should not sit down facing them.

Spatial behaviour is used to indicate dominance or status in a rather different way. It is shown by occupying seats or other areas which have symbolic value, for example sitting at the head of a table, or in one of the front seats. A further feature of spatial behaviour is the establishment of territories. Like animals, we often mark areas of space, such as library tables and parts of offices, by the manipulation of furniture, leaving property about, and so on. Lastly spatial behaviour is used to start and stop encounters; it is much more effective to change one's conversational partner at a dinner table by a shift of orientation than by saying, 'Please stop talking to me, I want to talk to this other person.'

5. *Bodily contact*. This is different from other bodily signals, in that it doesn't stand for anything else, but is the ultimate behaviour associated with various interpersonal relations – sexual, aggressive, nurturant, dependent and to some extent affiliative. There are elaborate cultural rules and restraints on who can touch whom and where. In our culture there is very little bodily contact outside the family, apart from greetings and farewells, the activities of tailors, doctors, barbers, etc. – which are defined as non-social events – and contacts in crowds and public transport, which are separated from any kind of social contact. For those who feel the need of further bodily contacts, there are encounter groups. Touching also occurs in many rituals and ceremonies, for example laying-on of hands, though the reason for this is not known.

6. *Gaze*. The main purpose of gaze is not to communicate but to collect information. However the very act of looking becomes a signal to the person looked at. Exline and others have found that people look more at those they like. Argyle and Dean suggested that looking is one of a number of alternative signals for intimacy; in support of this theory we have found that when two people are further apart they look at each other more, as is shown in Figure 5. Kendon has shown that looking acts as a synchronizing signal, in that speakers look up at the ends of their utterances; if they fail to look up then the listener fails to reply. Here the terminal look functions for the speaker as a means of collecting feedback, and for the listener as a signal that the speaker is coming to a stop.

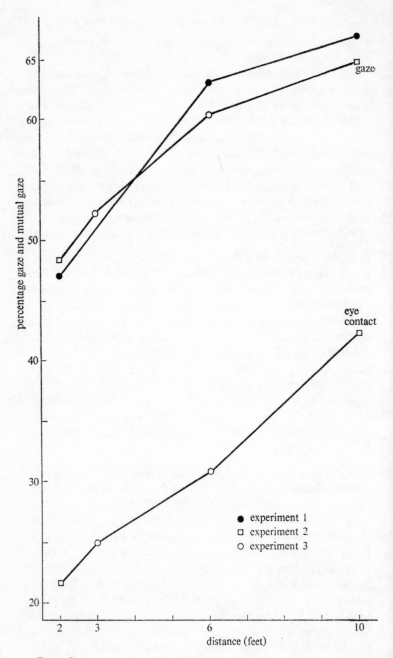

Figure 5

We were able to separate these different functions of looking in an experiment in which two persons conversed across a one-way screen, as shown in Figure 6.

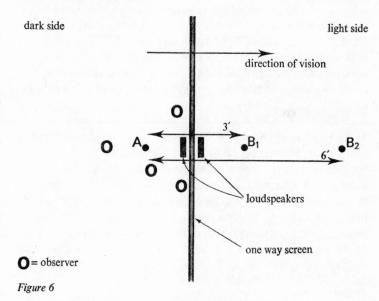

Figure 6

It was found that A (who could see) looked 65 per cent of the time, while B (who could not see) looked 23 per cent of the time. We deduced that A is looking to collect information, while B is looking to send information. A looked more during ordinary conversation than during a monologue, when he looked only 47 per cent; we assume that the difference is due to the need for synchronizing signals during a conversation.

Practical applications

I regard the possibility of making some use of research findings as a kind of further verification that useful progress is being made. I shall consider here only those applications which depend on the detailed results of experiments in some way.

1. *Inter-cultural communication*

A lot is known about cultural differences in bodily expression. For example Arabs stand closer, orient more directly, touch and look more, and speak louder. Peter Collett at Oxford found that an Englishman trained to act in this way got on better with Arab subjects. In recent surveys we have been trying to find out whether prejudice towards members of various minority groups is due to interaction difficulties. We have found that there are distinctive difficulties with each minority group, and that in some cases this appears to be the cause of dislike. We hope that this may lead to retraining either of minority group members or of other people.

2. *Social skills training*

Much training in social skills is directed towards non-verbal communication, because people are often not aware of this side of their behaviour. Role-playing with videotape playback is probably the most effective method. It is being used in the training of teachers at Stanford University, and by our group at Oxford in the training of mental patients who have interpersonal difficulties. While many mental patients have such difficulties, for some of them it seems to be the main cause of their trouble, and results so far suggest that they can be greatly helped by this form of training.

3. *Use of space*

Sommer and others have shown how space can be redesigned to influence interaction. For example Sommer rearranged the furniture in an old people's home so that instead of long rows of chairs against the wall there were circles of chairs around tables; this led to a great increase in the amount of interaction. Duncan Joiner found that senior civil servants and managers (but not university teachers) placed their desks in a way which created a barrier and a status difference between themselves and their visitors. I have found that there are clear rules for the placing of chairs for different kinds of conversation: for two male colleagues they should sit between an angle of 45° and 90°, and from 2′ to 5′ apart knee to knee.

4 *Visual communication problems*

Research at the Joint Planning Centre at University College has been directed towards the design of video-phones, and ways of creating the impression of mutual gaze. Other research is in hand in connection with the communication problems of the deaf and the blind. It may be suggested for example that the blind would be helped by more use of touch, and also if others would speak to them as they normally speak on the telephone.

Conclusions

There has been a great deal of experimental research on bodily communication, but there are a lot of unsolved problems, which need more and better research to solve them. The main new point which I have tried to make here is that there are a number of separate communication systems involving bodily expression, which have different properties, but which use the same parts of the body, often at the same time. None of these codes alone is as complex as language, but when three to five of them are operating at once in an interlocking way, and are combined with language, the system becomes quite complex. I have also tried to indicate how a number of individual and social problems would be solved if we learnt to use these codes better.

Argyle, M., *Social Interaction*, Methuen, 1969.

Argyle, M., *The Psychology of Interpersonal Behaviour*, 2nd edn, Penguin Books, Harmondsworth, 1972.

Argyle, M., ed., *Social Encounters: Readings in Social Interaction*, Penguin Books, Harmondsworth, 1973.

Birdwhistell, Ray L., *Kinesics and Context: Essays on Body-Motion Communication*, Allen Lane The Penguin Press, 1971; University of Pennsylvania Press, Philadelphia, 1971.

Goffman, E., *Relations in Public: Microstudies of the Public Order*, Allen Lane The Penguin Press, 1972.

Hinde, R., ed., *Non-Verbal Communication*, Cambridge University Press, 1972.

Knapp, M. L., *Nonverbal Communication in Human Interaction*, Holt, Rinehart & Winston, New York, 1972.

Mehrabian, A., *Nonverbal Communication*, Aldine-Atherton, New York, 1972.

David Crystal

Paralinguistics

The preliminary prospectus about this series (see p. 5) drew a clear contrast between the study of verbal language in man and the study of the expressive resources of the body as a whole. It was suggested that, compared with the rigorous attention paid to man's linguistic behaviour (particularly in the last two decades), his non-linguistic communicative abilities have been badly neglected. In the light of such an emphasis, it may not be immediately obvious why there should be a paper on a branch of linguistics within a volume ostensibly devoted to what is clearly not linguistic. But it is appropriate that linguistics should make its presence felt here. For one thing, many areas of non-linguistic study derive much of their stimulus and method from the linguistic theories and techniques of the 1940s and 1950s. And there is also the fundamental point that to wholly ignore the linguistic component is to commit as mortal an omission as the one which this series is trying to make good. Understanding man's expressive potential requires the concurrent study of both linguistic and non-linguistic modes of behaviour. Only a distorted picture can result from too rigid a separation between them.

But in any case, this paper is about 'paralinguistics', not linguistics – about 'paralanguage', not language. Paralanguage is in fact generally seen as a kind of bridge between non-linguistic forms of communicative behaviour and the traditionally central areas of 'verbal' linguistic study – grammar (in the sense of syntax and morphology, or accidence), vocabulary, and pronunciation (or, in the case of written language, spelling and punctuation). The study of the pronunciation system of a language is generally referred to as phonology, and within this the bulk of the linguist's effort goes towards the analysis of the vowel and consonant units, or phonemes, which constitute the identifiable syllables, words and sentences of meaningful communication. Over and above these 'central' properties of speech, however, there remain certain vocal effects which are qualitatively very different from phonemes or words, but which nonetheless seem to have an important role to play in the communication of meaning. These effects are often referred to popularly as 'tones of voice' – a convenient phrase which summarizes a complex functioning of the vocal apparatus, in which pitch, loudness, speed of speaking and many other vocal qualities are used in distinctive combinations – but in the literature on human communication, these features of pronunciation are subsumed under the heading of paralanguage. This term was originally chosen to reflect a view that such features as speed and loudness of speaking were marginal to the linguistic system – 'at the edge of language', as it was once put. It is a view which is no longer universally held, as we shall see, but the term 'paralanguage' has remained in general use nonetheless. Actually, there is considerable difference of opinion as to exactly what should be called paralinguistic in the communicative behaviour of a culture, and how it should be analysed. Not all the vocal effects to be mentioned below would be labelled paralanguage by everyone. Some scholars, also, include aspects of visual communication under this heading – facial expressions, for instance, and characteristics of writing (such as layout and spacing). There is indeed an important overlap between paralinguistic and kinesic function (hence the view of paralanguage as a 'bridge'); but in view of the emphasis on the visual in the rest of this volume, I propose to restrict the present paper to the vocal factors involved in paralanguage, which are a complex enough matter in their own right. I shall, however, be taking the broadest possible view of paralinguistic phenomena, including under this heading *any* meaningfully contrastive sound-effect which cannot be described in terms of the segments, or phonemes, in the sound system of a language, but which extends over stretches of utterance at least a syllable in length.

Paralanguage shares one thing with the study of other forms of body expression – namely, that it has been much neglected, even within linguistics. Indeed, the series on linguistics sponsored by the I.C.A. in 1971 made no mention of it.[1] There has in fact been a generally dismissive attitude towards the study of paralinguistic phenomena in the context of communicational analysis – an attitude which is perhaps reinforced by the etymological conditioning of our thinking arising out of the 'para-' prefix. There is the suggestion that tone of voice is a secondary facet of communication – a kind of optional 'extra', which does not affect the basic meaning of an utterance. Some of the reasons for this way of thinking will be discussed below; but before this, it should be emphasized that these attitudes have recently come under attack on a number of fronts, work in social psychology, psychiatry, sociolinguistics and elsewhere coinciding to suggest that the vocal effects called paralinguistic may be rather more central to the study of communication than was previously thought. Birdwhistell, another contributor to this volume (see p. 36), was one of the first to appreciate this point. In a 1959 paper called 'The frames in the communication process', he said: 'It is all too easy to assume that there is in any social interchange a *central*, a *primary*, or a *real* meaning which is only modified by a redundant surround . . . Our temptation so to classify certain aspects of a transaction as the central message and other aspects as serving only as modifiers rests upon untested assumptions about communication.' Certainly, observations of people's everyday reactions to language suggest that paralinguistic phenomena, far from being marginal, are frequently the primary determinants of behaviour in an interaction, sometimes pushing the so-called 'cognitive' or 'denotative' aspect of the utterances used into a secondary role. 'It's not what he said, but the way that he said it which upset/surprised/ . . . me' is the most widely-quoted phrase used in support of this point; but the importance of paralanguage can be similarly shown from a variety of other comments besides: 'Say it as if you mean it', 'You don't sound like a lawyer', 'You can keep that tone of voice for your secretary', and so on. If we begin our analysis of the communication situation by asking what features of the vocal stimulus account for the response behaviour, it is clear from such examples that paralanguage cannot be given anything other than a central role.

Once we look in detail at the various communicative functions of paralanguage, this point becomes more cogent. The most widely recognized function is for emotional expression. The traditional view in psychology, for instance, is that verbal language communicates 'cognitive' meaning, whereas the non-verbal code (which covers my sense of paralanguage, amongst other things) communicates 'affective' meaning – anger, sarcasm, surprise, emphasis, excitement and so on. This is certainly an important role for paralanguage, and it is perhaps its most obvious role; but it would be wrong to assume – as some scholars have done – that this is its only function. On the contrary: far more important and pervasive than its affective function is the use of paralinguistic features as markers of an utterance's grammatical structure. The intelligibility of written communication is in large part due to the conventions of spacing and punctuation we adopt; in like manner, the grammatical intelligibility of speech is largely a product of the way in which we organize a stream of noise into structured units (sentences, phrases, words, etc.). Intonation – the systematic use of pitch in a language – is the most important factor here. More than any of the other variables which constitute tone of voice, intonation is used to segment and structure stretches of language, expounding contrasts in meaning which are sometimes almost as clear-cut as the contrasts signalled by phonemes or word-order. For example, the difference between stating and questioning may be signalled by a change in pitch, from falling to rising, as in

He's coming   He's coming

(The interlinear transcription represents the direction of movement of the pitch of the voice. The large dots indicate strong, or stressed syllables.) Another example is in the 'tag-questions' of the following two sentences:

He's coming, isn't he   He's coming, isn't he

The first sentence has a falling tone on the tag-question, and this usually means that the speaker is expecting his listener to agree with him. The second sentence replaces this with a rising tone, and the meaning consequently changes: here the speaker is usually making a genuine request for information. These contrasts can be quite unambiguous. What makes intonation different from, say, the word-order differences of syntax (where statement versus question may also be expressed, as in 'He's coming' versus 'Is he coming?') is that sometimes in speech the contrast does not emerge so clearly ('Are you asking me or telling me?', one might hear), and sometimes, for a variety of reasons (not all of which are yet fully understood), one of these intonational tunes may be used with the semantic force of the other, as in the context:

He's coming, isn't he – I'm asking you, damn it!

Here the falling tone is used where, from the above examples, the rising tone might have been expected – presumably on account of the specific attitude adopted by the speaker.

But despite the 'fuzziness' which may surround intonational contrasts, there are enough clear cases to show that pitch *can* be used with a function corresponding to the cognitive use of word-order or morphological inflection in grammar. Moreover, it is not just pitch which works in this way. Increasing the speed of speaking, for example, is an important means of indicating that what one has just said was unintentional – a mistake – and to be replaced by the part of the sentence which was speeded up. In the sentence 'Those of you who aren't happy *aren't ready* for this announcement should . . .', the words in italics would normally be spoken more rapidly (and usually louder) than the surround, to indicate that a restructuring of the utterance has taken place. However, speed, rhythm and other tone-of-voice variations are not used as systematically for this purpose as are contrasts of pitch (and also those contrasts in loudness generally referred to as 'stress'). It is for this reason that some scholars take the intonation and stress systems separately from other paralinguistic characteristics, considering them to be more 'central' features of language.

Paralanguage has other communicational functions apart from the affective and the grammatical. It may be used as an index of our intentions, for instance: if we wish to show that we want to persuade, or irritate, or joke, then it is paralanguage, along with the appropriate facial expressions, which acts as primary exponent. In a similar, though less deliberate manner, paralinguistic effects are of major importance as indicators of social psychological states, such as dominance, submission, leadership, and so on. A great deal of research has been done into the nature and social correlates of such notions as 'brisk' and 'authoritative' voices, and stereotyped interpretations of a number of paralinguistic voice 'settings' have been studied in some detail. The range of paralinguistic effect used in television advertising shows this function very clearly: different types of product correlate with different types of voice – two well-recognized categories are the 'hard-sell' approach, with its dramatic, tense and rapid syllables, and the 'soft-sell' approach, with its gentle, melodious, leisurely tones. And it is this function which underlies Stephen Potter's recommendation about 'plonking' (*Lifemanship*, p. 43): 'If you have nothing to say, or, rather, something extremely stupid and obvious, say it, but in a 'plonking' tone of voice – i.e. roundly, but hollowly and dogmatically ... if properly managed, the tone of voice will suggest that you can afford to say the obvious thing, because you have approached your conclusion the hard way, through a long apprenticeship of study.'

A related function of paralanguage is to indicate a speaker's professional background. Most professions in which speech is an integral part of the professional activity have a distinctive paralinguistic style – though some are more distinctive than others. Barristers, undertakers and clergymen are traditionally supposed to be most distinctive in this respect, but there is rarely any difficulty in distinguishing many others on the basis of a sample of tape-recorded speech – drill-sergeant, street vendor, disc-jockey, sports-commentator, lecturer, policeman ('*Your* car, sir?') ... Professional comedians and satirists are well aware of the importance of paralinguistic features when they 'put on' a particular voice, either that of an individual, or that of a stereotyped social group or class; and the point has long been appreciated by teachers of speech and drama as an essential aspect of routine training.

'Style is the man' is a maxim which was largely viewed in relation to the written language. When we consider speech, it is paralanguage which is the man, as far as social identity is concerned.

More detailed illustrations will be found in the books listed at the end of this essay. But just from the above, it would seem that paralanguage has a complex function in communication, conveying grammatical, attitudinal and social information. If, then, it is such an important aspect of behaviour, why has it been so neglected? The reasons are very similar to those underlying the neglect of other facets of body behaviour. To begin with, there was the difficulty of getting hold of reliable samples of data for scientific study. The real range and complexity of paralinguistic phenomena emerges in informal conversational situations, and tape-recorded material of this kind is by no means easy to come by. Put a tape-recorder in front of the participants in a conversation and their interaction ceases to be normal: their language becomes more formal and less fluent, and their paralanguage alters radically. If the microphone and other equipment is hidden, then the paralanguage stays natural, but of course the quality of the recording may be poor. Quite sophisticated techniques are needed to get around these problems; and it is not surprising, therefore, that progress in this area has been slow. The tape-recorder itself, we must remember, is a relatively recent invention; and tape-repeaters (which provide convenient repeat listening to a piece of language, to ensure maximum phonetic accuracy in transcription) are still not widely used.

But assuming that some reliable data have been collected, the analyst has to face the problem of how to set about describing paralinguistic effects. And how do you identify and classify a tone of voice? The difficulty here is that linguistic techniques available for language description have been almost completely orientated towards the study of the segmental and verbal units of articulation and construction – the consonants, vowels, syllables, words and so on. The tradition in linguistics which makes the linguist look at language and see it as a sequence of discrete, non-overlapping entities (such as sounds, words) does not readily apply to phenomena such as speed of speaking or intonation. It is not so easy to specify the minimal units which are to form the sequences; and it is not so easy to establish the set of sequences which constitute the language's permissible pronunciation patterns. What is a falling-pitch pattern, for instance? How high may it start? How low may it finish? And how long may it take to get from one point to the other? Let us imagine a situation in which someone says 'No' in a fairly neutral, matter-of-fact way, in a low pitch-range, and then repeats it in a progressively more excited and emphatic voice, letting his pitch get higher and higher – as if he were reacting to someone who was continually querying the truth of his answer. If the first version of 'no' were then played over alongside the last, there would be a clear contrast in form and meaning – a distinction between 'low' and 'high' falling tones, which we might interpret semantically as 'neutral' versus 'excited' (or in some such terms). But in between, there is a continuum of gradation, which makes it extremely difficult to decide where one meaning ends and the next begins. And if we decide to set up a 'high falling tone', with the meaning 'excited', then we immediately find difficulties. Not only do the physical limits of this tone vary considerably from one utterance to the next, and from one speaker to the next, with no obvious change in meaning; the meaning itself becomes extremely difficult to pinpoint. The same high falling tone may on one occasion help to indicate excitement, but on another it may be part of an attitude of anger, or surprise, or joy. Context conditions our interpretation here in a way which never happens with the segmental and verbal sides of language. There, the meaning of a word or sentence is much more readily definable and much more stable. There too, the formal basis of a contrast is more definable and stable: there is no continuum of gradation between two words, or structures, or phonemes, like that illustrated above. *Is he* does not gradually merge into *He is*. A /p/ does not gradually merge into a /b/. It is for such reasons that paralinguistic features have been referred to as the 'greasy' part of speech.

To some linguists, these difficulties of identification and semantic interpretation are evidence that the effects being described are not matters of language at all – that the prefix 'para-' should be taken literally, as it were. But this does not follow. Just because this area of behaviour is difficult to describe and quantify, it does not mean that it lacks system altogether. Perhaps the reason for our difficulty is simply that we lack appropriate techniques for handling gradience between phenomena, for evaluating affective meaning and so on. I would in fact want to argue that this is the case. Our understanding of paralinguistic phenomena will not be increased as long as we approach the area assuming that unless we can see the sort of structure that we are used to seeing in verbal language, then there is no structure there at all. This is the kind of attitude that underlies the view, already criticised, that para-language has a secondary role to play in communication, that it has a 'merely' affective function, and the like. The argument also takes other forms – for instance, that paralinguistic effects are universal, being a product of nervous tension. It is sometimes said that, as we can always recognize a foreigner when he is being angry (for instance), expressive vocal behaviour must be outside the linguistic system, must be unlearned and culturally neutral. But these arguments embody fallacies, stemming from an over-simplified view of the complexity of paralanguage. We have already seen how paralinguistic effects have other roles than the affective – roles in which nervous tension can have little or no part. Cross-cultural studies, moreover, as they increase in depth of detail, bring to light more, not less paralinguistic difference between communities and cultures. And the fact of the matter is that it is *not* always easy to see that a foreigner is being angry – or sarcastic, or upset, or embarrassed. On the contrary: it is a very common reaction to misinterpret a foreigner's paralanguage – to assume that he is being rude, or belligerent, or sarcastic on the basis of his tone of voice, whereas in reality what we are respond-ing to is unintentional interference from the paralinguistic features of his mother tongue. For example, flat, level tones in English regularly connote boredom or sarcasm:

'I thought it was marvellous'

spoken with a final level tone generally means the reverse! In Russian, on the other hand, the level tone is much more widely used with a neutral, matter-of-fact interpretation. The danger for the Russian learning English, then, is that he produces English sentences with too many level-tone endings: to his ears, the sen-tences sound intonationally neutral; but to the English listener, they sound uninterested and often rude. Other examples? In some oriental languages, giggling is a normal indication of embarrassment on the part of adults, whereas in English it either relates to humour, or it is considered childish. In some varieties of Arabic, speaking with the tongue retracted ('velarization', as in much Liverpool or Birmingham speech) is an indication of masculinity; non-velarized speech is effeminate – which can lead to difficulties for the unsuspecting, non-velarizing male tourist!

The complexity of paralanguage can only be seen by attempting to carry out a systematic classification of the features within a number of languages. One's general aim is to set up an 'alphabet' of vocal effects, each of which is capable of altering the (affective, grammatical, or social) meaning of an utterance when it is substituted for another effect within it. Ultimately it would be necessary to classify the effects into categories, based upon their formal distribution and typical functions; but in the first instance, what we are concerned with is to establish the range of effects which are capable of being used by a language with *any* kind of semantic force. Some of these effects will accordingly be more obvious than others; some will be easier to describe than others; but these problems, as suggested above, are secondary.

In this way, it is possible to distinguish a number of variables within the human vocal apparatus which are regularly used in the production of tones of voice. (There is space for the briefest of examples only. To facilitate recognition, I will restrict the examples to English. Further illustration is provided in the accompanying bibliography.)

Pitch. In addition to the examples already given, one might illustrate from words or phrases spoken in a higher or a lower pitch range than normal, as when extended low pitch is used as a marker of parenthesis (e.g. 'My cousin – *you know, the one who lives in Liverpool* – he's just got a new job').

Loudness. Speaking words or phrases louder or softer than normal, in various degrees, is one of the more obvious systems of paralinguistic effect – used, for example, as an indication of rhetorical climax in public speaking, or as a marker of increased emphasis ('I want the *red* one, not the *green* one').

Speed. Words or phrases may be spoken faster or slower than normal, as when 'Really' is spoken in a drawled, meditative manner, or when an increase in speed of speaking is conventionally interpreted as one of a small set of 'meanings', e.g. that the speaker wishes to forestall an interruption, or to suggest that what he is saying need not be given careful attention.

Rhythm. Pitch, loudness and speed patterns combine to produce contrasts in the rhythm of speech which have paralinguistic force, as when a sentence is spoken with a more marked metrical beat than normal to suggest irritation, e.g. 'I *really think* that *John* and *Mary* should have *asked*.'

(The range of effects thus far outlined is sometimes studied separately from all other paralinguistic variables under the heading of 'prosodic features' – a term which reflects the traditional interest in the study of metre, where stress and syllable-length in particular were considered to be central. Those who make use of the distinction between 'prosodic' and 'paralinguistic' effects use the latter term for such other variables as the following.)

Larynx effects. Whispered speech is one of the more obvious paralinguistic effects originating in the larynx – one of its most conventional interpretations being to indicate a 'conspiratorial' situation. Another example would be 'husky' speech, in which the throat is constricted to produce a hoarse effect, commonly used to connote disparagement (as when 'Never!' is spoken forcefully in a low pitch-range).

Oral effects. Increased lip-rounding ('labialization') is an important feature contributing to a number of paralinguistic effects, e.g. dislike, scorn or (most obviously) as a feature of intimate vocal play (as in talking to babies or animals). A muscularly tense, precise mode of articulation is commonly used as an indication that the speaker is becoming increasingly irritated.

This is by no means a complete classification. In addition, one could refer to various kinds and degrees of resonance of articulation, contrasts in register (e.g. normal versus falsetto voice), spasmodic articulations (e.g. giggling, tremulousness), nasal effects, and many more.

What should be clear from even this brief illustration is that it is important not to underestimate the range and subtlety of the para-language that we can all intuitively interpret and produce ourselves as mature speakers of a language. This, as we have seen, is particularly evident during the process of foreign-language learning, where, characteristically, these are the features of one's mother tongue that it seems most difficult to eradicate. Even highly motivated foreign-language learners seem to find it almost impossible to replace their own paralinguistic system by that of another language. Why should this be? Doubtless it is something to do with the early age at which these features are learned. Paralinguistic features seem to be among the first language specific vocal contrasts produced by the child. It is normally assumed that a child begins to communicate in its own language when its 'first words' appear – usually around the end of the first year. But for several months before this, the child has already been using certain of his language's paralinguistic features. At around seven months, biologically conditioned babbling ceases to be random and un-differentiated: the vocalization becomes gradually organized into 'sentence-like chunks'. Long before one can identify specific vowels, consonants or words, there is an impression of organiza-tion and meaningfulness in the babbling, recognized by the parent in such comments as 'Baby always says that when his brother comes into the room'. The basis of this parental awareness is in the emerging intonational, rhythmic and other patterns which the child is introducing into its utterance. Babies respond to adult tones of voice very early indeed – from around two months; and it is these which are the first effects to emerge in their own produc-tion – from as early as seven months. It is at about this time that one can begin to tell children from different language backgrounds apart. Of course, the child takes many months to learn, control and use the whole range of his language's paralinguistic features; but the basic point is that during the first year he is well on his way to becoming an extremely competent paralinguist – which makes it hardly surprising that such features, being learned so early, are the most difficult to uproot later.

But much of this is speculation. We are still a long way from the stage of being able to state with confidence the facts of first- or second-language learning. It is but recently, after all, that para-linguistic phenomena have been studied at all in sufficient detail to warrant the formulation of testable hypotheses about their acquisition. But progress is being made. It is at least now possible, using a general phonetic framework, to define and classify all the tones of voice that the human vocal apparatus can produce, and a number of descriptions of particular languages are well under way. Progress in studying the variety of functions in paralanguage is much slower, but even here information is accumulating, as the references below make clear. There is still a considerable gap, however, between our intuitive ability to recognize and interpret paralinguistic effect – our 'natural' sense of linguistic appropriateness and taboo – and our ability to state in clear terms what it is that we perceive. The spectre which still haunts papers on paralanguage, including this one, is the extraordinary difficulty of putting into words and diagrams what it is that we hear, in order that the effects described be as meaningful as possible to the reader. Nor is it at all obvious, at present, how paralinguistic information is to be correlated with the data derived from the study of other modes of expressive behaviour. But at least, these days, we are beginning to have some precise ideas about exactly what it is that has to be correlated.

1 Published as *Linguistics at Large*, ed. N. Minnis, Gollancz, 1971; Viking Press, New York, 1971; Paladin Books, 1973.

Crystal, David, *Prosodic systems and intonation in English*, Cambridge University Press, 1969.

Crystal, David, 'Prosodic and paralinguistic correlates of social categories' in E. Ardener, ed., *Social Anthropology and Language*, Tavistock, 1971, pp. 185–206.

Lyons, John, 'Human language' in R. A. Hinde, ed., *Non-Verbal Communication*, Cambridge University Press, 1972, pp. 49–85.

Sebeok, T. A., Hayes, A. S., and Bateson, M. C., eds., *Approaches to Semiotics*, Mouton, The Hague, 1964.

J. A. V. Bates

The Communicative Hand

'. . . other portions of the body merely help the speaker, whereas the hands may almost be said to speak. Do we not use them to demand, promise, summon, dismiss, threaten, supplicate, express aversion or fear, question or deny? Do we not use them to indicate joy, sorrow, hesitation, confession, penitence, measure, quantity, number and time? Have they not the power to excite and prohibit, to express approval, wonder or shame? Do they not take the place of adverbs and pronouns when we point at places and things? In fact, though the people and nations of the earth speak in a multitude of tongues, they share in common the universal language of the hands.'

We can now give an explanation of Quintillian's observation in A.D. 80.[1] Though superficially different, there are similarities at a deeper level between acts of communication through the voice and the hand. Both the sounds we produce and the gestures we make are caused by precise adjustment of length and tension in a particular combination of active muscles. At some place in our brains, shouting 'Hi' and pointing with our index finger are similar. They are both acts whose goal is to attract attention; both are the result of a prior selection from a 'library' of inherited and acquired patterns or programmes for the activation of selected muscles. It is not surprising that speech and gesture have features in common. At the level of physiological mechanism they both depend on the selection of patterns of innervation in similar muscular mechanisms to achieve similar goals.

One obvious similarity between speech and gesture is that the 'meaning' of an item of each may be greatly affected by its context.

The phoneme 'Hi' is not the same as 'high', and the gesture 'thumbs-up' is not the same as 'thumbs-down'. The meaning of a finger posture can be affected by the position of the forearm and elbow, just as the meaning of a word can depend on its context. This essay is concerned with finger postures which have a large element of meaning independent of context in the above sense, and with static finger postures rather than movements. This is a purely practical restriction. There is no vocabulary of movement other than a few verbs of action. But although the vocabulary is limited, simple postures can be studied in the large amount of material available to us in representational art.

The most primitive representational drawing makes clear that the hand with fingers fully extended was some sort of communicative symbol. There are hundreds of such hands in prehistoric cave painting,[2] and one of the earliest representations in Egypt shows each ray from the sun ending in a hand.[3] Metal hands, possibly as lucky charms, have been found in Etruscan graves[4] and through succeeding ages there are carved, modelled, drawn, painted and, most recently, photographed hands. This is a large body of data, and the problem is to assemble it into some sort of order. If we start from the central idea that the finger posture is the signal in an act of communication between its owner, 'the sender', and an observer, 'the receiver', we find that hand postures can be ordered into groups like colours of the spectrum.

In so far as we are senders, the spectrum has at one end hand postures which are rare and special signals, postures which initially require the owner's concentrated attention, and which are produced at first by the tensing of more muscles than are strictly needed. The receiver of these special signs will instantly see some special significance. At the other end of the spectrum, we find hand postures which occur without attention to any of the details and with only the minimum of muscle action. Observers may find postures of this sort ambiguous, or doubt that they are signals at all.

Starting at the top end of the spectrum (Group 1 of Table 1), we would have the most unusual finger postures, for example the freak finger postures mastered by Hindu temple dancers only after years of practice starting in childhood. Equally special and bizarre are some of the finger postures devised for spelling and counting which go back at least to the Greeks. If the illustrations of these are reliable, the ancients acquired by practice far more different and repeatable postures of the fingers than we can master.[5] I will

Table 1 *Varieties of the Communicative Hand*

Postures of the thumb and fingers	State of the sender	State of the observer
Group 1 Special signs needing much practice	Concentrated attention	Instantaneous perception
Group 2 Common signs needing little or no practice		
Group 3 Postures signalling social status or mental attitude		
Group 4 Postures signalling the physiological state	Complete inattention	Doubtful perception

not consider these in detail. Each finger posture has one-to-one correspondence to a number or letter in some symbolic system of notation, and each posture has a simple equivalent sound in a speech vocabulary.

In the next group (Group 2), there are three postures with variations which have a long history.

The Manu Pantea

The Manu Pantea is a finger posture found in three variations[6]. In varieties a and b in Figure 1 it had a significance for the Romans, another for the early Christians and a secular significance in more recent times. This change with time in the meaning of a finger posture is similar to the change in the meaning of words. We can be confident that the Manu Pantea had some special significance in early Roman times, because a hand in posture b mounted on a plinth was found at Pompeii.[7] But its use in Southern Italy goes back at least several centuries, because it is represented on Greek vases from Apulia of the fourth century B.C.[8] It is the finger posture commonly found on the sarcophagi of Roman consuls and in this context it seems to have some meaning, such as 'I am

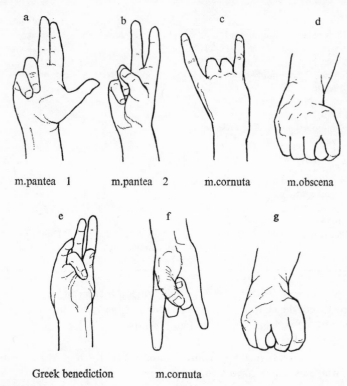

a	b	c	d
m.pantea 1	m.pantea 2	m.cornuta	m.obscena

e	f	g
Greek benediction	m.cornuta	

Figure 1

wise', 'I am a judge' or 'I teach'. It was described as a gesture for orators by Apuleius in the second century A.D.[9] The Christians took over the images of imperial Rome and the Manu Pantea is seen in the earliest Christian sarcophagi.[10] The Emperor Constantine III is portrayed giving this sign on a coin which can be precisely dated A.D. 385.[11] By the sixth century at Ravenna, the Manu Pantea appears in a variety of portraits of religious personages from the Godhead downwards[12] and it is established as the

Christian sign of benediction. In the Middle Ages, the religious association was carried to particular detail and the Manu Pantea became a formalized representation of the Trinity. The thumb represented God, the index finger the Holy Ghost, standing between the Father and Son. The third finger represented the divine nature of Christ and the fourth the human nature of Christ.[13] In a manuscript of about A.D. 1000[14] reference is made to the three fingers representing the Trinity as if it was then common knowledge. However, the pre-Christian secular meaning of the Manu Pantea was never quite lost; in France it was known as *le main de justice* and in Germany it can still be seen in oath-taking ceremonies. The Manu Pantea is still on sale in Italy as an amulet or lucky charm against all manner of human disasters.

The separation of the two extended fingers to form a v is a variation in the Latin Benediction sometimes seen between the eighth and twelfth centuries. Winston Churchill was probably not the first to use the Manu Pantea in a pun. Variety in meaning of the same posture in different societies is illustrated by reference to the Italian dictionary on manual gestures, from which we learn that Churchill's v-sign is the way Neapolitan schoolchildren indicate a call of nature to their teachers.

The Greek Benediction (Figure 1e) is a variant of the Manu Pantea, dating from the early fifth century. In this posture the thumb and four fingers spell out the four letters of the abbreviated Greek form of the name of Jesus Christ (ICXC). The X (Chi) is formed by the thumb crossing the bent fourth finger.[15] A typical example with the Greek letters above can be seen in the mosaic in the apse of the cathedral in Cefalù, Sicily, dated about 1148 (Plate 9).

To summarize: one can discover six different meanings of the Manu Pantea at different places and different times. A statement equivalent to 'I rule' or 'I judge' or perhaps 'I speak' as given to personages of imperial Rome and later to the Ruler of Heaven; a statement of benediction, 'I bless you in the name of the Trinity'; in the Greek form, 'Jesus Christ'; in oath-taking, 'I will speak the truth'; with Churchill 'I will bring you victory'; in the Neapolitan classroom, 'I want to be excused.'

The Manu Cornuta

The next finger posture from antiquity is the Manu Cornuta, in which the little and index fingers imitate horns. Like the Manu Pantea, it is pre-Christian, Christian and non-Christian. The posture was certainly current in Roman times and a single carved Cornuta hand was found in Herculaneum.[16] In post-Roman times it was a protection against bewitchment or the Evil Eye. When the horned hand is pointed at the supposed possessor of the Evil Eye, it neutralizes his malevolent magic. It may have had some similar meaning to the Romans and is seen in grave reliefs from Palmyra of about 240 A.D.[17] The early Christians used the Manu Cornuta as a sign of banishing evil.

Plate 10 shows the hand of St Luke from a sixth-century Ravenna mosaic where the Manu Cornuta also appears in the hand of God accepting the offerings of Abel and Melchizedek. It appears occasionally in religious illustration up to the fourteenth century.[18] The Manu Cornuta had a secular use throughout Europe at least up to the seventeenth century – when pointed at a man it insulted him by implying that he was a cuckold[19] – and like the Manu Pantea it is still on sale as a lucky charm. The undoubtedly strong signalling-power of the Manu Cornuta is used in contrary meanings, that of protection on the one hand and of aggression or insult on the other. We find the same alternative meanings between extremes in our speech. For example, the word 'bewitched' had an exclusively unpleasant meaning up to the fifteenth century. It then began to be used with both this meaning and the opposite, to express delight and enchantment, and this second meaning is the one it usually has now. A similar example is the word 'agony', which can now be used in the sense of 'awkward'. It looks as if a reaction can set in when a communicative signal by gesture or speech becomes too unpleasantly powerful. We remove its sting by giving it a feeble alternative meaning.[20]

The Manu Obscena

The last hand in this group, the Manu Obscena, was named and described by Roman writers including Ovid. It is called in Italy today the *mano fica* or 'fig hand' ('figs' was the Roman slang for haemorrhoids) and has a similar name in France, Germany, Spain and elsewhere. In England we have an expression of contempt, 'I don't care a fig', but we do not now name this gesture, so far as I know. A colleague who was a boy in Cape Town thirty-five years ago tells me that this gesture was the rudest one schoolboy could make to another. But in contrast another colleague, who spent her childhood in Vienna, tells me that this was a gesture which one girl would make to another to wish her luck in examinations. Thus in having simultaneous contrary meanings of insult and protection it has had a similar history to the Manu Cornuta.

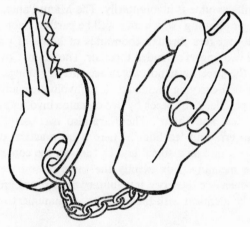

Figure 2 A suggested present for the newly wedded

Recognizing this finger posture and knowing its various meanings, it was with some surprise that, on a recent visit to a laboratory in Yugoslavia, I saw people smiling at a cartoon (Figure 2) stuck on a notice board. The words underneath were translated for me from the Slovene and the joke was not apparent. I was told that the finger posture means an absolute, emphatic negative. The point of the cartoon is that a newly married couple will never get a home of their own because of the cost of houses. Here we see a finger posture of classical antiquity still with much communicative power but with a new meaning in a non-superstitious culture. If the people in Yugoslavia were to go to Rio de Janeiro they could buy exactly what the cartoon says they need. In Rio, the Manu

Obscena is sold today as a lucky charm to protect against losing the key.

This group of postures could be called the 'speech-equivalent' hand because of the close equivalence between each posture and an item of propositional speech. The Pantea, Cornuta and Obscena are finger postures which can be assumed by anyone almost without practice and one may well ask if they are not, therefore, assumed involuntarily, that is without the intention to communicate. The answer is that they are. The Manu Obscena is sometimes a preferred position of the hand at rest, and the tendency is said by Wood Jones[21] to run in families. I would guess that about 5 per cent of adults assume it involuntarily. The Manu Pantea appears in 'two-finger pointing' which may well be partly a habit acquired by cigarette-smokers through thousands of hours of practice in using these two fingers extended together. The Manu Cornuta can be seen in the street in hands which are carrying things, particularly of women carrying handbags. The involuntary adoption of postures is paralleled in speech by two common involuntary speech utterances, 'er' and 'hum'. There are also two useful verbs in English, 'to err' and 'to hum'. There is no practical confusion between the sound as a signal and as 'noise'; the context distinguishes the meaning. For exactly the same reason we are not confused when we observe involuntary finger postures which happen to be identical with those used as communicative signals.

The 'physiological' postures

We now turn to look at the other end of the spectrum (Group 4, Table 1). In these postures the artist is using our intuitive awareness of the normal hand in a subtle way to send out a powerful message. Each of us acquires in the course of our daily life, a store of information about normal human finger posture. This store is common to us all and it enables artists to communicate in subtler ways than the depiction of finger signs. To receive the artist's message requires some sophistication and effort on the observer's part. The point can be illustrated by studying the finger posture of Christ in early religious illustrations. The illustrator of Christ has a problem with acute theological overtones. Is Christ to be shown in every way within the normal limits; or alternatively as a normally earthbound human but with abnormal skills and habits; or even as a being beyond gravity and thus obviously outside any standards of human normality? Specifically, is Christ the Infant to be shown with finger skills which imply supernatural endowment, and is Christ the Crucified to have hands in the posture of any human corpse? Circumstances force the illustrator to place the fingers somehow, and in no way can he avoid a charged theological statement whichever position he puts them in. Dorothy Shoor, in her work *Devotional Images of the Virgin and Child in Fourteenth-Century Italy*, used the different kinds of activity of the Infant's right hand and the direction of his gaze as the basis of her classification. These two parameters alone give her ten main types, further divided into thirty-five sub-types. She shows that there is a change as the fourteenth century progresses from a hieratic deity figure, with the fingers of the right hand giving the Latin Benediction, via an intermediate type who seems perplexed about what his right hand should be doing,[22] towards a type of infant whose hands do human things. This shift in illustration accompanies a shift of theological position instigated by the Franciscans who, in order to spread the Gospel to the poor, invented homely episodes in Christ's childhood and these were seized on by illustrators. Perhaps the most positively human thing the Infant can do with his fingers is No. 32 of Dorothy Shoor's types, namely to suck them, and particularly at the wrong moment. There is, therefore, no doubt at all on which side of the theological fence Ambrogio Lorenzetti stands, when in 1342 he depicts the story of the Infant Jesus being presented in the Temple to St Simeon (see Plate 11). The same emphatic means of statement was adopted by one of the young revolutionaries of Renaissance Florence, Masaccio, who in his Pisa *Madonna* now in the National Gallery has the Infant not with just two fingers in his mouth, but with the two fingers with which he has previously given the Roman Benediction (see Plate 12). The significance here is that these particular two fingers are not the ones commonly chosen by an infant for its sucking pattern, nor are they the fingers that an infant would use for stuffing grapes from Mary's right hand into his mouth, although the picture has this reference to the Passion.[23] But by choosing the index and middle finger Masaccio seems to communicate the signal from Jesus: 'You see I'm an ordinary infant, not the superhuman prodigy who gives you a blessing with these two fingers.'

The illustrator of Christ the Crucified has a similar problem; will he depict the normal or the supernatural? In an era when the corpse was less concealed from public view, it would be common knowledge that the fingers begin to curl inwards about eight hours after death, and remain fixed in semi-flexion. Now if Christ's fingers on the Cross are shown in any position other than that of rigor mortis, a signal is sent out that we do not see a human corpse obeying natural laws. Christ on the Cross is first shown as triumphant over death and his fingers are straight. From the end of the thirteenth century he is shown as after a death in suffering. His fingers are curled in rigor mortis, and this slight change makes the point of his humanity in a subtle but emphatic manner.[24]

Our knowledge of the normal can be used in other ways, for example, when the illustrator selects an unnatural posture to attract the viewer and stir his emotions by a sombre reference to the future. In *Madonna with Sleeping Child* by Bellini (Plate 13) we know that no normal baby would sleep on his mother's knee like this for more than a few seconds. The unnatural stretching of the nerves that run into the upper arm quickly brings on pins and needles which would wake up the infant. Bellini's intention is to make us sigh knowingly and recall his *Pietà* (Plate 14). Bellini's two pictures put side by side make the reference perhaps rather too easy and obvious. Bellini influenced Dürer in the same direction and looking at the Infant's left arm in Plate 15 one perhaps needs to remind oneself that Dürer was a complete master of naturalistic drawing, and there is no chance at all that this left arm is the incompetent mess-up it seems to be. So what message is this obviously unnatural child communicating? Dürer is referring you to the left arm of Eve holding the apple in his engraving of the Fall of Man (Plate 16). Note also the odd position of the fingers of the right hand of the Infant, with the third finger emphasized by its position outside the Virgin's collar. This is surely no accident, for the third finger, as I remarked above, symbolized the divine nature of Christ in the Latin Benediction.[25]

We have now examined the two ends of the spectrum, and are prepared to consider in some detail a finger posture which falls somewhere between the two ends. The posture has no name that I can discover, and so I call it the 101 ('one-o-one'). It is illustrated in Figure 3.[26] The 101 refers to the gap–no gap–gap sequence between the four extended fingers. The 1X1 refers to a variation of the 101 where the middle pair are crossed. The history of this finger posture appears to be as follows.

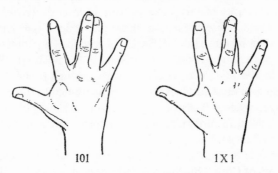

101   1X1

Figure 3

My researches show it first in the middle of the twelfth century. I have so far been unable to find evidence for it in Egyptian, Greek, Roman or early Christian representation.[27] Its first appearance seems to be in Sicily, in the mosaics of the cathedrals built for the Normans; these mosaics were made by Greek or Byzantine craftsmen around 1150. In the figure already illustrated in Plate 9 we can look at the left hand which is holding a book for us to read the text at the words '*Ego sum lux mundi* . . .' Do the fingers look natural? Would it not be more usual to have them more equally spaced? With the question in our minds we can go fifty miles to Palermo to the rich mosaics of the Palatine Chapel of Roger and there we see the three Fathers of the church, St Gregory, St Basil and St John Chrysostom (see Plate 17). Here St Gregory and St John are giving the two different versions of the Greek Benediction, but what is St Basil saying to us with his spindly Byzantine right hand? The hand of the central figure must be supposed to convey some message, and these fingers show the 101 spacing. The left hand of the apse figure in Monreale, a short distance away, holds the book in the same finger-spacing as in Cefalù. These mosaic craftsmen, working between 1140 and 1170, were in no sense artistic originators. They worked from pattern-books, and perhaps Byzantine examples of earlier date could be found.[28]

If we go next to Torcello, near Venice, we see the Virgin on the west wall of the basilica, in the orant posture (see Plate 18); both her hands show the 101 spacing as in the St Basil in Palermo. This mosaic cannot be dated more precisely than the twelfth or thirteenth centuries. If we leave Venetian mosaic and go to Tuscany, we find examples of this finger posture in three different kinds of twelfth-century work. First in Byzantine-style *Virgin and Child* panels, then in the hand of Christ in crucifixes attributed to the School of Berlinghieri which flourished in the region of Pisa and Lucca in the middle of the thirteenth century (Plate 19). The 101 hand is in most surviving crucifixes attributed to this School.[29] The finger spacing is also found in carved marble pulpits of the Pisano School towards the end of the thirteenth century in Pisa, Pistoia and Siena.[30]

Around 1290 to 1300 the 101 posture suddenly vanishes from the fingers of Christ, his Mother and his earthly servants. There is not a hand showing the 101 in the works of Giotto and his followers, and I have not found it in works in the international Gothic style nor in works of the early Florentine Renaissance.[31]

We have gone forward 130 years, and it now appears in an unexpected place, but in a circumstance where it is fortunately datable, conspicuous and clearly intentional. The 101 finger posture appears in the left hand of the Infant Jesus, in *St Luke Painting the Virgin* by Roger van der Weyden (Plate 20), and datable to 1435. This finger posture is not found in any surviving works of masters of the early Netherlandish School, which can be given a prior date. Van der Weyden's source for this posture and his reason for using it might be discovered by further research.[32]

From 1435 onwards there are many examples in the work of masters working in the Netherlands, the Rhineland and the north of France between 1435 and 1460; these men were the younger contemporaries of van der Weyden and were influenced by him. In an *Annunciation* in the Metropolitan Museum in New York the hands of a Virgin are undoubtedly in this posture, and there is agreement in attributing this painting to an immediate follower of van der Weyden working around Amiens in 1450.[33] In a famous altarpiece now known as the Avignon *Pietà* (Plate 21) the hand of St John is in the 1X1 position. The date of this picture is around 1460. The fact that the buildings in the distance have been identified as Byzantine is of interest in view of the earlier history of the posture.

Thus, the revival of the finger posture began in the Netherlands in 1435 and during the next twenty-five years spread locally eastwards and southwards. I can find no examples across the Alps before 1465; by this time the posture was well established in the second-generation Netherland masters Memling, Bouts and Joos van Ghent.

The evidence seems to be that the Italian School was introduced to the 101 and the 1X1 by Zoppo and others in Bologna in 1465–70 (Plate 22).[34] The court of Ferrara with which this group of artists was associated had particularly close contact with the Netherlands, and there is evidence, albeit disputed, that van der Weyden worked there in 1450, as did Joos van Ghent at some time, so the influence could be first-hand. It had not yet spread to Florence or Venice by the 1470s but in the 1480s its use in both these cities is evident. There are three examples in Botticelli's work, all datable around 1485 (Plate 23) and Verrocchio and his School adopted it in the 1480s.[35] In Venice the leading painter was Giovanni Bellini; he puts the hand of St Francis into this posture in the San Giobbe altarpiece, which can be firmly dated to 1485 (Plate 24).[36]

So the posture of the 101 hand is re-adopted in Italy rather abruptly in the twenty years between 1470 and 1490. It is seen in reliefs as well as in paintings, and seems particularly favoured in the Virgin's hand, to a less extent in other saints, male and female, but not, so far as my present records go, in a minor character earlier than 1500.

The detailed documentation of the 101 and 1X1 in the next 100 years is beyond the scope of this essay, but its appearance in a few conspicuous highlights of the High Renaissance and Mannerist periods will be enough to show what happens. Around 1500, Michelangelo was in his twenties; it is no surprise to find it in the right hand of the *Pietà* in St Peter's. But in 1508 he begins to use it in minor characters in the Sistine Chapel ceiling. Raphael ignores the posture until about 1515 but uses it freely in the last few years of his career, notably for the important hand of the Virgin in the Sistine *Madonna* (Plate 25). Meantime, his associates Giulio

Romano and, especially, Sebastiano del Piombo take to it avidly for portraits and scatter it about in the conspicuous hands of players of minor roles. Italian art in the sixteenth century becomes dominated by elements which emphasize a higher emotional key. One way is by an exaggerated refinement in deportment and posture, and in this climate the 101 is rapidly devalued as an item of communicative currency. Titian uses it for the conspicuous hand of the ascending Virgin in the Frari *Assumption* (1516), but he also uses it for the extended hand of the Apostle. In portraiture, Titian uses it in the right hand of an unidentified pretty girl later called the Repentant Mary Magdalene, and Bronzino gives it to all possible subjects, male and female, young and old.[37] The 101 quickly finds its way to the Fontainebleau School (Plate 26). Niccolò dell' Abbate (1509–71), who worked in Fontainebleau, in a drawing now in Chatsworth, gives it both to the madam who keeps the brothel and to the client whose exploring fingers most blasphemously mock the Virgin's hand on the naked body of Christ (Plate 27).

Thus, by the 1570s the communicative value of the 101 had been reduced to nothing.

There is no point in following the 101 through the ensuing centuries, since for 350 years its value has stayed where Niccolò dell' Abbate put it. You can see it today in Carnaby Street[38] and Oxford Street (Plate 28), and in the West End theatre belt where 'Christ' has his fingers in the 1X1 clasping the microphone (Plate 29).

This is a brief review of the data about a single posture which, as far as I know, has not before been collected together. The problem is what can we infer from it?

Starting at Cefalù the evidence between 1150 and 1300 makes it difficult to avoid the conclusion that the 101 finger posture is a sign. But of what? One would expect, and indeed hope, that some German scholar of the last century would have gone into the problem in much greater depth than I am able to, and found mention of it in Byzantine theological writing. I still feel that such a scholar must have done so, but so far I have no evidence of his existence.

Professor C. Mango and Professor H. Ladendorf, who has reviewed *The Hand in Art* with an extensive bibliography,[39] have both replied to me that they have no knowledge of any reference to this posture. In the circumstances all I can offer is the following speculation. In the Middle Ages the middle finger represented Christ as a Divinity (in the Trinity), and the ring finger represented his human nature. The conspicuous fusion of the two fingers could be a finger sign of the dogmatic statement that Christ was both human and divine.[40] When the two fingers not only touch but cross, this could be an additional reference to the cruci-fixion.

The use of the posture abruptly vanishes after 1300 along with the successful drive in the fourteenth century to humanize Western Christianity, and when the 101 returns in 1435, van der Weyden may have got it direct from Byzantium or via Sicily or Tuscany. I must suspend judgement on whether the 101 was a sign with a universal meaning when it spread round Italy in the 1470s and 1480s. But clearly thirty years later it was a cliché, a way of emphasizing elegant otherworldliness. And from this point it rapidly degenerates in significance, just as any over-used impreca-tion becomes a mild swear-word. The 101 is still retained in our culture and, I imagine, is secure because it is a slightly unusual position for the hand and so calls attention to itself. But like some words – 'awfully' for example – it is now in currency with a very vague meaning ('look at my hand'), or with none at all.

Summary
I have selected a very small sub-subject of 'The Body as a Medium of Expression', namely static finger postures and their com-municative power. The reason for this selection is a purely prac-tical one: data for study exists ready-made in representational art.

There emerge from the study clues to basic principles which govern some aspects of expressive human behaviour. One can call them basic principles with some confidence because the same prin-ciples seem to apply to finger postures and speech communication.

We inherit a bias towards adopting some patterns of finger position rather than others, just as we are born with a tendency towards uttering certain phonemes in infancy such as 'dad' and 'mum'.

We can acquire special postures through daily practice just as we acquire the special phonemes of an adult language.

A special finger posture can become a sign as soon as it occurs consistently in the same context.

Variation in the posture of the wrist, elbow and shoulder can have the same effect on meaning as variation in related words can have to meaning of a word.

There is abundant evidence of the change in meaning of a posture with passing time, and of different meanings at different places at the same time.

Some finger postures which are capable of being a signal are on other occasions assumed unconsciously and are then like 'noise' – the same applies to some common words which phonemically are identical (e.g. 'err' and 'er'). A finger posture, like a word, can be weakened by the simultaneous adoption of two meanings, a feeble and a strong.

An example is given of how a slight unusualness in spacing of the fingers can be used as a sign, evolve into a mannerism, and degenerate to worthlessness as an item of communication.

The similarity between speech and finger posture derives from the basic fact that the body behaves as an integrated whole. The variety in behaviour is merely the expression of countless millions of possible combinations of patterns of lengths and tensions of the muscles, and the principles which underlie all modes of expression are, for this very reason, essentially similar.

1. *Quintillian M.F. Institutio Oratoria* XI, **3**, pp. 85–7 in Loeb Classical Library, Tr. H. E. Butler, vol. 4, p. 289.
2. e.g. the painting or stencilled hands in the Castillo caves; see M. Raphael, *Prehistoric Cave Painting*, Bollingen Series 4, Pantheon, 1946, fig. 31.
3. Representation of celestial power by a symbolic hand in the sky starts with the Sun God of the Ancient Egyptians (see F. T. Elworthy, *The Evil Eye*, John Murray, 1895, p. 244) and reappears in Semitic art a century before Constantine (A. Grabar, *Christian Iconography*, Princetown University Press, New York, 1968, p. 40). In the Middle Ages two hands, a right and left, are occasionally shown in the sky. It is striking to see how the symbolic value of the hand is degraded when it becomes a slightly more obvious human appendage (see L. Twining, *Symbols and Emblems of Early and Mediaeval Christian Art*, Longmans, 1852, fig. 2).
4. Illustrated in F. T. Elworthy, loc. cit. p. 241, figs. 96–101.
5. G. Austin (*Chironomia*, 1806, Ed. M. M. Robb and L. Thonessen, Carbondale Ill., 1966, p. 27) shows twenty-seven different finger positions for representing the values 1–9, 10–90 and 100–900. One could imagine that

after much practice any number from 1 to 999 could be signalled by three consecutive finger postures in a second or two.

6. For a fuller discussion of the history of this finger posture with many references, see M. Heuser, *Gestures and Their Meaning in Early Christian Art*, D. Phil. Thesis, Radcliff College, Harvard University, 1954 (available on microfilm at the Warburg Institute library).

7. Illustrated in Elworthy, loc. cit., p. 293, fig. 136.

8. Illustrated in E. Pfuhl, *Maleri und Zeichning der Griechen*, Munich, 1923, vol. 3, fig. 369.

9. Quoted by W. W. Artelt, *Die Quellen der Mittelalterlichen Dialogarstellungen*, Ebering, Berlin, 1934, p. 9.

10. A. Grabar, loc. cit., fig. 90, *Christian Iconography*, Princetown University Press, Bollingen Series 35, 1968, fig. 90.

11. A. Grabar, loc. cit., fig. 98.

12. See e.g. the hand of God and of one of the three angels in the Ravenna S. Vitale mosaic of the episodes in the life of Abraham.

13. The earliest authority I can find for this is Guillaume Durand, or Durandus (1230–96), quoted by A. N. Didron, *Christian Iconography*, vols. 1 and 2, 1841, Tr. E. J. Millington (1851). Republished Ungar, New York, 1965, vol. 1, pp. 408–9.

14. The following is a quotation (kindly supplied by Mr Geoffrey Needham, University College, London) from Alfric, 'Homily on the exhortation of the cross', translated A. S. Napier, in *The Legend of the Cross*, 1894, p. 104: 'Though a man wave about wonderfully with his hand nevertheless it is not a blessing except he make the sign of the cross, and forthwith the fierce fiend will be terrified on account of the victorious token. With three fingers must a man make the sign and bless himself for the Holy Trinity, which is a glory-ruling God.'

15. This is a simplified version of the instruction given in the *Byzantine Guide to Painting*, translated and reprinted by Didron, loc. cit., vol. 2, p. 395. The date of the original guide is uncertain, perhaps the tenth or eleventh century.

How to represent the hand in blessing.

When you represent the hand in blessing do not join the three fingers together; but cross the thumb by the fourth finger, so that the second, namely the index, remaining upright, and the third being slightly bent, they may both form the name of Jesus (IC). Indeed, the second, remaining open, indicates an I (iota), and the third, when curved forms a C (sigma). The thumb is placed across the fourth finger; the fifth is also a little bent so as to indicate the word Christos (XC); for the junction of the thumb and the fourth finger forms a X (chi), and the little finger by its curvature forms a C (sigma). These two letters are the abridgement of Christos. So, by the divine providence of the Creator, the fingers of a man's hand, whether they be long or short, are so placed that it is possible for them to figure the name of Jesus Christ.

Heuser, loc. cit., p. 162, notes that this sign is one of the few to be a Christian invention and to be original. It appears first on an ivory carving of an emperor on horseback (Barbarini diptych, Louvre, Paris), dated around 500, probably from Constantinople. It is arguable that when the tip of the fourth finger just touches the tip of thumb, the two represent Eternity by making a circle. The whole finger posture would then become a sign of the eternal Trinity.

The position of the fifth finger in the Greek Benediction is variable. It can have the slightly flexed position as recommended by the writer of the guide. It can also be fully extended or fully flexed – see the hands of St Gregory and St John Chrysostom in Plate 17. The semi-flexed position seems the most difficult of the three to adopt, the other two seem more 'natural'. In my opinion the different positions may well indicate three different shades of theological opinion, but if so they have still to be unravelled. It seems unlikely that the difference represents artistic licence, or the fashion of a certain school, or the blind copying of previous work, but there is no way of settling the matter at the moment.

16. Elworthy, loc. cit., p. 264.
17. This posture can be seen in a number of the grave reliefs on display in the British Museum, and also in a Mother and Child in the Fitzwilliam Museum, Cambridge. It would seem that the mother is using this sign to protect her child, although the Museum catalogue suggests that the fingers of her hands are being used to 'adjust her dress'.
18. e.g. by Andrea Orcagna in the Strossi Chapel Altarpiece dated 1357 (Florence, S. Maria Novella). St John on Christ's left has his right hand in the Manu Cornuta. Heuser considers that this may be a variant of the Greek blessing, in which case it would be a rather elementary error by the artist.
19. For discussion of this with references see Elworthy, loc. cit., pp. 262–3.
20. The reverse process also occurs. 'Holy' words can be degraded by use simultaneously as a mild swear word, and the Manu Pantea, a sign of blessing in the name of the Trinity, can become, with a little rotation of the fore-arm and a slight upward thrust, an obscene gesture.
21. F. Wood Jones, *Principles of Anatomy as Seen in the Hand*, 2nd edn, Baillière Tindall and Cox, 1941, p. 152.
22. e.g. In an adoration (Carrand Diptych, Franco-Flemish School, Bargello, Florence) the infant sucks his right index and blesses with his left hand!
23. This is the explanation given by Hendy in his notes on this picture in the National Gallery (Thames and Hudson, 1963, p. 94). The bambino sucking two fingers is also seen in a Madonna with Saints attributed to Masaccio from S. Giovanne a Cascia (Reggello, Florence).
24. Two crucifixes attributed to Deodato Orlandi can be compared to make this point. The first dated 1288 in Lucca (Pinaco) has the outstretched fingers; the second dated 1301 from the Convent of St Claire San Miniato al Tedesco has the fingers curved.
25. This observation seems to exemplify what Didron wrote in 1841: 'Christian archeology, to become a science, requires like botany and other natural sciences, to be scrutinised even in its most minute and microscopic details: in fact the true science exists only in those details.'

26. The use of the binary notation 1 and 0 to signify existence and non-existence of the gap between the fingers enables one similarly to name other finger spacings as the '100', the '001' and the '010'. Each of these has a definite history in representational art. The '010' is found in some early Flemish painting, particularly of the Master of Flémalle (see Panofsky, *Early Netherlandish Painters*, figures 100, 205, 209 and 211).

27. This statement is based on working through three large photographic collections as well as searches in museums and elsewhere. A single exception is in the hand of a Disciple in the S. Pudenziana mosaics, Rome. These mosaics are dated before 420, but fortunately for my generalization the relevant section of the mosaic was restored in the sixteenth century!

28. The Byzantine style and iconography started to spread round Europe in the middle of the twelfth century. The 101 hand is to be seen in both the Virgin and Child in the Westminster Psalter (London, British Museum, Royal M.S. 2A XXII). Although it is not possible to establish the exact date of this it is probably before 1200. There must have been earlier examples in Byzantium, but the 101 is not present in the mosaics of Daphni and Hosios Lukas of 1080–1120. Unfortunately there seem to be no surviving Virgin and Child panels datable around 1100.

29. To date I have records of the 101 in nine Altarpieces and Virgin and Child panels painted in Tuscany in the second half of the thirteenth century. Also in fifteen painted crucifixes from the same area and period. The attributed problem is a subject of dispute between experts, and at least one of them has remarked on the 101. E. Sandberg-Vavala (in *La Croce Depinta Italiana* vol. 2, p. 555) notes its presence in the hands of St Francis in the Pescia Altar of Bonaventura Berlinghieri and in the Crucifix in the Villa Basilica, Lucca. She inclines for this reason among others to attribute them to the same hand. Besides appearing in the hands of Christ and the Virgin and St Francis it appears in the hands of various other Prophets and Saints. Giunta Pisano and his followers in Siena were disposed to use it rather freely.

30. It is to be seen in nine of the sculptured panels in five of the pulpits of the Pisano's. Only in the hands of Christ and the Virgin, not in the numerous other persons present.

31. This sweeping statement needs qualification to the extent that the 101 is put into the hand of the Virgin clasping the upright shaft of the Cross in a crucifixion attributed to Orcagna (Florence, Uffizi, No. 3515). It is occasionally used by minor fourteenth-century masters who seem to be continuing in a more heiratic and counter-Giotto attitude for example by Tino di Camiano (Florence, Bargello, No. 434) and a few of the followers of Duccio (Siena, Pinaco. Naz.).

32. There were close political and trading contacts between Flanders and the tottering Byzantine empire in the early fifteenth century. Roger could well have redrawn the Infant's rather stiff and forced position from an icon he had seen.

33. The work referred to (No. 32.100.108–111) is fully discussed in the

Metropolitan Museum Catalogue of French Paintings, XV–XVIII Centuries, pp. 1–7.

34. Marco Zoppo used the 101 in the Virgin's hand in New York (Metropolitan No. 1414). Carlo Crivelli similarly uses it in the Virgin's hand in London (National Gallery, No. 724), New York (Metropolitan, No. 49.75), Boston (Museum of Fine Art) and Milan (Brera).

35. For example in two Virgin and Child works in Florence (Bargello, Nos. 296 and 116), and also in a Baptism (Florence, Uffizi).

36. The use by Bellini of this posture for the hand of St Francis is not original, St Francis is given it in Tuscan works of the second half of the thirteenth century (see note p. 186). It is interesting that Bellini does not use it for the Virgin's hand, and elsewhere in his work its use is very muted.

37. The Titian referred to is the well known portrait in the Pitti, Florence, and there are several other copies. I have records of the 101 in ten portraits by Bronzino.

38. In a fashion article in the Evening Standard of 6 March 1972 there was a photograph of the latest belt-clasp. This was a shiny metal hand in the 101 lying nicely on the model's front below her waist line!

39. Ref. *Zur Hand in Medicine et Artibus*, Festschrift for Professor W. Katner, Triltsch Dusseldorf, 1968, pp. 61–90.

40. It is of interest that the first appearance of the '101' in Sicily was not in the hand of the Saviour, but also in the hand of St Basil in Palermo (see Plate 17). This is St Basil the Great who in 370 succeeded Eusebius as Bishop of Caesarea and who was influential in writing against Arianism. The Arian theology was based on the absolute transcendence of one God the Father, alone uncreated, unbegotten, and eternal. In logical consequence the Saviour was assigned by the Arians to a subordinate position, created by God, finite, and though sinless, at least in their theology, liable to sin. The opponents of Arianism were equally emphatic that the Saviour was divine, and this doctrine had been formally expressed in the Nicene Creed of 325 – for a fascinating account of the verbal jugglery see Kelly, *Early Christian Creeds*, pp. 205–62. Eusebius's position at the Council of Nicaea is generally interpreted to have been placatory, and Basil is said to have been generous and sympathetic to opponents. It might thus seem consistent with his nature and reputation that he should be depicted giving the sign of a compromise theology, namely that Christ was simultaneously divine and human.

Aaron V. Cicourel

Gestural-Sign Language and the Study of Non-Verbal Communication

The Problem of Context-Free Norms in Non-Verbal Communication

The concern with language origins and manifestations of language in auditory, pictorial or gestural forms points to the cognitive basis for using and understanding movement and sound as communicational systems. Communicational systems achieve considerable power when detached from their context of use. But these context-free communicational systems interact with thinking and memory activities to create a data base for processing inputs from various sensory modalities. The creation of ideal typical forms of language categories, be they gesturally or auditorily based, is central to an understanding of how context-free forms of communication develop and are used in everyday exchanges. These ideal forms of language provide a context-free matrix that can be imposed on everyday interaction to create beliefs and consensus or agreement on semantic issues. The context-free forms also enable various members of a group or society to make judgements about other members, thus establishing grounds for normative or socially acceptable agreement.

We do not have such ideals for non-verbal communication. In the United States, however, American Sign Language is emerging as an ideal normative system of gestural signs. This formalization of gestural language has relied on oral-language conceptions of grammar, but this development is possible because of the existence of organized native gestural signs as used by the deaf socialized in deaf families. The study of gestural signs affords us a basis for understanding the role of non-verbal communication among the hearing despite the fact that such communication remains residual for speaker–hearers. Gestural systems, like oral systems, seem to have normative features peculiar to a particular culture. Hence the non-verbal forms used by the hearing in a particular culture can be related to the gestural forms developed by the deaf.

Gestural-sign language and language origins

A broad spectrum of researchers – interested in language origins, language acquisition and use, and semantic information-processing – have found common ground through studies of verbal and non-verbal communication. A recent paper by Gordon Hewes (1973) refers to work on teaching some form of gestural- or pictorial-sign language to chimpanzees to trace the possible gestural origin of language. Hewes refers to papers by Hockett (1960) and Hockett and Asher (1964) to indicate how conditions basic to the development of language like productivity, displacement, the designation of semantic qualities, and the like, can be found in a gestural system. Hence language need not have started as a vocal or acoustical system. Hewes, like others before him, argues that a gestural language was probably more appropriate to the form of life of early hominids. He notes how the complexity and form of life would give rise to cognitive abilities associated with a particular form of language development. Hence during man's early use of verbal language, forms like embedded nouns, and passives, were probably not developed. Recent studies of present-day hunting and gathering groups reveal, of course, complex oral language forms. Therefore, we must not extrapolate too readily from present conditions to those that might have existed for early hominids. The central point is that language development is said to have evolved according to the complexity of man's cognitive and social life. Complex social institutions, therefore, presuppose important cognitive and linguistic foundations.

Hewes notes that although we cannot 'go back' and capture the nature of early language development in hominids, we can seek evidence based on neurophysiological development, brain capacity, tool-making and use, and the like, to piece together how language developed.

A number of researchers (cf. Hewes) have suggested that

vocalization was probably not the basis for propositional language, but primarily for emotional displays. In primate studies it has been claimed that vocalizations have been used for territorial markings or spacing to set off local troops, but there is no implication that a propositional format was involved. They appear to be situational and triggered by internal and external stimuli that do not come under the animal's explicit control.

The studies of teaching some form of gestural- or arbitrary pictorial-sign language to chimpanzees (Gardner and Gardner, 1969; Premack, 1971) are cited as possible evidence for the gestural origin of language. Hewes notes that in these studies the chimpanzees do not originate signs, nor do we know whether they could teach such signs to other chimpanzees. The generative aspect of language – not in Chomsky's sense, but in a broader sense that would include interaction settings and specific cognitive structures – is what is at stake here. Present-day gestural language as used among the deaf does not require any use of the vocal–auditory channel of communication, and this system of manual signs can be communicated to deaf children or hearing children with ease in the same 'natural' sense as when we talk of the hearing–seeing child who acquires oral language.

A recent paper by Stokoe (1972) answers Hewes's suggestion that gestural-sign language does not contain the complexity that oral language possesses. Stokoe notes that unlike oral signs, gestural signs have more information attached to them than the vocal sign and also act as indicators of more details. Gestural-sign language includes many connotations that become marked in the context of using manual signs. Stokoe refers to primate studies to note the importance of feedback when an animal could see its own hand move. The movement becomes a signal to the recipient of the movement as well as to the sender. He stresses the point that when a tool is used and then displaced with a gesture that simulates the use of the tool, the movement or gestural sign becomes an icon representing the use of the tool. But the issue of what kind of cognitive development is needed for the animal to receive such information, and act on it, is not clear.

The general thesis explored by Hewes is that gestural language is prior in evolution to or independent of oral language. Studies of deaf communities reveal that man has always been capable of developing a gestural system of language regardless of which system, gestural or acoustical, comes first. The study of gestural-sign language sheds new light on information-processing systems by stressing the role of several modalities and different levels of analysis.

A general point is that if auditory language began to displace some form of gestural system (if this thesis is to be believed), then the gestural significance of language would become less organized as a codified system of gestures used propositionally, and therefore more and more residual as an index of the informational particulars available in everyday social interaction. The representational context would become radically altered. The considerable information we can experience through several modalities as modified by our thinking, and the interaction that occurs with our memory, become compressed into sequential auditory–verbal expressions whose limitations are seldom examined. Thus we find non-verbal communication is always present in everyday interaction but inadequately indexed by acoustical forms. Our accounts of our experiences, therefore, must always be represented by unexamined limiting factors associated with speech. The context of interaction becomes crucial for understanding the role of non-verbal communication. This is not simply a question of how context-free expressions presuppose ethnographic details, as articulated in particular settings, but how the idea of social structure requires a model that is not limited by the verbal accounts of members, despite our reliance on such accounts to claim findings. The general problem is how to represent a broader conception of everyday life by recognizing and formalizing non-verbal activities in interaction, while also examining the limitations of verbal accounts for understanding everyday communication. Additional constraints are introduced because of having to speak sequentially while experiencing information from several modalities simultaneously. Finally, the study of gestural signs forces us to re-examine whether morphemes or morpheme-like units, much less sentential structures, provide necessary and sufficient conditions for the analysis of everyday human and primate communication.

We need to study how the emergence of social organization is related to the development of cognitive and communicational skills regardless of the specific form of language that is used. The development of pictographic notational systems provided considerable complexity to forms of oral culture and history. Verbal languages can be quite complex in the way they can displace iconic features that must be imagined by user and receiver. The development of Chinese, Egyptian and Sumerian hieroglyphics provided iconic or pictographic information, but we do not know what kinds of oral-language forms accompanied the emergence of pictographic forms, though researchers in this area all insist that the pictograph forms were independent of speech. Some pictographic forms were later accompanied by notations indicating speech cues (Sturtevant, 1917; Friedrich, 1962; Gelb, 1952; Jensen, 1970; Diringer, 1968). But to communicate across time and space with pictographic art-like forms must have been cumbersome, and presumably a script that could be written more quickly became more and more dominant. The initial pictographic forms were dropped. The script became a kind of shorthand and lent itself to standardization. These later stages of cultural evolution were already quite complex and obviously cannot be related to earlier hominid forms. The problem of teaching 'language' to primates would have to clarify the evolutionary status of early hominids, and the complexity of their everyday existence, before using a language derived from more complex group life where verbal forms had become quite elaborate in displacing various types of information over time and space.

Hewes and Stokoe and others stress that the use of gestural signs involves more than the gestures or signs themselves. They involve the ethology of the group involved and their lived experiences with each other (Cicourel and Boese, 1972a; 1972b).

We can shift here, for the moment, to the idea that earlier pictographic forms (American Indian, Chinese, Sumerian, Egyptian systems) are word-signs that are pictures with presumably some independence from speech. Because we know very little about how culture structures the connection evident between these pictographic forms and speech, we make unexamined assumptions about what we are teaching primates and the kind of structure attributed to gestural signs.

Presumably, oral languages achieved some of their formal structure through a written idealization process that presently cannot be discerned in gestural-sign language, for the latter does not possess this form of representation. A way of approximating this evolution of writing systems by seeking a notational system for gestural signs will be discussed later in the paper.

Language socialization and the deaf

In my study of British gestural-sign language and verbal communication among the deaf I have stressed my attempts to create a context for the analysis or description of materials. This creation of a context is necessary to suggest what the meaning of the materials might signify. Hence what particular gestural signs mean in some dictionary sense is of less interest to me than how I come to appreciate their production by observing their manual generation and their verbal description by others and myself. In using a story (presented later) about a married couple discussing their next holiday, I structure the kinds of gestural signs to be used from my perspective as a hearing–seeing person. By creating a hypothetical story from the perspective of a hearing–seeing person who can speak normally, I compromise my contact with the world of the deaf because of numerous assumptions and conceptions about the meaning of the oral-language terms I use in the story. The meanings I assume are not readily available to the deaf subjects who must somehow interpret the intentions of the story. The gestural-sign language produced, therefore, becomes oriented to an oral conception of social reality. This oral-language orientation forced upon the deaf by the hearing world is not to be equated with a deaf person's interpretation of some event explained to him by another deaf person using gestural-sign language.

The way in which hearing–seeing children learn to represent their thought and remembered experiences through an oral modality remains unclear, despite the fact that they initially rely on the perception and processing of information from other modalities to satisfy their everyday activities. The activities I want to outline are as follows.

The child's acquisition of communicational devices is assumed to begin at birth, though we cannot pinpoint the time at which these devices can be used competently in an adult sense. The use of different modalities is integral to the child's receiving information about social orientation, nourishment, physical security, emotional security, etc. A vast array of potential information can impinge upon the child. Depending on his culture, the child must convert experiences from several modalities into oral representations and also interpret verbal signals as signifying various types of details available from other modalities.

What is the relationship between sound and the representation of everyday experiences? The sound system presumably characterizes the experiences and thought processes, including non-verbal forms, through an arbitrary set of acoustical signals. If our experiences and thought processes can also be represented and indexed by iconic or pictographic forms, then we can have two competing or complementary types of representational abilities. This interpretation presumes the dominance of an acoustical interpretational system for mediating our experiences and thought processes in everyday exchanges, as well as relying on the oral modality for representing non-verbal activities.

Humans are obviously capable of creating communicational systems that do not depend on an acoustical representational system. Exploratory research on hearing children born to deaf parents whose first language was gestural sign (Cicourel and Boese, 1972a; 1972b) supports the idea that having normal hearing does not lead to an automatic acquisition of oral language. Both languages can be learned fluently.

The next obvious point is to ask how much of our non-verbal capacity for communication is facilitated, masked or distorted by our exposure to oral forms. This is difficult to study but the use of video-tapes in the study of children in testing and classroom settings (Cicourel, 1974; Mehan, 1971; Jennings, 1972) reveals an informational disjuncture between oral expressions and non-verbal activities in the same interaction setting. What is not clear is which modalities are being attended to when the actor attaches interpretative significance to what is being experienced. Recent research (Cicourel *et al.*, 1974) in primary-school settings reveals how talk is often misleading because the teacher is engaged in activities of a non-verbal sort that undercuts what she is saying, or makes what she is saying irrelevant because her talk seems to be redundant or marking time while she engages in other activities. Further, her gestures or touching of children, her glances, communicate information that is not marked clearly in her speech or not marked at all. After a formal lesson the teacher was asked to describe the event. Her descriptions frequently relied on unclear glosses or truncated expressions that made use of standardized language categories. But these categories often can transform or distort or obliterate details that can be discerned from the video-tape.

There is another problem here. We can easily acknowledge that a hearing–seeing child often cannot represent his intentions or understanding by verbal means. But it is difficult to obtain clear measures of this problem because any description of the child's difficulties entail references to a setting whose features require adult description (and condensed description at best). But descriptive statements of the child's activities are available and are not unusual. What is difficult to assess is what the child seems 'to know' despite not being able to represent himself or herself verbally or through some kind of oral expression. Acting out the meaning of sentences provides some basis for revealing compre-hension, but the problem persists in classroom settings where the teacher must make a judgement she cannot objectify for others and where the demands of the educational bureaucracy require that the child should demonstrate his or her comprehension through oral activities or verbal activities that are written. The child's written expressions can provide indirect evidence of his thought processes and their relationship to some of his verbal skills.

In the case of the deaf child the problem is more complicated, and perhaps more interesting because the deaf child can seldom express himself verbally with the same proficiency as the hearing child. Hence the deaf child's written expressions can be important for understanding concepts that have been presented in an oral form through lip-reading, and then in written form. A child who has learned gestural-sign language at home as a first language and from peers in school may use this gestural system to mediate the verbal information he or she receives. This implies differences in how information is received, organized, stored and retrieved. There are several issues here. Some researchers are interested in the organization of manual-sign language and how it can be seen to possess a structure that is similar to or different from oral-language structure. The hearing researcher's conception of lan-guage is based on his own and others' conception of oral-language syntactic structure and the role of phonology and semantics. Hence the prior significance of the oral model is paramount.

Another problem is the extent to which all gestural-sign language-users today are educated in orally dominated contexts, and how much of their use of gestural sign is a reflection of oral-language syntax and semantic interpretations. Gestural signs are described and compared to oral-language structures in a context of communicating results and an understanding of what is produced for consumption by a hearing audience. The oral dominance is unavoidable despite the hearing researcher's strong interest in the elements of 'natural' gestural sign as used by persons born deaf whose first language is manual sign.

Deaf communication and gestural-sign language

Everyday communication between hearing and deaf persons raised in a hearing–speaking world is constrained because the deaf lack the usual exposure to intuitively acquired linguistic rule systems for understanding casual and formal speech acts and rules said to govern conversational exchanges. For the deaf, this has meant that their efforts to communicate with hearing persons requires them to learn a system of rules that originated with acoustical properties that are represented formally by a standardized orthographic system; yet they have no direct exposure to the vocal–auditory system that gave rise to the grammatical rules and categories. Even when the deaf are exposed, from an early age, to the vocal–auditory rules or their representation as written symbols, it is not clear how this oral-language system is being mediated by the deaf person and what kind of thinking is involved. For persons born deaf in deaf families, the problem is different because these persons are usually exposed to a manual- or gestural-sign system that may have borrowed elements from oral-language rules, but the gestural signs can stand as an independent language system. What is important about the gestural-sign system is that it is self-contained, needing no help from the oral-language system, and hence is a generative system that can be passed from one generation to another.

To orient the reader further it is necessary to distinguish between what can be called native gestural-sign language as a first language that deaf persons born into deaf families acquire within the same household, and gestural-sign language, which we can call second-language gestural signing (Cicourel and Boese, 1972a; 1972b). Most deaf communities in Western societies produce both kinds of signers. The first group, or native gestural signers, are invariably deaf unless hearing children of deaf parents, while the second group, or second-language gestural signers, are hearing persons who have learned to use gestural signs. A third group includes the deaf born to hearing parents. Depending on their education and age of exposure to deaf groups fluent in the use of gestural signs, this third group may approximate native signing or second-language signing. The second-language-signer, however, can seldom avoid using his knowledge of oral-language rules when interpreting and generating gestural signs. Many deaf persons born to hearing parents and educated almost exclusively in schools stressing oral methods may also make use of oral-language gram-matical rules and meanings when using gestural signs, but some of this latter group can switch to a native sign code when signing with deaf persons whose knowledge of oral-language syntax is minimal.

When we describe deaf sign language as a system of organized gestures having all the qualities of oral language despite being more context-sensitive and not having an abstract orthographic system to represent its structure in a context-free way, we must not forget that our interpretation of the gestures is dominated by a hearing–speaking conception of what a 'language' should be like. This point is important when trying to describe the meaning of gestural signs because there is a tendency to reify the significance of different movements and to assign interpretations that are based on an understanding of the significance of grammatical rules in oral language. Our orientation to oral language makes it diffi-cult to sustain the idea of a different way of using, organizing and storing information for the deaf, when we make inferences about the linguistic structure of gestural-sign language.

All language expressions are indexes of a broader context of meaning that is both linguistic and extralinguistic, and the extra-linguistic meanings are integral features of any interpretation of clearly marked linguistic elements. Hence the description of gestural-sign language is complicated by the same difficulties that plague the analysis of oral language: the selective attention and memory of the participants and the observer operate continuously to create different data bases for both the participants and the observer or analyst. Specifying a data base, therefore, is always a problematic and practical issue. In studies of oral language we tend to resolve this problem by conventional (normative or socially designated) ways of representing sentences and conversational exchanges that often reify the data base because non-verbal activities are either completely eliminated or ignored when making inferences of a syntactic, phonological or semantic nature. What is stressed are formal rules of speech and conversational exchanges despite the fact that the organization of the data base is often unknown *vis-à-vis* its significance in a larger population of language-users. In studies of gestural-sign language the problem is complicated because we do something similar but always in a context where the oral-language representations are viewed as passive vehicles for describing the gestural signs. Further, the dictionary meanings of oral-language lexical items invariably become a hidden resource for the researcher, despite the fact that such meanings are often limited for understanding spontaneous conversational exchanges among hearing–speaking–seeing persons.

I want to underline the significance of the interactional setting as a complex resource of potential verbal and non-verbal meanings that are only partially indexed by the oral or gestural signs used by hearing and deaf persons. For the deaf the non-verbal communication involves visual information that is consistent with their use of gestural signs and thus fits into the general presentational modalities that serve as informational resources for them. For the hearing, the picture is more complicated because they do not have a formal way of generating and interpreting gestures or other non-verbal communication. The study of deaf gestural-sign language can be central to our understanding of non-verbal communication among the hearing, just as oral language is used to construct formal properties about gestural-sign language. Our biggest problem is not to allow either to reify the interpretation of the other. Researchers (Furth, 1966; Conrad and Rush, 1965; Conrad, 1970; Bellugi and Siple, 1971) have suggested that memory and the organization of oral communication seems to be different from the memory and organization of gestural-sign usage. This would explain some of the difficulties experienced by hearing persons when describing non-verbal forms of communication. A similar problem exists for deaf persons' use of oral language; they experience difficulties with its formal properties. Deaf persons born to hearing parents and raised in hearing–speaking settings can acquire a fairly strong, but not a native command of oral-language syntax.

Problems of method in translation and transcription

My analysis of the video-tapes of the story (Figure 1, p. 209) reveals the same cognitive problems I seek to describe in the study of verbal and non-verbal communication. I could not process the gestural-sign visual information while selectively attending the simultaneous oral translation that accompanied the picture. Neither source of information was adequate for understanding the audio-visual setting. My informants also found that the gestural signs were often unclear unless they could attend to the oral-language translation or the lip-movements or finger spelling that accompanied the gestural signs.

A key person in the adult story exercise was Le, an adult born in South London who became deaf as a child after acquiring a normal command of oral language. He produced five versions of the story. He not only used manual signs that were supposed to be translated versions of the written story, but he also spoke the story as he signed. A second-language signer, Ce, a hearing adult who has had years of gestural-sign experience with the deaf in South London, provided formal translations. Ce's voice was picked up by two microphones that recorded her interpretation of the signing being done by Le. The audio portion of the video-recording contains Le's spoken version of the story, and two audio versions by Ce, spaced a second or two apart. This made listening to the soundtrack quite difficult and confusing. Ce's translation includes more than an oral English gloss of the gestural signs used by Le. Her translation also incorporated her perception of Le's lip-movements and occasionally his voiced interpretation of the story. A third translation, done a few weeks later, was provided by Pe, a hearing person born and raised in South London of deaf parents. Pe's first language was gestural sign.

The uninformed viewer must attend to the oral-language translations by Le and Ce to interpret the gestural signs. I found that my memory of the story as signed was inadequate to translate the gestural signs with the sound turned off. Having to contend with two slightly spaced translations did not help my attempts to transcribe the gestural signs because I had to separate what I heard from what I could see. The discrepancy was obvious immediately. Le produced gestural signs and finger spelling that did not correspond to the written version of the story. The gestural-sign versions did not correspond clearly to his oral rendition of the story, or the versions supplied by Ce. Some of the finger spelling was so rapid that it was difficult to tell what was being spelled until after many viewings were completed. Some signs were not translated by either Le or Ce.

Because of the technical difficulties associated with the change from British video standards to American standards, some eighteen months elapsed before I could study the tapes. As my recognition of British Sign Language (B.S.L.) began to return, I could begin to separate what was being said from what was being signed, but the confounding was quite obstructive at times. I had to suppress some details to understand others. I could not write down the oral version each time while simultaneously comparing what I heard with the gestural signs on the video-screen. I had to remember what I thought I perceived and then re-wind the tape once again to view the section I had transcribed from the oral part to confirm or note differences between the oral rendition, the gestural signs and the original written story. I found myself listening to a section of translation while watching the signing, quickly re-winding the tape and then trying to ignore the glossed speech version but retaining its basic information while then trying to decide which signs could be interpreted by reference to my memory of the spoken version. I could not co-ordinate the sound-track and visual information because the selective attention required to understand the spoken version of the story made it difficult to follow the gestural version simultaneously. If I focused on the gestural version it was difficult to follow the spoken version carefully.

Hearing–seeing subjects find it difficult to identify non-verbal features when responding selectively to spoken language because no convenient vocabulary exists for describing such activities (Cicourel, 1973). My viewing of the video-tape leads to a reconstruction of the original experiences as now constrained by the video-camera's perspective.

The problem of description is complicated by the fact that different types of gestural signing occurred and the oral-language renditions of the gestural signing also changed over the course of the exercise. The assembly of my analysis, therefore, is the problem. When I first planned the exercise I had hoped that Le would employ native signing, or the gestural signs that the deaf use amongst themselves when signing informally. A few days before the exercise Le informed me that he would not employ native signing for the video-tape session because it would not be grammatical in an oral-language sense, and hence could convey a negative image of gestural language. He further stated that the translator (Ce) might be embarrassed because of difficulties she could encounter translating native gestural signs.

During the first part of the exercise the first signer, Le, attempted to provide careful oral-language spoken and gestural versions of the story to the second signer. He found it necessary to produce additional versions because the second signer had difficulty comprehending the signing. The second signer found it difficult to sign the story to the third signer. The first signer felt he should repeat the signing to the second signer and to the third signer because of their 'nervousness' and apparent inability to follow the story. The second-language and native gestural signing are captured by the camera and illustrate the problems of translation and transcribing. The video-tape reveals changes in the iconic structure of the signs as they are progressively rendered for a native gestural-sign language audience, rather than for a hearing group expected to know second-language gestural signing, finger spelling and lip-movements associated with oral-language speech and syntax.

The first signer (Le) was asked to read a story written in good English (Figure 1) and simultaneously translate the contents into gestural signs. The following elements were involved.

1. The subject first reads the oral language written text.
2. The subject encodes the written version into gestural signs and finger spelling of words for which no gestural signs exist or which are seen as difficult for the deaf to understand because the context is not restrictive enough.

3. The subject shadows the written version with subdued speech, making it possible for the translator to have access to the auditory rendition, the lip-movements and the gestural signs–finger spelling representation.

4. Finally, the gestural sign–finger spelling translation produced by the subject emerges initially with oral-language syntactic word-ordering.

I have a story I want to tell you from the newspaper.

A man was arrested in America last week because he threw his wife into a public fountain. The newspaper said the wife told her husband she was anxious to swim on their holiday. The husband then pushed his wife into a fountain they were walking past. The wife was not hurt but had the husband arrested. It seems they had been arguing all morning about where to take their holiday. Last year the husband had promised to take her to the seashore this year. But the man now said he wanted to go camping in the woods. They continued to argue while walking to a friend's house and were passing the fountain. The wife kept insisting that she wanted to go swimming on their holiday. Suddenly the wife was pushed into the fountain by the husband. The wife was not hurt but the husband spent the night in gaol.

Figure 1. Adult sign language story

In the discussion of the video-tapes that follows I focus on the five interpretations rendered by the first signer (Le), the second-language translator (Ce) and the earlier and later translations of a native gestural signer (Pe). I will only provide the reader with a few lines from the first part of the story to illustrate my analysis of the video-tapes. The later parts of the interpretations and translations are often more supportive of my inferences, but the first part of the story provides an adequate basis for showing a shift in interpretation of the story upon which my analysis hinges.

I have put together several levels of meaning. The different levels were derived from different scans of the video-screen and my perception of the verbal reports. My knowledge of the original story prejudiced my attending to details on the video-screen, or available through Le's and Ce's oral translations. The translations seemed 'obvious' during the initial viewings, only to be reinterpreted later on when I continually discovered discrepancies between the written text and the gestural signs used. My attention to different parts of the video-screen and to different elements of the verbal reports sparked various interpretations of the text. The constraints of editing and integrating my analysis often masks the retrospective–prospective reasoning that produced my description.

Verbal representations of gestural signs

Compare the first three lines of the original story (Figure 1) with the first (Le) signer's initial version as described orally and as translated officially (Figure 2). The first signer, Le, altered the opening line slightly by dropping 'I have' but appropriately retaining the reference to 'a story'. The term 'public' was dropped

Figure 2. First three lines of first signer's initial version of story *

**Oral interpretation by
first signer (Le)**

I want to tell you a story from the newspaper.
A man was arrested in America last week because he threw his wife into a fountain. The newspaper said the wife told her husband he was anxious to swim on holiday.

**Second-language signer
oral translation (Ce)**

I want to tell you a story from the newspaper.
A man was arrested in America last week because he threw his wife into a fountain. The newspaper said the wife told her husband he wanted to (pause) he was angry (pause) something about a holiday in America.

Written literal translation

I want tell/say/you story newspaper.
-A- man w-a-s- arrest A-m-e-r-i-c-a America last week because you/he/ throw wife/husband/in fountain water drink water throw.
T-h-e- newspaper say t-h-e- wife /husband/tell/say/yours/her/ husband/wife/you/he/w-a-s anxious t-o swim when holiday.

Native signer oral translation (Pe)

I want to tell you a story from the newspaper (pause).
A man was arrested (pause) in Amer . . . when he threw his wife into a fountain water he threw.
The newspaper said that the wife told her husband that he was anxious to go swimming on holiday.

---

*Brackets indicate alternate interpretation possible.
Dashes between letters indicate finger-spelled word.

in the second sentence but otherwise follows the original text. The third sentence by Le contains a discrepancy in the use of pronouns with 'he' being substituted for 'she'. The translator (Ce) picked up this confusion, repeated it, and then paraphrased the rest of the sentence, altering its meaning simultaneously by substituting 'angry' for 'anxious' and adding 'America'. The second-language signer (Ce) and the native signer (Pe) translations are consistent in their following of the first signer's changes, and provide consistent oral interpretations. The written literal translation substains a sentence-like form, but the second sentence of Le's first version contains 'water drink water throw', and implies some ambiguity in the signs employed. The pronoun confusions in the third sentence are not surprising because their gestural-sign existence is quite limited, and indicates additional ambiguities in providing a gestural-sign representation of the oral-language written text.

The first oral version of the story is displayed consistently in Figure 2 (except as noted above). The word-order of oral English is preserved. The context provided an implicit basis for deciding the appropriate use of pronouns despite the error made by the first signer in saying 'he' rather than 'she' in the third sentence. The native signer noted that he had to guess what was intended because no formal way of designating feminine and masculine pronouns exists in B.S.L. The signer must make the sign for husband or wife, by having the right hand simulate the placement of a wedding-band and then add the sign for either 'man' or 'woman' to designate which spouse was being referenced. The initial dominance of oral English syntactic rules is evident from interpretations by Ce and Pe because they both trade on prior knowledge of the story and lip-reading to decide on an 'appropriate' translation of the gestural signs for a hearing audience.

The confusion over the sign for the appropriate spouse becomes more obvious in the second version (Figure 3) of the interpretations of the first three lines of the story. In the third sentence the first signer Le provides confusing oral designations of 'husband' and 'wife' and a confusing use of the appropriate pronoun. Le's interpretation, however, was essentially correct, including the reference to 'anxious'. Ce alters the first sentence by putting it in the past tense. In the third sentence she maintains the incorrect reference to the husband but alters 'said' to 'told'. She then

provides a correct oral gloss for the confusions produced by Le.
The literal signed version reveals the various confusions previously
described and suggest that Le is having difficulties producing a
second-language gestural-sign version of the story. The oral

**Oral interpretation by
first signer (Le)**

I have a story to tell you from the
newspaper.
A man was arrested in America last
week because he threw his wife into
(a) fountain.
The husband said the wife was all
/pause – Signer shakes his head as
if he were wrong and starts to sign
and talk again./
The newspaper said the husband
told her husband she was anxious to
swim on holiday.

**Oral translation by second-language
signer (Ce)**

I have told a story from the
newspaper.
A man was arrested in America last
week because he threw his wife into
a fountain.
The husband told the wife (pause)
mistake (pause)
The newspaper said the wife told
her husband she was anxious to
swim when on holiday.

Written literal translation

I want tell/say/story implied/
newspaper.
-A- man w-a-s arrest i-n America
last week because you/he/throw
wife in water/water drink ?/
fountain.
T-h-e husband say t-h-e wife tell
h-e-r husband/subject stops and
begins again/
T-h-e newspaper t-h-e- husband
/spoken as husband/tell you/her/
husband w-a-s anxious t-o swim
when holiday.

Oral translation by native signer (Pe)

I've seen this from newspaper.
A man was arrested in America
last week because he threw his
wife into a water fountain.
The husband said the wife told
her no (pause) the newspaper
(pause) the wife told her
husband was anxious to swim
when on holiday.

Figure 3. Second version of first three lines of story

English syntax shows indications of being altered. The native signre
also provides a different interpretation of the first sentence. Pe's
interpretation of the third sentence is similar to the gloss produced
by Ce though he has deleted the pronoun 'she' before 'was

anxious'. There is slightly less information in the second version of the literal-sign interpretation and the interpretations by Ce and Pe. Despite the confusions in the third sentence of the literal-sign interpretation, the first signer's oral rendition is consistent with the original text.

In the third oral version (Figure 4) the first signer again ad-

---

**Oral interpretation by
first signer (Le)**

I read a story from newspaper.
A man pushed his wife into
fountain they were walking past.
(Pause to look at script.)
Her husband said (pause) the
newspaper said the wife told
her husband she wanted to swim
on holiday.

**Oral translation by second-language
signer (Ce)**

The story from the newspaper.
A man pushed his wife into a
fountain (pause) they were
walking past and arguing
(pause)/now reading the script/
The husband said, no, the
newspaper said the wife told her
husband she wanted to swim on
holiday.

Written literal translation

I tell you story from
newspaper.
-A- man wife push yours
/his/wife in water/pool?/
fountain fall.
T-h-e-y walk past argue
/subject stops. Can't seem to
remember story and asks for script
which he reads from as he continues
signing./T-h-e husband/spoken and
basis for transcription/say newspaper
say, t-h-e wife tell yours/her/
husband you/she/want t-o swim
holiday go swim.

Oral translation by native signer (Pe)

I said story from newspaper.
A man (pause) husband pushed his
wife into fountain (pause) they
walked past arguing.
Husband said, newspaper said wife
told her husband she's wanted been
go swimming holiday.

Figure 4. Third version of first three lines of story

dresses the second signer and begins without looking at the script. He immediately alters the story by simplifying the first sentence, leaving out the reference to being arrested in the second sentence, and adding the information 'they were walking past' after 'fountain'. Le then looks at the script, adds 'Her husband said' (not in original script), pauses, and then provides an almost correct oral version of the script after substituting 'wanted' for 'was anxious' and deleting 'their'. Ce's interpretations include a condensed version of the first sentence, she then adds 'arguing' in the second sentence, and acknowledges a mistake ('no') in the third sentence. The literal sign interpretation includes a premature reference to 'argue' in the first part of the third sentence, and also provides a less coherent oral English syntactic rendition of the third sentence ('The husband say newspaper say, the wife tell her husband she want to swim'). The interpretation by Pe, the native signer, also indicates a less coherent ('wanted been go') syntactic rendition of the third sentence.

The fourth oral version (Figure 5) of the first three lines by Le are altered, more telegraphic and simplified. The oral English

---

Oral interpretation by first signer (Le)

The newspaper story.
A man's wife walking argue, argue, argue about holiday.
Wife want seaside because husband promised her last year.
Wants to swim.

Oral translation by second-language signer (Ce)

A man's wife walking along arguing about holidays.
The wife wanted seaside because husband promised last year.
Was interested in swimming.

Written literal translation

I tell newspaper story/then two hands simulate holding newspaper/story.
/Modified sign for story/
Man wife walk go argue, argue -a-/bout/holiday.
Wife want you/her/sea/side/ because husband promise sea[side].
Want swim.
Husband change think/mind/.
Want sea/side/don't/not/.

Oral translation by native signer (Pe)

Newspaper story (column it could be).
Man walking along walking argue wife want go to sea.
Husband promise sea.
Wife want swim.

Figure 5. Fourth version of first three lines of story

account includes elements that occur later in the story. The interpretation provided by Ce leaves out the reference to 'newspaper' but is coherent and condensed. Ce's account now reflects an informal use of spoken English. The literal-sign version includes a simulated visual depiction of someone reading a newspaper and a modified sign for 'story'. This version strongly resembles native gestural-sign language structure. The interpretation by Pe supports this observation despite the fact that a reader could argue that subject–verb–object structure is maintained for Ce and Pe's interpretations. Both Ce and Pe, however, are trying to preserve an oral English syntactic framework for a hearing audience. Le, the first signer, however, does not preserve oral English syntactic coherence in his oral and gestural-sign renditions. *I want to stress the importance of the constraints imposed by the use of written versions of oral- and gestural-sign language glosses. These glosses make it difficult to represent the visual significance and internal consistency of native gestural-sign language.*

In the fifth version (Figure 6) of the first three lines (based on Le's recollection of the story) there are a few modifications of earlier interpretations. Le's oral remarks are more coherent than in the fourth version, perhaps because he is not addressing the second and third signers with whom he experienced the considerable difficulty that led up to the native signing of the fourth version. Le paraphrases the story extensively by bringing in elements from later parts. Ce's rendition is coherent but does not duplicate Le's remarks completely. This raises the question of whether she is reading Le's lips this time or remembering the story from previous occasions. The literal translation retains a few elements of the native signing of the fourth version, like the modified (condensed?) sign for 'about' and the telegraphic quality of the gestural signs. The significance of the fifth version is to be found in the contrast between the oral gloss by Le and the literal interpretation of the gestural signs. It is as if Le had finally managed to deal with the two activities on parallel tracks such that the qualities of both would be satisfied. This interpretation supports the idea of two types of memory organization and matching languages. My reasoning is that Le became more and more concerned with getting the story across to the second and third signers by the fourth version, and felt he should employ native gestural

Oral interpretation by first signer (Le)

I'll tell you a story from the newspaper.
A man pushed his wife into a fountain.
The newspaper said they had been walking, arguing, all the time, about their holiday, but the wife said her husband promised to take her to the seaside because she was anxious to swim.

Oral translation by second-language signer (Ce)

I will tell you a story from the newspaper.
A man pushed his wife into a fountain.
The newspaper said they were walking and arguing, walking and arguing for a long time about their holiday.

Written literal translation

I tell you something from newspaper.
-A- man push yours/his/wife in pool/drink/water.
T-h-e newspaper say t-h-e-y walk, argue, walk, argue, long time, a/bout/holiday.

Oral translation by native signer (Pe)

Tell you story from newspaper.
A man pushed his wife into fountain (pause) ring water.
Newspaper said they walk argue long about holiday.

Figure 6. Fifth version of first three lines of story

signs. This problem of getting the story across to the signers seems to be a necessary element in the gradual alteration of the forms of communication used by Le. But these conditions did not seem to affect the two translators. The native signer's translations approximated the literal gestural-sign interpretation more than the second-language signer's translation. He is bilingual and can sustain the reasoning and memory organization needed for using the two systems of communication. Despite continual oral cues the gestural signing changed dramatically by the fourth version and underlines the significance of differences in information processing.

Almost six weeks before the actual video-taping of the exercise I asked my native gestural-sign informant to go over the story with me and to provide native signs and an oral literal gloss of the kinds of signs that could be used if he were to sign the story to a deaf

Researcher	Pe
1. I have a story I want to tell you.	I have story. I want tell you. I want tell story.
2. A man was arrested in America last week.	Last week man in America arrested.
because he threw his wife into a public fountain.	because he threw wife into water fountain, (then we'd have to) public 'open' (its) 'fountain open.' (I might add) 'open people look,' 'fountain,' (you know, you do a sort of mime). (You'd say) 'water' (or) 'fountain water.'
3. The newspaper said the wife told her husband	(We have to make the transition from the actual incident to the paper. We'd have to put that sort of in, that it was 'told out' or published, not exactly word (?), 'told out in print paper, in print paper'.)
Told out?	Told out, in print paper.
Okay. The newspaper said the wife told her husband she was anxious to swim on their holiday.	Newspaper said wife told man husband want swim holiday.

Figure 7. Hypothetical translation of story by native signer before communication exercise.

adult. Some of the transcript from this exchange also reveals differences in how the transition from oral-language representation to the use of native gestural signs suggests two types of grammatical organization and memory systems.

In Figure 7 the native signer provided many verbal glosses for which no signs were generated. He sought to preserve some semblance of oral-language syntactic structure despite the fact that I had asked him to provide only verbal glosses for the signs he used. The adverbial shift ('last week') in the first part of the second sentence does not alter the subject–verb word-order, and is not uncommon among deaf signers, but this should not imply that there are similar underlying syntactic structures. The native gestural signer is constrained by what he knows about oral-language syntax if he is to provide a gloss for a hearing recipient. The details about how to sign 'water fountain' imply giving the deaf recipient adequate clues about the visual appearance of the object being discussed. The informant felt it was necessary to distinguish between the imaginable event of 'throwing the wife into the public fountain', and how what the newspaper said requires signing something like 'told out in print paper', 'in print paper'. There is an example of optional word-order when the native signer says 'want swim holiday' in the third sentence and later in the translation used 'want holiday swim'. Our oral-language orientation dominates our reaction to the word-order reversal. The reversal of the word-order complicates the meaning of the bounded sentence for a speaker–hearer. 'Want holiday swim' could mean wanting a vacation anywhere that permitted swimming. The exchange contains various other material suggestive of different thinking on the part of deaf when generating native gestural signs. Here are two additional examples from the story.

RESEARCHER : The husband then pushed his wife into the fountain they were walking past.

PE : They argue (better make picture here) past water circle fountain (describe the fountain [using signs]) husband saw water push wife in water fountain.

RESEARCHER : But the man now said he wanted to go camping in the woods.

PE : Man now change. Want different. Sea no. Camp in woods.

It is not simply changes in word-order or expected variations in representational forms that are of interest here, but the implication that different ways of organizing information are operative both in processing what is received and in producing native gestural signs. The informant indicates something of the reasoning the deaf would use based on features that would explain to a deaf audience unstated assumptions of oral-language syntax use which would not be obvious to a native gestural signer but which we assume native oral-language-users know intuitively. In the first sentence it is the visual information that the native signer wants to mark gesturally to provide the deaf with details ('better make picture here' and 'describe the fountain') assumed to be relevant to their understanding of the intent of the story. In the second sentence ('But the man now said he wanted to go camping in the woods') the native signer feels the sentence must be broken up to reveal the complex oral-language presuppositions that accompany the verbal representation. Hence the native signer feels it is necessary to point out that 'man now change', 'want different, sea no' but 'camp in woods' should be signalled. I am not certain if 'want different' is casual redundancy, or if these terms must be signalled to clarify how different chunks of information spell out particulars implicit or presupposed in the use of oral syntax. I am conjecturing that the informant was taking pains to indicate how information communicated by oral-language syntax would best be 'chunked' if it is to be received and processed by deaf subjects who may think differently. The surface structure of the oral sentences seems to require more than a different representational form (gestural signs). The possible meanings of the content of the message for speaking–hearing subjects require translation commitments that assume knowledge of deaf intuition about language. The fact that different chunks of gestural-sign information are created implies that the boundary conditions of the model sentences used in the formal analysis of oral languages by linguists are inappropriate, despite our reliance on these oral or written glosses to describe gestural-sign language.

When the first signer, Le, paraphrases the story in Figures 5 and 6, and the native signer, Pe, breaks up the oral-language sentences in Figure 7, two different processes are implied. The paraphrasing requires cognitive reorganization and hence exceeds the representational structure of model sentences for processing and understanding the intent of the story. This general point is not specific to gestural-sign language, but indicates the necessity of incorporating processes like selective attention and memory into an understanding of language-use in everyday communication. Breaking up the sentences means that the oral-language sentence information contained in the story can vary and is not readily transmitted to the deaf.

The modified oral versions of the story by Le and his use of more native gestural signing with each succeeding version of the story (especially in the fourth version) has been described as indicative of two systems of memory organization and grammatical representation. Researchers of gestural-sign language assume that syntactic rules in gestural-sign language exist that can be contrasted with oral-language rules. These students of gestural-sign language seek a standardized set of rules based on a native signer's intuition. The native use of gestural signs in B.S.L. is responsive to organizing principles, but may best be described at this time as being constrained by the particular social contexts of delivery and what is assumed to be 'common knowledge' by the participants of objects and events inside and outside the setting.

Discussion

The two translations provided by Pe (one version was done before the video-taping and the other is based on the tape) underline the importance of native gestural signing because he stresses the additional signs necessary for a native signer to understand the relevance and meaning of the story. Pe provides details on the organization of gestural signs that suggest how the deaf think differently from the hearing. Furth (1966) has argued that thinking does not require language if by language is meant the use of verbal symbols. Furth is referring to the deaf and their lack of oral-language facility. So when he discusses the kinds of symbols the deaf employ in their thinking, he is referring to this lack of oral-language facility, and this leads him to suggest that thinking may not involve language as verbal symbols. Research by Conrad and Rush (1965) and Conrad (1970) on deaf subjects educated in the oral method of lip-reading and finger spelling indicates that the deaf do use 'symbols' in memorizing, but their nature remains open to empirical study. The deaf are capable of acquiring a highly developed system of gestural language and a use of 'symbols'. Hence their thinking does involve language. Conrad's research with profoundly deaf adolescents suggests how memory is related to thinking and the language used, by noting that memory errors of the deaf are different from those of hearing subjects and seem to be consistently patterned.

The broader questions seem to involve the existence of different memory bases for visual and auditory information. If these memory bases are related to different language systems, then a hearing–seeing person who is raised in a deaf home will learn to process information initially like the deaf and use gestural signs, while learning at a later time to speak and process oral information like a hearing person. We do not know if the deaf who learn to speak are making use of linguistic memory as Haber (1968; 1969; 1970) describes it, or whether they are using a visually based linguistic memory. For the hearing–seeing person the question is how do they recode non-verbal information into an acoustical language system? But hearing–speaking–seeing persons can develop both types of memory and language (e.g., the hearing child born to deaf parents). How is their interface negotiated? An interface occurs but the two systems seem to operate in parallel.

We cannot explain the development and parallel use of two normative representational systems only by reference to their formal properties. The parallel systems for gestural and oral languages are similar, but they are also different, because the oral system contains an explicit contrast between a normative or ideal system of rules that the linguist infers from model sentences which he uses to study formal syntactic and semantic structures, and the more complex language we use in everyday social exchanges. Gestural-sign language in the United States and Israel have only recently been subjected to this type of formal analysis. The same cognitive system, however, presumably allows the actor to tune into either the gestural–visual or auditory–verbal system of communication, but this tuning-in seems to involve different forms of memory organization. Because of the extensive formalization of oral-language syntax, a context-free story in oral language does not translate into gestural language without considerable negotiation.

An understanding of gestural communication is not simply a matter of describing how particular gestures resemble some previous or present iconic form that can be identified in the everyday world, or some sign to represent an emotional state or abstract idea in a particular culture. How I produce an analysis is an integral part of what is to be described as 'elements' of non-oral or gestural communication. An analysis is always selective but should show the reasoning and tedious observational procedures the researcher used to make the video materials and actual scenes he witnessed visible to the audience or reader. When the video-tapes are not available to an audience or reader, elements of the communication process cannot be described adequately by my oral or written representatiòns. The video-tapes allow the audience to absorb fleeting aspects of the countless particulars that I have reacted to and interpreted in creating my analysis, but which are difficult to index, or are not available to the audience for an understanding of my interpretation of the materials.

If two systems of memory organization, language principles and normative representational frameworks are operative in the use of native gestural and oral languages, then explaining the different versions of the story becomes more feasible. The initial stimulus conditions consisted of a hypothetical story about a man and a woman arguing about where to spend their holiday. I organized the story as a native speaker of oral American English, but tried to satisfy lexical differences between English as written in America and England. The oral shadowing, and the progressive switch from second language (B.S.L.) to native signing by the first signer over the course of five independent versions of the written story, provide evidence that something 'different' is taking place in the various representations. I am asserting that the 'differences' in oral and gestural-sign glosses cannot be attributed to recall problems associated with the story, but are due to the interface between parallel systems of communication. By the third version the first signer seemed to be troubled by his inability to get the story across to the second signer and unsuccessfully tried to shadow and sign the story from his memory of the script. This could account for the truncated version presented, but I would prefer to argue that the first signer's inability to produce convincing materials for the second signer led to native gestural signs which then sparked further modifications. After two sentences into the third version he asked to see the script again and proceeded to complicate his oral rendition of the third sentence. The interpretations by Ce and Pe, the second-language and native signer respectively, became somewhat ambiguous because both the oral glosses available for lip-reading and the gestural signs by Le provided confusing displays.

As noted previously, the fourth version of the story was attempted from memory and seems clearly oriented to a deaf recipient despite the representational bias inherent in the use of written English lexical items. I have claimed that the first signer transformed the initial data base of the written story into a native gestural-sign language representation in the fourth version, because he encountered deaf recipients who could not follow his oral-language syntactic versions of the story as available from lip-reading and second-language signing. The materials presented do not reveal the frustrations and delays experienced by everyone involved in the exercise. The first signer's concern with getting the story across to the second signer, and his frustration observing the second signer trying to recall the story for the third signer, resulted in the use of more native signing. This was not planned. I had hoped that similar results or native gestural signs would emerge from the other signers' versions of the story. The exercise kept breaking down because the second and third signers seemed rather uncomfortable and claimed not to understand what they were being told.

Gestural signs and the origin of writing systems

The study of non-verbal communication among hearing persons cannot be monitored carefully under present circumstances because although experienced visually, the information is often coded for representation by the verbal–auditory modality. A normative visual information processing system is needed for designating non-verbal communication because such a framework would provide a formal basis for subsuming experiences of a non-verbal sort under more general rules. We can benefit from the formalization and also monitor the problems associated with the reification that normative systems achieve when used to describe practised and enforced activities (Cicourel, 1973).

Creating a formal notational system for gestural-sign language means preserving elements of the native signer's intuition. Monitoring the creation of such a formal system and its evolution would clarify both the tacit processes associated with the acquisition of communicative competence, and also how all formal systems can reify and distort or transform the emergent elements of everyday communication. Current linguistic models are highly sophisticated normative systems that only address the evolutionary development of speech and writing from the most recent period of man's use of language. Hence attempts to teach primates 'language' stress conceptions involving sophisticated structures whose evolutionary status remains unclear and possibly misleading for understanding the learning and use of language by early man. An understanding of language-use by early man could help us devise strategies for the study of the language capabilities of present-day primates.

Some of the basic conditions for creating a formal notational system for gestural-sign language could, as a first step, involve the use of a luminous substance on the hands and face so that a film or video-tape would provide a pictorial display of where gestural signs begin and end. The role of the face and the space immediately above the waist up to the top of the head would have to be indexed. The idea is to have a trace of the different positions that the hands and fingers assume *vis-à-vis* different spatial arrangements, and how facial expressions are used, or how different parts of the face are touched during the execution of key elements of the signs. Preliminary work on problems of spatialization, the role of the face and the problems of designating the beginning and end of a gestural sign have commenced in several research centres (Stokoe at Gallaudet College; Bellugi and co-workers at the Salk Institute; Cohen, Namir and Schlesinger at Hebrew University).

The film or video depictions would be reduced to schematic form to capture the iconic or pictographic features of the gestural signs that can be designated as 'essential' for native signers. The general idea is akin to the early creation of Chinese characters and early hieroglyphic forms used by the Egyptians and Sumerians. These forms bore a striking resemblance to the objects and activities of the everyday life of the times. Deaf native signers would have to decide how characters can be created in conformity with their sense of what are appropriate movements and the distinctive features of individual signs. How something like 'sentences' would be created requires some arbitrary decisions that would then become reified in actual use by the deaf to establish preferred orderings of gestural signs. Approximations of these pictographic forms can now be found in books on gestural signs that are intended to teach signing to hearing persons. The face and simulated hand- and finger-movements are represented with arrows to indicate movement and direction. Unless the native gestural signer's intuitive conception of 'appropriateness' is incorporated into the pictographic characters, the system will quickly degenerate into another version of oral-language notation and syntax.

The evolution of present-day written languages can be simulated by the formalization of gestural sign to reveal how the orthographic forms gradually assumed shapes that did not match pictographic or acoustical patterns as originally developed, but instead facilitated their depiction by a brush or pen or pencil. This would provide evidence on how written forms displaced information that was marked initially pictographically as well as by the prosodic features of the speakers.

The creation of a normative or socially organized notational or orthographic system that would be expected to evolve into script forms, similar to changes in early Chinese characters and hieroglyphic forms, can be very important in establishing relationships between native gestural signing and the formal syntax of oral languages. This development would enable a deaf gestural signer to compare the two notational systems, but such an interface should preserve the independence of both forms.

The development of a formal notational system for gestural signs would enable hearing persons to learn a framework based on the processing of information by persons with a different representational system for organizing non-oral communication. Hence the residual status of non-verbal communication in studies of everyday exchanges would be gradually eliminated as researchers of hearing persons learned to supplement their verbal descriptions with an organized notational system based on visual information-processing. The development of a normative gestural-sign notational system would organize non-oral communication according to visual principles that would not depend on verbal memory and representational systems. This development would be consistent with the idea presented by Atwood (1971) of an executive thought-processing activity that regulates the interface between information coded by vocal auditory and visual memory systems.

Throughout Western civilization vocal–auditory communication has dominated our representation of the processing of information experienced from several modalities, as well as how we evaluate an individual's intellectual capabilities. The residual status of non-verbal information and communication has not been enhanced by the use of linguistic approaches to its notational depiction, and the implicit attribution of oral-language syntactic principles to characterize visual experiences, gestures and facial expressions. The idea of an executive thought-process that regulates the interface between the vocal–auditory and visual systems underlines the idea of coding information from different modalities into separate compatible memory-reasoning processes. This would facilitate the use of notational systems that do not force experiences from one modality to be channelled into coding schemes developed for other types of information. One consequence for researchers of everyday social interaction is that the two notational systems would provide more powerful ways of marking and understanding distinctive features than can be attended to with audio-visual recording devices. The deaf could be provided with a formal system with which to code their normal way of attending to their environment and communication with other deaf persons, while simultaneously giving them a different basis for understanding the structure of oral-language syntax. The deaf have always been exposed to oral-language syntax as if it was *the* natural language of man. If the deaf were to have a formal notational system that attempts to map their intuitive knowledge of gestural-sign language, then they could begin to appreciate the misleading features of all notational or orthographic systems when we seek to describe our experiences of visual and vocal–auditory information. The gap between the formal principles of oral-language syntax that the deaf learn and a native speaker–hearer's intuitive use of the same system would be clarified by an examination of the idealization of gestural signs. The key roles performed by practical reasoning and glossing practices in everyday communication would be seen as integral features of claiming knowledge through formal descriptions. The use of practical reasoning and the normative idealization of experiences would then be recognized as basic features of the researcher's methods and his claims to knowledge.

Conclusion

The impact of a dominating oral-language normative model for recording visual information and visual imagery is often not appreciated by linguists because they are seldom interested in non-verbal communication as a self-contained or generative language system. We do not possess a formal or normative model for recoding auditory–vocal information into visual gestural signs, facial displays and body-movements. But it should be clear that the deaf possess a system that can organize non-oral information efficiently despite the fact that everything specifiable by hearing–speaking–seeing persons cannot be recoded in present-day gestural signs as native signs of the deaf as used with other deaf persons. The principles that organize visual information and visual imagery in memory for the deaf are not available to hearing persons because the structure of gestural-sign language is relatively unknown and cannot be used as a resource for understanding context-sensitive non-verbal information among the hearing.

The adult gestural-sign language experiment reveals a number of curious problems of translation and transcription in moving from a written transcript to auditory and simultaneous visual representations of the story. The first gestural signer gradually seemed to drop the auditory–oral reasoning that organized his initial gestural signing, and began switching to an apparent implicit model of deaf native gestural signs to communicate the story to the second and third signers. Communication by educated deaf persons is usually subordinated to auditory–oral language organization because of deaf educational practices that stress the use of syntactic forms derived from oral language. Thus the apparent confusions of transcribing and translating the video-tapes can be explained by the dominance of the auditory–oral categories and reasoning used to interpret the gestural signs. As the native signer Pe explained, the simultaneous method of speaking and signing is being used and even he is biased by the lip-movements and what he can hear of the translations by Le and Ce. Yet the native quality of the gestural signs were dramatically revealed in the fourth version of the story and in Pe's independent translation of the story prior to the video exercise.

I am not concerned here with the problem of whether verbal categories have low or high abstractness, which is the problem addressed by Atwood. I am focusing here on the task of making available a formal, normative system for organizing non-oral information as developed by the deaf using native gestural-sign language. Atwood's model of the higher-level thought processes is used by him to illuminate cognitive problems, and he does not investigate the question of representation by new types of system. Nor is he concerned with how the evolution of one (the oral) as a self-contained, self-embedding and self-referencing system has made difficult the recognition of a second, a gestural-sign system with powers similar to oral language. Hence the organization of non-verbal information remains residual for hearing-speaking persons even though clever strategies that rely on oral-language structures (Hall, 1966; Birdwhistell, 1970) have been devised for describing such activities.

Can we relate the structure of sentences or gestural signs to the ways in which information can be received by hearing or deaf subjects as chunks, and then processed for comprehension? If we assume that 'chunking' oral language syntactically is different from the way the deaf organize their visual gestural signs according to implicit principles, then we should not equate gestural signs to words or lexical items, but recognize that signs index and organize other unmarked information differently. The problem is analogous to the way a grand master chess-player is said to 'chunk' more information after years of experience than a B player, and hence to perceive and comprehend a chess-board differently (Chase and Simon, 1973). The native gestural signer would be expected to 'chunk' visual information into signs differently or with more embeddings than a second-language signer. If gestural signs involve different memory principles and semantic 'chunks' yet lack a formal structure and notational or orthographic system, then we must be careful in our use of formal oral language to describe its structure and use. A formal model of gestural-sign 'sentences' based on a representation of the visual properties of gestures is needed for an interface with an oral-language model.

This paper has followed the suggestion (Bower, 1969; Paivio, 1969) that two alternate coding systems in cognition exist for visual imagery and oral symbolic processes. Atwood (1971) proposes that an interface between the two systems is accomplished by executive thought-processes or higher-order cognitive organization. The existence of higher-order executive thought-processes that can enrich the visual or auditory–oral systems presumes that cultural and normatively organized learning experiences provide a basis for 'chunking' or coding or recoding information.

The chunks acquire labels to index them conveniently for members of a group, and become a member's data-reduction device to facilitate intersubjective communication and claims of consensus or agreement.

Our discussions of non-verbal information are often naïve because we do not possess crisp, socially organized categories for identifying activities independently of social interaction settings. The ability to 'chunk' or code or recode non-verbal information under a general rule or into classes of objects by the use of a gestural-sign system would permit generalizations based on cultural or normative conceptions of what is 'appropriate' and 'normal'.

Non-verbal communication between hearing members of a group remains an *ad hoc* enterprise that is basically situated and implicit despite the availability of ambiguous oral indexes of such activity. The broader status or significance of non-verbal communication requires a model that can specify how gestural movements and facial displays fit into the general perception of visual experiences. A formalization of gestural-sign language and its facial and body-movements can provide a normative organization comparable to oral–auditory language. Gestural signs can be the basis of a writing system which uses the iconic or pictographic elements of gestures, facial displays and body-movements to develop idealized communicational strategies. The consequence of developing such a writing system based on gestural signs and paragestural qualities like facial displays and body-movements is that visual information-processing would be elevated to a level of importance comparable to oral–auditory processing. This elevation would enhance the interface between visual and auditory–oral systems.

The formalization of gestural-sign language would seek to stimulate something of the history of Chinese, Egyptian and Sumerian word-signs as a generative, self-contained basis for describing visual information. The visual system would not be subordinate to the auditory–oral system. The interface would permit higher executive thought-processes to make maximum use of both systems of information-processing to allow for independence and switching between systems.

The dominance of one modality for hearing and deaf persons

has been outlined. A related problem exists for the blind because of difficulties in using auditory–oral categories that presuppose vision (Ima, 1972). In each case the representational system revolves around the modality that is intact, though many deaf can learn to use the verbal system fairly well if raised from infancy within the oral tradition. But these deaf will not become native speakers of the oral language though they can become proficient second-language speakers depending on the conditions of their early training. The formalization of gestural signs and their interface with oral-language rules could conceivably offer to both the blind and the deaf a rule-based access to methods of communication with which it is presently difficult for them to achieve proficiency.

The executive thought-processes of the hearing–speaking–seeing persons would channel sensory information through the dominant language representational system. The hearing–speaking–seeing person would be capable of developing and utilizing both systems and would negotiate the interface to take advantage of the organizing principles of the two forms of language and their respective memory structures. The analysis of non-verbal behaviour would then acquire an elegance and power that is now denied to speaking–hearing–seeing persons. The application of the interface between the two systems would permit more powerful teaching techniques for the blind and the deaf, and enhance their communicational abilities across communicational modalities.

*

The research discussed in this paper was done in London during 1970–71 while the author held a National Science Foundation Senior Post-doctoral Fellowship at the Sociological Research Unit of the University of London Institute of Education. A small grant from the Faculty Research Committee, University of California, San Diego, facilitated its completion. The video recording was made possible through the generous assistance of the staff of the University of London Audio-Visual Centre, and its Director Michael Clarke. I am grateful to Percy Corfmat, Leonard Kent, Celia Shakeshaft, Ivor Scott-Oldfield and many others who wish to remain anonymous for their help in making this part of my study possible. I am pleased to acknowledge the helpful suggestions

of Robbin Battison and Carl Hopkins that were incorporated into
an earlier draft of the paper.

Atwood, George, 'An experimental study of visual imagination and memory'
Cognitive Psychology, 2, 1971, pp. 290–9.

Bellugi, U., and Siple, P., 'Remembering With and Without Words', International Colloquium of C.N.R.S., Paris, 1971, p. 283.

Birdwhistell, Ray L., *Kinesics and Context: Essays on Body-Motion Communication*, Allen Lane The Penguin Press, 1971; University of Pennsylvania Press, Philadelphia, 1971.

Bower, G. H., 'Mental Imagery and Associative Learning', Fifth Annual Symposium on Cognition, Carnegie-Mellon University, 1969.

Chase, William G., and Herbert, A. Simon, 'Perception in Chess', *Cognitive Psychology*, 4, 1973, pp. 55–81.

Cicourel, Aaron V., 'Some basic theoretical issues in the assessment of the child's performance in testing and classroom settings' in Cicourel *et al.*, *Language Use and Classroom Performance*, Academic Press, New York, 1974.

Cicourel, Aaron V., *Cognitive Sociology*, Penguin Books, 1973.

Cicourel, Aaron V., and Boese, Robert J., 'Sign language acquisition and the teaching of deaf children' in C. Cazden, D. Hymes and V. John, *The Functions of Language in the Classroom*, Teacher's College Press, New York, 1972.

Cicourel, Aaron V., and Boese, Robert J., 'The acquisition of manual sign language and generative semantics', *Semiotica*, 5, 1972, pp. 225–56.

Cicourel, A. V., Jennings, K., Jennings, S., Leiter, K., MacKay, R., Mehan, H. and Roth, D., *Language Use in Testing and Classroom Settings*, Seminar Press, New York, 1974.

Conrad, R., 'Short-term memory processes in the deaf', *British J. Psychol.* 61, 1970, pp. 179–95.

Conrad, R., and Rush, M. L., 'On the nature of short-term memory encoding by the deaf', *J. Speech Hear. Disorders*, 30, 1965, pp. 336–43.

Diringer, David, *The Alphabet*, Hutchinson, 1968.

Friedrich, Johannes, *Extinct Languages*, Peter Owen, 1962: New York, Philosophical Library, 1962.

Furth, H., *Thinking Without Language*, Collier-Macmillan, 1966.

Gardner, R. A., and Gardner, B. T., 'Teaching Sign-Language to a Chimpanzee', *Science*, 165, 1969, pp. 664–72.

Gelb, I. J., *A Study of Writing*, Routledge & Kegan Paul, 1952.

Haber, Ralph N., ed., *Contemporary Theory and Research in Visual Perception*, Holt, Rinehart & Winston, New York, 1968.

Haber, Ralph N., ed., *Information-processing Approaches in Visual Perception*, Holt, Rinehart & Winston, New York, 1969.

Haber, Ralph N., 'How we remember what we see', *Scientific American*, 222, 1970, pp. 104–12.

Hall, E. T., *The Hidden Dimension*, Bodley Head, 1969; Doubleday, New York, 1966.

Hewes, Gordon W., 'Primate Communication and the Gestural Origin of Language', *Current Anthropology*, 14, 1973, pp. 5–24.

Hockett, Charles F., 'The origin of speech', *Scientific American*, 203, 1960, pp. 88–96.

Hockett, Charles F., and Asher, Robert, 'The Human Revolution', *Current Anthropology*, 5, 1964, pp. 135–68.

Ima, Kenji, dittoed manuscript, 1972.

Jennings, K. H., 'Language Acquisition: The Development and Assessment of Rational and Rationalizable Skills', dissertation, University of California, Santa Barbara, 1972.

Jensen, Hans, *Sign, Symbol and Script*, George Allen & Unwin, 1970.

Mehan, H., 'Accomplishing Understanding in Educational Settings', dissertation, University of California, Santa Barbara, 1971.

Paivio, A., 'Mental imagery in associative learning and memory', *Psychological Review*, 76, 1969, pp. 241–63.

Premack, David, 'Language in chimpanzee?', *Science*, 172, 1971, pp. 808–22.

Stokoe, William C., 'Motor Signs as the First Form of Language', American Anthropological Association Annual Meeting, Toronto, 1972.

Sturtevant, E. H., *Linguistic Change*, University of Chicago Press, London and Chicago, 1917.

Paul E. Willis

The Expressive Style of a Motor-Bike Culture

The following analysis will not be limited to the unequipped body as a medium of expression, but will take bodily style, clothes, social interaction and the human use of functional and expressive artifacts as further manifestations of non-verbal expressivity. This essay is based on a research programme that concentrates on the role of pop music in the life-style of two groups – 'hippies' and 'motor-bike boys' – in Birmingham, England. I intend to publish a much longer work on this subject. The fieldwork on which this article is based was conducted at a motor-bike club in Birmingham during 1969–70. The club has now closed and the group of motor-bike boys I worked with has dispersed. I have changed the names of all individuals referred to.

The fundamental argument I want to put forward is this. Whereas 'deprived' minority cultures do not use verbal codes to express their meaning, they do have complex feelings and responses which are expressed in their own culturally resonant way. Essentially these groups have forms of expression quite as varied and rich as those in apparently more 'accomplished' cultures, but in a mode which make them opaque to verbally mediated inquiries and therefore vulnerable to gross minimization in conventional accounts. The conclusion of this essay pushes this line of argument further to speculate that it is *because* these codes of expression are largely passed over, or misinterpreted, by the middle classes and their agencies of control that they can, and are allowed to, play such a vital part in the generation of minority cultures with critical stances towards the dominant culture.

For the moment, however, it is enough to approach our

subject-matter with the view that certain styles and activities within a minority culture, far from being meaningless or random, may in fact perform something like the same expressive function that language does in the more familiar (to the middle classes) culture. Indeed, in so far as these expressive styles are based more organically and intricately in the living processes of everyday life than are verbal communications (especially of the distanced, abstract type taken as the 'educated style') they may well be superior to those of the middle-class culture. It is interesting that within the dominant culture itself there has been increasing disillusion with the traditional high-art heritage, and an unmistakable call for art that is more 'living', 'participatory' and 'relevant'.

In this essay I shall indicate what some of these 'opaque' expressive styles are in the case of the motor-bike boys, and go some way towards unpacking their meaning in relation to the central life-values of the motor-bike culture. But first, two caveats concerning the whole project of analysing non-verbal communication via language. In the nature of things, new meanings will be imported, and old meanings misrepresented, especially in the sense of becoming cerebralized. The hope must be that such meanings are gone through merely to arrive at a final sense, a final 'taste', of the original phenomenon, which does not rely mechanically on the language used to achieve it. Secondly, I have used the words of the actors themselves at times in the following presentation. This might seem strange in a context addressed to non-verbal communication, but generally I have used the actor's statements as documents *about* activity, rather than as *direct* examples of expression.

Clothes as Expression

The dress of Bill-the-Boot, Sammy, Slim Jim and Bob (a group of bike-boys within the larger motor-bike culture that I studied) was not primarily a functional exigency of riding a motor-cycle. It was more crucially a symbolic extension of the motor-bike, an amplification of the qualities inherent within the motor-bike. The strict motor-cycle apparel, i.e. that most designed to eliminate the discomforts of riding the motor-cycle, had the opposite effect. It tended to close down and minimize the natural qualities of the motor-bike. Thus, the conventional clothing of Percy consisted of a helmet, goggles, waist belt, tightly closed-in neck, gloves and large woollen socks. The helmet clearly protected against head-injury in an accident, the goggles prevented eye-irritation from dust or high winds. The belted waist and tightly closed-in neck prevented wind from entering and ballooning the clothes at high speeds. The gloves protected the hands and, by overlapping the jacket, prevented wind from travelling up the sleeve. The large woollen socks prevented air from pocketing, and kept the feet warm. Generally, this conventional gear was watertight and warm, to minimize the obvious discomforts of driving in the English climate. Also, it was generally free from all but essential accoutre-ments, and was pulled in tightly without open flaps, so as to minimize wind-resistance. In this conventional dress Percy was thus tightly packaged in, and given the maximum protection from the inherent dangers and discomforts of the motor-bike. The special characteristics of the motor-bike, its openness to the ele-ments, its instability, its speed, the free rush of air, were minimized as far as possible, so as to render the motor-cycle a neutral form of transport.

The other members of the group, the motor-cycle boys, kept the same basic elements within their style but *transformed* them by small though crucial modifications. To start with, helmets and goggles were never worn. They knew quite well that helmets were advisable for safety, if only because a national safety campaign of the time, with posters across the nation, was aimed at encouraging motor-cyclists to wear helmets. The slogan read 'You know it makes sense'. (Helmets have since been made compulsory in Britain.) The reason they did not wear them was that helmets and goggles would have significantly limited both the *experience* and the *image* of motor-cycling. Helmets and goggles destroy the excitement of the wind rushing into the face, and of the loud exhaust-beat thumping the ears. The point of fast driving was the experience, not the fact, of speed. Sports cars, though of similar speed-potential to motor-bikes, were despised. For those who have never ridden on a motor-cycle, it may not be clear that high-speed riding is an extremely physical experience. At high speeds the whole body is blown backwards; it was a common way of com-municating speed at the club to say that 'I was nearly blown off'.

When even a slight bend is taken at high speed, the machine and the driver need to go over at quite an angle in order to compensate for the centrifugal force which threatens to throw the rider off, and topple the motor-cycle away from the direction of turn. Novices find this an extremely precarious situation to be in, and can panic. The experienced fast motor-cyclist will not take a complete amateur on the back of the motor-cycle, in case a lean in the wrong direction on a fast bend upsets the precise balance, and sends them both hurtling towards the tarmac. The experienced driver becomes part of the motor-cycle and intuitively feels the correct balancing at high speeds. If there is anything wrong it is the motor-bike's fault.

The dangers and the excitement of bodily wind-pressure exist of course for the conventional motor-cyclist too, but he is partly removed from the rawness of the experience by the protection of his face and eyes and hands from the wind. He is, in a sense, contained and sealed by his gear, so that he makes decisions, and controls the motor-cycle, at one remove from the direct experiences which make the control necessary. Thus, he must lean with the machine around corners, and he will feel the force of the wind blowing his body backwards along the motor-bike, but these senses are both blunted and mediated by protective clothing. The clothing is also as streamlined and smooth as possible to prevent unnecessary drag. The experience for the motor-cycle boy such as Slim Jim or Bill-the-Boot is very different. The absence of gloves, goggles and helmet means that the equivalent of a high gale-force wind is tearing into exposed and sensitive flesh. Eyes are forced into a slit and water profusely, the mouth is dragged back into a snarl, and it is difficult to keep it closed. There is no disjunction whatsoever between the fact and the experience of speed, and physical consequences are minutely articulated with control decisions of the motor-bike. There is no sense in which the rider is protected by a panoply in which he has some calm to make protected decisions about events in the world out there. The motor-bike boy is in the 'world out there' and copes with handling his motor-bike at the same time as feeling the full brunt of its movement in the natural physical world. Furthermore, the motor-bike boy makes no attempt to minimize the drag effect of the wind. Jackets are partly open and are not buttoned down around the throat, belts are not worn, there's nothing to keep the jacket close to the skin, trousers are not tucked away in boots and socks, there is nothing to prevent wind tunnelling up the sleeves. Adornments of the jacket and free-flowing neckties add, although fractionally, to the total drag, an unnecessary drag that would be avoided by conventional motor-cyclists.

The Motor-Cycle as Expression

The motor-cycle itself was not designed for aerodynamic efficiency. All of the motor-cycle boys in the group, except Percy, preferred large cattle-horn handlebars which required an upright sitting position with hands and arms level with the shoulders. This considerably increased drag, and ironically limits the top speed of the motor-bike. But it improves handling ability and increases the sensation of speed dramatically. The conventional motor-cyclist does exactly the opposite: he lowers the handlebars and puts the foot-rests further back, so that the body can lie virtually flat along the bike and present the minimum surface for wind resistance; tiny windscreens about the handlebars are often used to protect what little frontal surface area of the rider is visible.

Thus the motor-cycle boys – that is Slim Jim, Bill-the-Boot, Sammy, Bob, in contradiction of the typical conventional motor-cyclist, Percy – were concerned to *open out* the inherent characteristics of the motor-cycle. The clothing and style and riding and acceptance of risk accentuated the physical exhilaration of speed, and the gut reaction to danger. With the conventional motor-cyclist, the qualities of the motor-cycle are closed down. The rider is completely impersonalized and hidden from view. The whole outfit is a carefully worked out, and carefully put together, attempt to muffle the effects and characteristics of the motor-bike; it is the technological answer to the problems technology has created – uniformity, anonymity, featurelessness encircle the rough, roaring, dangerous qualities of the motor-cycle. The motor-cycle boys accepted the motor-bike and allowed it to reverberate right through into the world of human concourse. The lack of the helmet allowed long hair to blow freely back in the wind, and this, with the studded and ornamented jackets, and the aggressive style of riding, gave the motor-bike boys a fearsome look which amplified the wildness, noise, surprise and intimidation of the motor-bike. The bikes themselves were often modified to accentuate these features. The high catttle-horn handlebars, the chromium-plated double exhaust pipes, the high exuberant mud-guards gave the bikes an exaggerated look of fierce power. More particularly, it was common practice to remove the baffles from the silencer box on the exhaust, in order to allow the straight-through thumping of the exhaust gases from the cylinder to carry their explosion directly into the atmosphere.

An alleyway led up the side of the church to the coffee-bar of the club. Members often parked their bikes along this narrow passageway, and stood by them talking, starting and revving their bikes, discussing technical matters or indeed, any matters at all. It could be extremely intimidating to walk up this narrow aisle. The noise was often overwhelming; the loud thumping of the motor-bike engines seemed to promise sudden movement and action – but none came, so that one could be unnerved by the continual imagined necessity to take evasive action against some fantasy explosion of movement and aggression. This feeling diminished after a time, but on a summer's evening, or on a crowded night, the walk up that thundering passage would always bring some unease.

That response illuminates a crucial aspect of the motor-cycle culture both in its image and experience. In this culture, human flesh and sensibilities exist in a very special relationship to mechanical power. Where the conventional motor-cyclist and car-driver are, to some extent, shielded from the ferocity of mechanical power, the motor-bike boy accepts it, controls it and attempts to make it his own. There are two things here: one is the flesh wrestling with and controlling mechanical power, precisely overcoming the unease produced by powerful machines; the other is the appropriation of that power within the human zone of meaning, the symbolic extension of the motor-bike into the human world. Essentially then, the motor-cycle was not prescribed by the limits of its functional use. It was accepted in the rawness of experience, allowed to make its full register on the human culture. Mechanical qualities were recognized, appreciated, extended and transformed into human qualities. This is not to posit a view of the relationship between man and machines which could be the beginning of some cybernetic nightmare of machines conditioning man, overriding his specifically human qualities. Rather it is the opposite. It is man's domination of the machine: the motor-cycle has to be controlled, the direct physical consequences of riding accepted, before the 'spirit' of the motor-bike can be appropriated and anthropomorphized.

Death as Expression

Death on the motor-bike held a particular awe and even attraction for the motor-bike boys; it held a privileged position in the symbolic world of the motor-cycle. Death on the motor-cycle was mentioned several times in our discussions. This is a selection of their comments on the subject.

BILL-THE-BOOT	I think it's the best way. I'll have a bike until I'm thirty-five, you know. I think it's the best way to die . . . I'd like to go quickly mind you, out like a light, 'bang' . . . fast like about a hundred miles an hour . . . hit a car, you know . . . smash straight into something.
P.W.	What are the chances do you think of having a serious accident?
BILL-THE-BOOT	Oh, well, I'm a nut-case you know on a motor-bike, it might do, I've had some near misses, you know, through crash barriers, and I've had concussion and things like that without a crash helmet.
P.W.	But did that make you think?
BILL-THE-BOOT	No, funnily enough it didn't, everybody else said 'I bet that's made you think' . . . You see that's why I think I may die on a motor-bike.
SAMMY	I'd like to die on, I'd like to die on a bike, that's the way I wanna go, fucking great. I'd hate to get old.
P.W.	Why?
BOB	The thing is . . .
SAMMY	Hang on you daft cunt . . .
BOB	I'd like to . . .
SAMMY	It would be a great sensation to croak out on

	a bike . . . I'd like a fucking smash, got to be a good one, or I don't want to go.
P.W.	Tell me why you'd like to croak out on a motor-bike then?
BILL-THE-BOOT	You'd hate to get old wouldn't you?
SAMMY	I'd hate to grow old, I see some old people and I think, fuck, if I was like you I'd go under the first bus.
P.W.	Well, why don't you finish yourself off with drugs and die that way?
SAMMY	Oh bollocks to that, I'd sooner kill myself on the bike any day. Just blast down the road, giving it almighty stick and fucking that's it. I don't want to know I was going to die, you know what I mean, but if I was going to die I wouldn't mind going on a bike – fucking great!

Such interest in the motor-bike should not be taken as signifying a morbid fascination with death, or as a random quest for excitement or kicks (as, for instance, in drug-use). This would be to misunderstand their relationship to the motor-bike. Firstly, it was *not* the case that they had a simple death-wish which the motor-bike could efficiently minister to. The notion of skill and experience on the motor-bike, which was widely valued, was precisely about *avoiding* unnecessary accident. To have died through stupidity or obvious incompetence would not have been meaningful. Death came only after physical limits had been pushed to the full, after the body had made massive attempts to control the machine. In an important sense, the culturally significant death was thus out of the rider's hands; he could do nothing more to save himself. This explains the kind of fatalism apparent in the way they talk about death on the motor-bike. They did not regard death on the motor-bike as a specific choice to be made with total free will. It is not, in that sense, even the acceptance of a wager, as in a bet, and certainly not the acceptance of odds unmediated by skill as in Russian roulette. Skill is important at all times, and when pushed to the limits of skill, if something quite beyond control happens to kill the rider, then that is the culturally significant death, that is 'the way to go'. The death in this case sums up and glorifies all the aspects of riding a fast bike well – those qualities which in fact, paradoxically, would make death less likely. The significance of death for the motor-bike boys is very much in *this* world, and not in any mystical 'other' world.

Thus they did not have a submissive attitude to the motor-bike, but an assertive attitude that stressed the importance of control over the machine; if the machine wouldn't be subject to the dictates of their will, then it was to be distrusted, not valued:

SAMMY   No . . . the motor-bike don't frighten you.

BILL-THE-BOOT   If the bike handles well, the bike will never beat you, if it handles bad, it frightens you, that's all.

P.W.   Frightens, what does 'frightens' mean?

BILL-THE-BOOT   No, scared, I mean. Like if I've got a bike and it don't handle well, I won't go fast on it, but if it'll do everything you want it to, well that's it you know.

Secondly, the motor-bike was not a random source of danger and excitement, but was located well within the commonsense world, and was responsive to ability and co-ordination in the physical world. Confidence in identity and the experienced unequivocality of the physical world expanded to envelop and control the ferocity of the motor-bike. This is quite contrary to the subjective vulnerability of a drug experience. Not only is the ontological security of the motor-bike boys demonstrated in their mastery of such an apparently alienating object as the motor-bike, but the qualities of the motor-bike itself are developed to express crucial aspects of this confidence in identity and unarguable reality. The motor-bike responds inevitably and concretely to a subjective will and skill, it accelerates to the point of blowing the rider off at the twist of a wrist. Control decisions are met immediately by the physical consequences of rushing air. The sheer mechanical functioning of the motor-bike, with the hardness of metal against metal, the controlled explosion of gases, the predictable power from the minutely engineered swing of machined components, underwrites a positive and durable view of the physical world. The boldness, dash and intimidation of the machine enhance a boisterous confidence in the identity of the rider. In several ways – in its image, in its difficulty of mastery, in its precise functioning, in its predictable response – the motor-bike puts beyond doubt the security and physicality of the motor-bike boy's world. In its ferocity, and undeniable presence, it contradicts the more abstract and formal structuring of the world.

Social interaction and bodily style as expression

At a simple physical level the bike-boys were rough and tough, certainly by conventional standards. Many social exchanges were conducted in the form of mock fights, with pushing, mock punches, sharp karate-type blows to the back of the neck. All of the groups (excepting Percy) had been in several fights and spoke of the occasions with some enjoyment. Slim Jim had been a Teddy boy in earlier years and had been involved in several fights during that period. He used to say that he could never understand why so many people seemed to take objection to him, and why he was so often forced into fighting. In more recent times he had been thrown out of other clubs for fighting. It was true of them all that they came to their particular club partly because other clubs, and often public cafés, would not have them.

However, their style was masculine and tough in more developed ways than the simply violent. This style, or ambience, within the culture could be described simply as the notion of 'handling oneself', of moving confidently, in a very physical and very masculine world. At one level this was the ability or potential ability to 'handle oneself' in a *real* fight situation. At another level, the same physical propensities were symbolically expanded into a rough kind of bonhomie. Movement and confidence in movement were the key to their style.

That the style and roughness of this 'bonhomie' was a *symbolic* extension of physical ability in a fight situation, and not a direct extension, is illustrated by the case of the dwarf. A dwarf used the club regularly; he was much too small to ride a motor-bike and he did not wear motor-bike gear. Clearly he was also much too small to be very effective in a fight situation. However, in a crucial sense he could 'handle himself' and was popular in the club, especially with Slim Jim and Bill-the-Boot. A common form of exchange with the dwarf was again the mock fight in which Slim Jim and Bill-the-Boot would go through an elaborate fight routine and suddenly pretend to be overpowered or mortally injured. An amusing situation was developed by the imaginary construction of a scenario which emphasised the gap between actual ability and the 'imagined ability'; the imagined ability was always a culturally approved ability. As well as mock fights, there were frequent jokes of the sort 'I'll set him onto you' when someone had apparently annoyed one of the motor-bike boys. The dwarf went along with these fictions. He would very readily stick his fists up, characterize the flashy footwork of a professional boxer and hit his adversary with what was probably all of his strength. The dramatic downfall of his opponent was greeted with puff-chested pride, strutting and baiting, aggressive shouts worthy of Muhammed Ali.

Although the dwarf clearly lacked physical strength and mastery, he more than made up for this with the symbolic masculinity and rough 'matiness' of his style. The jocular treatment of the dwarf was entirely playful, and in the end protective. In a way the rough masculinity with which the dwarf was treated, because of his cultural appropriateness, was turned, in the end, through an excess of good feeling, into a fatherly protection and support of the dwarf. He was, in a way, the mascot of the motor-bike boys; he could hold certain values of the motor-bike culture, without threatening them with any kind of outside values and, importantly, without having the actual physical strength to usurp the crown himself. It was this ability to *embody symbolically masculine qualities*, without the actual ability to be threatening in the masculine mode, that made him popular and even cherished in a way that culturally respected figures such as Bill-the-Boot were not. To have extended this kind of warmth to Bill-the-Boot might just have resulted in 'having your head punched in' for being too patronizing.

To be quite clear about the nature of this masculine style, it must be stressed that it owed nothing to the conventional notion of the healthy masculine life. Participation in organized sport, for instance, held very little attraction for the bike-boys; their view of the appropriate manly scope of action did not include the wearing of shorts and the obeying of formal rules, nor was athletic ability taken as evidence of masculinity. Attempts to channel their aggressive and robust style into formal sports situations generally met with disaster precisely because it misunderstood the nature of, and the difference between, the two kinds of masculinity. Where individuals did become involved in sport, by and large it was to spoof the whole thing. Rules and conventions were ignored, old sweaters and jeans were often worn instead of neat sports clothing. This was not due (as can so often be thought by the liberal establishment) to material or social deprivation; but to a conscious unwillingness to even begin to be trapped by the paraphernalia, the artificial external definitions of what masculine activities should be like. They would not engage in any safe channelling off of agressive feelings that might have endangered the normal course of life. That would have been dishonest. Masculinity and aggression were mixed in with normal life. To have syphoned these things off in a formal and organized way would have been to deny their identity.

A crude, completely unorganized kind of football was played in various situations, in the factory yard, or the patch or, occasionally, in the coffee bar in the club. However, this was completely unstructured and the boys had total control over the game, so that it could be moulded to their own special needs. Formal football enthusiasts may well have been alarmed by the delinquent and violent overtones of these fluid informal games, where a ball against a window, or a ball bouncing around an internal room, gave considerably more pleasure than a well-executed penalty shot. Nor did the bike-boys have much interest in spectator sports. Participation in formal games held little interest for them, and watching such games even less. Again, their mode of masculinity was different from that expressed even in sports that have developed away from the 'wholesome' notions of masculinity, such as professional football. So far as those boys were concerned, in professional spectator sports there are still the rules and regulations, still the narrowed scope of masculine behaviour, still the stereotyped symbols and clothes of the game disguising fundamental identity, denying spontaneous expression.

An official report notes the lack of interest in sporting programmes when a television set was installed in one of the spare rooms:

One point of significance that I have noted is the lack of interest in the sporting programmes, which one might have felt, in a strong physical environment, heavily orientated in the male direction, would not have been the case. This is probably because, with our current clientele, the niceties and skills of professional and amateur sport are basically lost and are therefore unattractive.

This report corroborates my view of the masculine style of the club members. It comments, at a tangent, on the disjunction between the two kinds of masculinity, and then offers its explanation. I should add that the 'niceties and skills' are lost because of the crucial kind of masculine style already articulated among the boys of the club. Their masculinity had a broader sweep than anything contained by the notion of *skill in a game*: the important skills were about preservation of life on a motor-bike, or survival in a fight situation. 'Niceties' was an alien concept altogether, that only managed to convey something of the distant claustrophobia of middle-class Sunday afternoons and china cups too delicate to handle, too small to satisfy.

Music and related activities as expression

The musical quality the motor-bike boys universally disliked was slowness and dreariness; the quality they prized in their preferred music was speed and clarity of beat – a general encouragement to movement and dancing. This is from a discussion of Ray Charles:

BILL-THE-BOOT   It's too slow and dreary isn't it? ... eh? I like music that makes you get up and do something like ...

BOB   You put the Beatles against them and you know straightaway don't you, or the Stones, you get the Stones or the Beatles with them, they're outclassed, ain't they? You can't understand a word he says ... and the beat, well there ain't one is there?

BILL-THE-BOOT   No, too dreary. You couldn't get up and dance to them.

The antidote to boredom was always movement, particularly dancing, and this in turn relied on the strong beat. As Bill said, 'that's all you need'. The importance of being able to dance to the music was stressed time and again. This is not to say however that music was always danced to, or that it could only be appreciated when dancing. Appropriateness to dance was meant as a description of a general quality of the music, that was quite as evident whether the music was actually danced to or not.

The consistent taste for strong beat, fast tempo and danceable atmosphere is a direct extension of the motor-bike boys' attitudes and style in general life. In a masculine, aggressive, extrovert world, relying above all on movement and confidence, the qualities appreciated in music were bounce, movement and exuberant confidence. Slower music became necessarily boring and formless, because there was no homological aspect of their interests and life-style that would have bitten into the music. Where one could move with the music, the music was relevant, exciting and *homological*. Slower, more introspective qualities in music were either totally passed over or registered as 'boring'.

The motor-bike boys' preference for singles as against L.P.s can be understood more fully in this light. Singles were responsive to the listener in the sense that they only lasted for two and a half minutes. If a particular record was disliked, at least it only lasted for a short time. It could also be rejected from the turntable more quickly without the difficulty of having to pick the needle up to miss a track on the L.P. and replace it a little farther on. Exact selection could also be made so that the order of records was responsive to individual choice. To play an L.P. was to be committed (unless you were prepared to go to a great deal of trouble) to someone else's ordering of the music. By and large, L.P.s are more popular with an audience which is prepared to sit and listen for a considerable period, and with a certain extension of trust so that unknown material can be appreciated and evaluated. L.P.s are a cheap way (as distinct from singles) of building up a large collection of songs within particular traditions. Often there will be tracks on an L.P. which have never been very popular but which are of interest to the expert, or the devotee, or the technician. Of late, L.P.s have also been produced which have been conceived as a unit, parallel in a way to the opera or extended musical piece. Dating from approximately 'Sergeant Pepper' by the Beatles, the progressive groups particularly have been concerned to produce L.P.s imaginatively conceived as a whole in this way, which are meant to be taken as a whole at one sitting. All this implies an audience which is *stationary, sitting, not engaged in other activities,* and prepared to devote a substantial length of time to the appreciation of the music alone. Of course, there are many exceptions, but it is generally true that the L.P. audience is stationary and mono-channelled towards the music. The motor-bike boys, by contrast, are usually moving, engaged in other activities and responsive to music only when it is not boring. Their preference for singles was overwhelming.

Another clear aspect of the boys' taste was their dislike of confusion, lack of clarity and lack of meaning. The boys were masters of their social, technical and physical environment, and they felt a full-blooded relationship with those things they could grasp. Abstraction, lack of clarity, confusion of styles threatened to hold off this grasp. In a sense their music had to be quite as graspable as the physical objects in their social field: the notion of an aesthetic or distanced artistic concern, or of concern with technique and formal structure, was simply not relevant. Their need to grasp the music in an *immediate* way is shown by their frequent comments that a record has to be liked immediately, or it was not liked at all.

There seemed to be an integral connection between rock music and riding fast. The experience of riding fast was incited by the feel of the rhythm in the head; all the qualities of fast dangerous riding, with the emphasis on movement and masculinity, summed up, and were part of, the similar qualities of the music. This became a generalized quality of the culture as a whole. Dancing had a similar, though less dramatic, function; it went with the music, it extended its range, expressed the same thing but in another mode. The same extension occurred from dancing to the bike; where dancing is stretched to the full, or is unavailable, then riding takes over as an extension of that mood and feeling. That mood or feeling would have remained basically suppressed, possibly in the end alienating, if it had not been for dance and riding.

BOB   I kind of get a rhythm in my head, and try and beat it on my bike kind of thing, you can hear a record in your head while you're riding.

BILL-THE-BOOT If you hear a fast record you've got to get up and do something, I think. If you can't dance any more, or if the dance is over, you've just got to go for a burn-up.

Here there is an explicit kind of statement about the escalation from dancing to riding for the same kind of emotional feeling. There were several half-explained, sometimes obscure, statements pointing in a similar way towards the connection between rock music and riding the motorcycle:

BOB   It helps like, the sound of the engine . . . try and get a beat in my head, and get the beat in my blood, and get on my bike and go.

SAMMY   If I hear a record, a real good record, I just fucking wack it open, you know, I just want to wack it open.

BOB   I usually find myself doing this all of a sudden [moving head up and down] with my feet tapping on the gear or something stupid like that.

BILL-THE-BOOT Once I've heard a record, I can't get it off my mind, walking or on the bus, humming it, or singing it you know. I think that's in your head . . . you know . . . if you were on a motorbike, it'd drive you mad that would, it's all in my head, you're bombing down the road.

It isn't the case simply, that either the music or the bike reflects or parallels their feelings. Both have become part of feeling, and those feelings could not exist without the music and the bike.

In a more violent way, and particularly for Sammy, fighting was an extension of emotion associated in the first place with music. In a telling comment Bill said of Sammy, 'he can't dance you see; I get up and dance, he gets up and hits.' For him fighting had a relationship with pop in the sense that fighting was a playing-out of emotion embodied by the music; it would not have happened without the music, in a sense *was* the music. There is here a distinctive sense of bursting through a block, of managing to communicate something deeply. Fighting is of course an entirely anti-social activity, and on other grounds this particular phenomenon may demand criticism, but within the terms of our analysis it was intrinsically related to pop music and can serve as evidence of the power of pop to take part in, become part of, a life-style. It may well be that a more articulate culture would find more 'socially acceptable' ways of expressing its meaning but, from at least one point of view, this would have been inferior and more dislocated. There would not have been the experience of an integral relation between living elements, but only a kind of sublimation of feeling: a blowing-off of harmless steam, rather than a concrete spontaneous extension. There were several comments about fighting and pop music, which clearly show that it is neither pop music nor fighting which is being talked about, but a fusion of the two in relation to a dominant feeling; remember again that aggression and 'handling oneself', movement, bravado and courage were in-group values. Fighting too, fired by a primitive rhythm, was a quintessential expression of those qualities:

BILL-THE-BOOT   ... if the dance is over, you've just got to go for a burn-up.

SAMMY   That's like me, we were at the Guardian Angel's dance and whenever a good record came on with a big beat I had to get up and hit some fucker, or do summat. It did, it sent me fucking wild ... It just sends me mad. I'll tell you one thing that used to send me fucking mad, that was 'Revolution', 'Revolution', any rock any one with a big beat in it, the fucking sound, I go fucking wild, I do. Me and Dave, you know, we got banned from a dance, and the police came practically every week because we used to fight every week, couldn't help it, it used to send us wild. There'd be a perfect stranger and Dave would go and punch his head in, he wouldn't get back up, only 'cause the records, certain records, they'd send us fucking mad, they would, they're old beat records ... If I hear a good record it ... fucking, you know, I go in a temper, it just puts me in a temper if I'm just there, so I have to thrash out, it sends me wild, that fucking 'Revolution' used to get me mad.

P.W.   When you said mad, though, you enjoyed it all
                the same?
SAMMY   Yeah, but it sent me fucking wild, if I was
                arguing with somebody I'd jump all over them
                and do some – couldn't help it – I think they
                ought to have banned some of them records I
                tell you.

This kind of relationship wasn't always predictable. Basically what
seemed to be involved was strength of feeling combined with
rhythm and an overwhelming need to externalize emotion.

SAMMY   Have you ever been in a dance and you get that
                tensed up over the record you feel like fucking
                lashing out on everything and everybody there?
P.W.   Well, I just have a pint and keep it in.
SAMMY   No, I don't drink, you do it the easy way, you
                can do it the other way, you can go and get
                pissed down the road and come back there to
                it, and then listen to the record.
P.W.   How about the bike?
BILL-THE-BOOT   Yes, give it holy stick down the road ...
                fucked up, I get like that, sometimes I fucking
                shiver with a record like that ... you get that
                tensed up, you know, you just let it, get it all
                out, you know, then your bike, or fighting
                somebody, takes the heat off you, doesn't it.

Drinking alcohol would be an 'easy way out', it would not recognize the nature of the emotion and the nature of the music. To
really 'listen' to the music meant taking in its full implications,
and these at once spilled over into action and real life movement.
There was a connection which it was dishonest to break.

   These are highly specific ways in which pop music played an
expressive role in the motor-bike culture. In much less definable,
but still real ways, pop music coloured the whole cultural style,
whose confidence and muscularity seemed to owe something to the
tradition of early rock 'n' roll.

Conclusion

I have suggested in this essay that in the motor-bike culture the body, clothes, interaction, functional and expressive artifacts are used to express, confirm and resonate a whole cultural world and its intricate meanings. None of these expressive modes would be thought of as 'cultural' by middle-class and received standards, and yet within their own matrix and precise location they can hold tight, complex feelings and responses. That these expressions are buried in a life process, and hidden from a casual view, does not invalidate them: rather it is a mark of their unpretentious role as truly participatory elements of a living human culture.

At a more general level I would like to propose a few ideas of a more provocative nature. They are only partly related to the preceding analysis, and I cannot bring to them here any weight of empirical evidence; but they may well serve to sharpen the debate provoked by this series of essays. I suggest that the expressive life of a minority culture, in opposition to the main and dominating culture, is likely to have certain specific characteristics:

1. It is likely to use a code which is not fully understood by the main culture.
2. It is therefore unlikely to express its innermost meanings in a verbal way. To do this would be to risk destruction or incorporation by the main culture which has the mastery of, and exerts its power through, language.
3. It is most likely to express its meanings through some configuration of the visual, the bodily, the stylistics of movement and interaction, the use of functional objects, and the appreciation of anti-high-art expressive artifacts.
4. It is likely to use these 'protected' modes of expression to state its opposition, marginal or full, to the main dominating culture. Its survival depends, in part, on the inability of the main culture, its agencies or commercial interests, to understand or reproduce those meanings and the style of their statement.
5. Though all the above elements may be present in a culture, it will not thrive and grow unless the expressive style allows a crucial sense of enhanced personal attractiveness and the development of some kind of collective mystique. The visual

non-verbal basis of such a culture is likely to be the basis of such attractiveness and distinctiveness.

To simplify even further in order to encapsulate in a sentence one of the themes of the present volume, I could speculate that the main middle-class culture is based on the head, language and cerebrality, and that minority opposition cultures are based on the body, style and the non-abstract. We must consider the possibility that the body is used in certain minority cultures (and if one thinks of black minority cultures in the West the case looks even stronger) to express coded, and partly hidden, opposition to the dominant culture surrounding them – in a way that language, even where it could be effectively used, would never be allowed to.

John F. Szwed

Race and the Embodiment of Culture

One of the ironies of this not-so-happy century is that although it was the first time in human history in which a concerted effort was made to discredit racist ideology, it was also the occasion on which an enormous number of lives were sacrificed in the name of race. Surely now we realize that science and humanism have scarcely scratched the primordial notion that people with bodies different from our own must also be different in culture and character; nor has the converse belief been touched, that people culturally different from ourselves must also have bodies of a different order from our own. So banal is the restatement of this belief in the equation between physique and behaviour, and so obvious its refutation in the world around us that it embarrasses me to mention it, even in passing.

Nevertheless, I'd like to try to say something different about race, or try to say the same things in a different way, just once, before we again find ourselves moving to an acceptance of the inexorable intertwining of race and destiny.

1.

Let me begin by calling up a few of the terms that we associate with race: physique, culture and stereotype.

First, far too much emphasis has been given by students of race relations to the idea of race as a cluster of physical features – skin, colour, hair form, nose shape, and the like. This they do because these seem to be the core of what people talk about when they speak of races. But physical features are also things that scientists can see, and feel that they can accurately describe and classify through systematic observations and measurements. For example, in order to better show who was or was not a member of a particular race or, on the other hand, to demonstrate that race was so unscientific a concept as to warrant abandoning it, scientists of the early 1900s relentlessly pursued tests and measurements with a single-minded goal of showing the laymen to be wrong:[1] nothing delighted an anthropometrist more than finding a light-skinned Negro or a dark-skinned Caucasian, unless it was the discovery that the odour of a vial of Caucasian perspiration was offensive to an Oriental. At its thinnest, then, the method was one of discovering racial anomalies or prejudices of non-Westerners towards Euro-Americans. Alas, as is too often the case with scientists, they were not in touch with the laymen. The average person is not so much bothered by the repulsiveness of physical differences, but rather with their seeming co-occurrence with behavioural differences. Exotic appearance accompanies exotic behaviour, or so it may seem. And where this is not true on the surface of things, where one may exist without the other, the equation is completed by fantasy.

Perhaps an example would be useful. A perusal of early English writings on the Irish shows that although the Irish were initially seen to be physically much the same as the English (as early illustrations show), Irish culture was seen as alien and threatening. In 1617 Fynes Moryson, for example, found the Irish more than a little offensive. Their language was crude, if indeed it was a language at all, their clothing almost animal-like, if they wore any at all: Moryson noted with shock an Irish lord, seated at the fire with his women, all of them naked,[2] or, again, corn being ground by nude maidens, 'striking off into the tub of meal such reliques thereof as stuck on their belly, thighs, and more unseemly parts'.[3] From the same period one also thinks of Edmund Spenser's bestial Irishmen[4] or of William Camden, who in 1610 recounted the profanity, cannibalism, musicality, witchcraft, violence, incest and gluttony of the 'wilde and very uncivill' Irish.[5] In fact, in many ways the Irish sound remarkably like Africans as described by the nineteenth-century English – sensual, slothful, affectionate, garrulous, excitable, humorous, etc.[6] – except that the English appear to have initially often found Africans preferable to the Irish.[7]

The unasked question for the Elizabethans was simply, were the

Irish, with their different culture, truly human? And the question was not to be settled quickly, as the following several hundred years show. But by the late 1800s the English physiologist James Redfield could distinguish the Irish as a lower form of life by reinterpreting even their most appealing human qualities in animal terms. Irish 'verbosity' for example:

Compare the Irish man and the dog in respect to barking, snarling, howling, begging, fawning, flattering, backbiting, quarrelling, blustering, scenting, seizing, hanging on, teasing, rollicking, and whatever other traits you may discover in either, and you will be convinced that there is a wonderful resemblance.[8]

In the same manner, it was common for the nineteenth-century English to see the Celts as apes, as cartoons in *Punch* (and in America, in *Harper's* and the *Atlantic*) showed the Irishman as a boasting, drunken, lower-level hominoid, bent on the destruction of civilization.[9]

It remained only for John Beddoe, President of the Anthropological Institute, to develop an 'index of Nigresence' which showed the people of Wales, Scotland, Cornwall and Ireland to be racially separate from the British. And to be more specific, he argued that those from western Ireland and Wales were 'Africanoid' in their 'jutting jaws' and 'long slitty nostrils', and thus originally immigrants from Africa.[10] The equation was complete: what was at first seen as behavioural (that is to say, cultural) difference between two peoples was now rooted physiologically, these differences having their origins on a distant continent, if not at a lower level of animal origin.

The fantasied equation works in reverse, too, as in South Africa, where special schools and curricula are required of those with 'black' identity, regardless of whether or not the student has a European or, for that matter, a European *and* African cultural repertoire; or in Nazi Germany, where cultural identity was assumed of those of Jewish descent, even though the Jewish 'race' was so poorly defined that special names and dress were required by law in order to complete the equation. This process of stigmatization is one which we meet again and again through history and across nations, and if we object to the process, one name we commonly give it is stereotyping.

It is generally agreed that a stereotype is a distortion or exaggeration of the facts.[11] It would seem then that if only positive stereotypes had emerged in the world we might well have never felt the need for the term. However, some decidedly negative characteristics have been subsumed under stereotypes, as the pejorative connotation of the word suggests. Thus it is worth considering that the process of stereotyping is not itself clearly distinct from the kind of everyday social typifications we make of individuals as members of classes such as 'Englishmen', 'educated', 'farmers' and so forth. All are forms of classification by which we quickly summarize the social information of human encounters as to render social life predictable, or at least less chaotic. And all social types are theoretically subject to correction and individualization as we get to know individuals through direct contact. But here we meet some differences between stereotyping and other forms of social typing. 'Everyday' typing characteristically grows out of interaction with individuals, where stereotypes, particularly those of races and foreigners, may often historically precede these individuals and are often a function of the physical or social distance between them and ourselves. Consequently we may simply never get close enough to the people we stereotype to correct or modify the original typification. And since there is some form of distance between ourselves and the others implied in this latter process, there is also typically some form of social hierarchy implied in the stereotype.

But so much about stereotyping is obvious. What is perhaps less obvious is that there are two distinct forms of typing operating within the stereotype. The first is the reading of a person or a group of persons as being known by a set of physical characteristics or behaviours which are quite concrete and subject to some kind of verification. Thus, a people may be said to have red skin, or blue eyes, or to be musically inclined, or to avoid facing each other when they talk. All of these can be measured or checked if we care to do so. But there is also a second level of stereotyping, one which offers observations about a people's laziness, ugliness, childishness, stupidity, dishonesty, lack of self-control and the like. In these latter forms, we see virtual moral ascriptions or accounts of deviancy, assessments of how far another people's behaviour is seen to vary from the observers', and even a sense of how much conflict seems implicit in these characteristics. Obviously in practice this second level of stereotypification is dominant, but related to the first, and forms with it a complex, myth-like whole. Any part of the whole, whether empirically 'correct' or not, tends to call up the whole ideological cluster.

Stereotypes also concentrate on the very domains of human behaviour and values that are basic to a society's performances and order. Thus they focus on work practices, health and eating habits, means and style of communication, sexual and kinship conceptions, notions of etiquette and law, notions of the supernatural and the eternal. And since relatively few people have ever been exposed to a wide variety of human behaviours, there is a tendency to view another society's behaviours as the polar opposites of one's own, even if they are in reality only small variations on a common human theme. Viewed as opposites, they are typically understood as a *lack* of those behavioural values.[12] Thus, a people may be seen as promiscuous (that is, lacking a sense of sexual propriety or a kinship system), or seen to 'babble' and 'jibber' (to lack a true communication system, to speak a 'broken' form), to be superstitious or fetishistic (i.e., to lack a real religion), and the like. And even where the people may be recognized as having certain domains of behaviour in which they excel – ritual, openness to friendships, musical or dance skills, whatever – these, too, are seen to have been achieved at the cost of 'proper', more important domains of human endeavour, such as rationality, order, discipline, work, etc. Thus it was that early writers on Africa and the slaves of the West Indies, while observing in great detail some of the exotic strengths of black people, seem to have concluded that these people lacked a proper human culture as well as a soul, much as St Augustine had once wrestled with the question of whether apes were worthy of salvation.

It might appear that I am saying, like most other commentators, that stereotypes are merely the results of lack of information or faulty perception of an alien and exotic people, or simply the natural reaction of an isolated and insular people to outsiders with different physiques and means of organizing their lives; in other words, xenophobia. From such a point of view, however, the function of the stereotype would be simply to *exclude* a people from one's perception. But the function is really *inclusory*; it seeks to explain the presence of other peoples in our midst or in the natural order of the world. In this sense stereotypes are one of the results of normal classificatory thinking, the practice of measuring alien characteristics against existing taxonomies of humanness. It is sobering to recall that such processes are not limited to Western explorers and imperialists. While Europeans were debating the humanity of their 'discoveries' in Africa, their discovered peoples were pondering the same questions in reverse. They were repelled by white skin, associated as it was with 'peeled' skin and leprosy, its ugly blue-veined surface shamefully covered by many clothes; these offensive-smelling Europeans with the wild-animal hair on their long heads, bodies and red faces, these savage-looking men who could live so long without their women, were seen to be cannibals.[13]

It should be obvious that stereotypical folk-notions of races arose out of early historical contacts in which it was found that an alien people not only looked different from oneself, but also performed differently, behaving in exotically stylized, recurring presentations of self. Never mind that another people's institutions – law, polity, family and the like – might be profoundly different, it was their use of their bodies that had the most impact.

To most people, then as now, motor habits – the way one moves, blinks eyes, stands and walks – the way one pitches one's voice, laughs, cries and collectivizes with others socially – are seen to be rooted in some mysterious racial, or at least 'instinctive' fact.[14] For who ever 'learns' such things? Who 'teaches' them? As easy as these things are to sense, they are even difficult to describe accurately. Surely, if anything was peculiar to the 'genius' of a race (as nineteenth-century writers put it) these things were. But as Professor Ray Birdwhistell[15] stresses (see his contribution to this volume, pp. 36–58) one of the great discoveries of the last twenty years is that even these micro-behaviours are systematically learned and patterned, even though, like language, at a very early age and largely out-of-awareness. Further, they can be unlearned or changed. But as we know them, they are the underlying communicative baselines of what we in the West at least consider to be the *real* communication, words. Thus, the finding of students of kinesics, paralinguistics, proxemics and microcultural behaviour is that the communicative and fundamental level of humanness is as plastic and variable as other forms of human behaviour – it is, in the fullest sense in which E. B. Tylor used the word, *culture.*

What makes this matter all the more complicated and interesting is that it is just this level of human cultural variability that also makes up the basis of what we call artful human behaviour. In *Folksong Style and Culture*[16] Alan Lomax has elaborated the argument that song, dance, ritual and other artistic performances are high-level statements of these very microcultural patterns. The arts rest not so much on words and ideas as on these largely out-of-awareness communicative codes. And since the arts are the supreme collective statements of what a people seem to think life is about and what they feel is their place in that life, artistic behaviour reaches down into the bases of communication which appear most mysteriously human. Further, since history demonstrates that the stylistic components of the arts are slow to change and difficult to destroy, it is often easy to feel that particular performances are 'natural' to particular races.

Let me give an example from Lomax's work. His studies of the styles of song and dance suggest that, far from it being the case that the world has as many different systems of these arts as there are peoples, there are in fact a limited number of ways in which these modes of artful communication may be expressed. Indeed, the world is characterized by a limited number of style areas and means of organizing and presenting performances. To use only one case, there are people whose song and dance performances are characterized by a high level of interpersonal synchrony, by great cohesiveness and complementarity of performers.[17] These are people whose performances typically include both men and women at the same time, whose songs are well-blended and rhythmically co-ordinated, who can organize relatively large groups into complex, multi-parted choruses and dance groups usually without leaders, whose members submerge their individuality into a precise collectivity. Perhaps the three most pronounced areas of the world in this respect are subsaharan Africa, Polynesia, and portions of Eastern European village areas. The same peoples use similar schemes and stylistic means for organizing work activities. When these people are compared in their performances with those of Western Europe, Euro-America and the civilizations of the Middle East – all of whom put emphasis on the non-complementarity of sexes, and either on individuality of performers or on highly stratified, collective performances under the rigid control of a leader, both in art and in work – then the degree of the stylistic contrast becomes apparent. Indeed, as Lomax has suggested, Westerners are people who find conscious synchrony – talking at the same time, walking in stride and the like – embarrassing, 'monkey-like' or childish, on the one hand, and on the other they reserve it for rather frightening and coercive mass events such as training soldiers for war.

Other kinds of stylistic variables offer similar societal contrasts: some cultures use heavily worded song texts, some use only sounds; some cultures articulate all parts of the body in dance, others use only the trunk and feet; some sing in unison, some in harmony, some in fugue, etc. And similar kinds of contrasts turn up in between the same societies' characteristics of work, ritual and speech events. All of this simply says that art symbolizes (and thus reinforces) 'non-artistic', everyday behaviour. And art styles, like behavioural styles, can be mapped across time and geography. What we may have thought of as behaviour caused by physical form is rather learned behaviour organized at many communicative levels, each cross-referencing the other. It is possible to see from this way of looking at the world that throughout history we have been confusing cultural styles with race.

2.

One advantage of looking at race conceptions and relations from a cultural point of view is that it opens up new ways of looking at old phenomena. Consider this: when two 'races' find themselves in close and relatively stable social contact, typically where one has power and high status and the other does not, two kinds of problems emerge for the high-status group. How, on the one hand, to maintain its genetic *status quo*, in order to prevent a dilution of the dominant racial group; on the other hand, how to prevent a dilution of the dominant group's culture? The first of these problems has been given considerable attention, and as a consequence we know that although racial 'dilution' and 'intermixing' occurs in bi-racial societies, there are elaborate and varied established means for maintaining the fiction of racial purity: to name just one technique, traditionally in the South of the United States the offspring of parents of different and unequal racial status are assigned to the descent group of the lower-ranking parent.[18] But surprisingly little attention has been paid to the second of these problems, the question of how to prevent the 'bastardizing' and 'mongrelizing' of the high-status group's culture.

If we can be sure of anything throughout history, it is that two peoples – regardless of the lines drawn and the barriers between them, whether socially unequal or not – will in the process of everyday close interaction learn and adopt some aspects of the other group's behaviour. And some of each group will become proficient to the point of being capable of assuming at least the *cultural* if not the racial identity of the other group. We are less conscious of the high-status member skilled at low-status behaviour and culture, perhaps, but it is just such skill and proficiency of low-status members in high-status culture that has drawn attention to inequities in the United States, Great Britain and elsewhere.

If the low-status member or group borrows from or learns from the high group (even where the high group may deny that true learning goes on, and may see it as merely imitative or 'apeing'), the high culture is said to become degraded, cheapened and misunderstood, and attempts are made to carefully guard it and institutionally lock it out of reach. But since more characteristically the high group considers the low as lacking such capacity, such efforts are not made until it is too late.

On the reverse side, the high group views borrowing and learning from the low to be so personally polluting, and to be such a naked recognition of merit in the low, that few – even the scholars of race contacts – even discuss the possibility. Nevertheless, it goes on. Again, hear the complaint of William Camden discussing the affects of Irish customs on the English: 'But the Irish are so wedded to those, that they not only retain 'em themselves, but corrupt the English among them; and it is scarce credible how soon these will degenerate: such a proneness there is in human nature, to grow worse.'[19] Even earlier, the preamble to the Statutes of Kilkenny bemoaned the fact that

now many English of the said land, forsaking English language, manners, mode of riding, laws and usages, live and govern themselves according to the manners, fashion and language of the Irish enemies and also have made divers marriages between themselves and the Irish enemies . . .[20]

Similarly, travellers to the colonies of the New World were fast to condemn the 'degeneration' of European and English culture there. A visitor to the United States in 1746 noted:

One thing [the American planters] are very faulty in, with regard to their Children, which is, that when young, they suffer them too much to prowl amongst the young Negroes, which insensibly causes them to imbibe their Manners and broken Speech.[21]

Even an American planter's child, however, could be aware of these cultural influences. Commenting on the influence of slaves' culture on whites, one Mississippi slaveholder's son wrote: 'It was as though another Civilization had been wiped out, and a set of Goths and Vandals with shaggy hides and wooden bludgeons were stalking around amid the ruins, in lieu of the inhabitants whom they had slaughtered.'[22] Occasionally, there even appeared a detailed chronicle by which one can trace at least the partial personal acculturation of a white European to slaves' culture. In the case of Matt Lewis, the English playwright and novelist who inherited a plantation in Jamaica, the process he recorded took only a year.[23]

But such public admissions are rare. So profound is the potential, so awesome its consideration, that the idea of high turning low is usually left to fiction that borders on myth. The corrosive effect of the stigmatized is richly documented in Joseph Conrad's *Heart of Darkness* or in William Faulkner's novels. And the madness of the first Mrs Montgomery in *Jane Eyre* was well understood by Brontë's contemporaries, who knew the corruption and degeneration likely in a Creole, a white person born in the Caribbean.[24]

But despite the fears, the high do learn and borrow from the low, and they have developed elaborate techniques and justifications to skirt the pollution and degradation involved in the transformation. Perhaps the best-known such technique is what might be called *minstrelization*, the process by which the low are characterized or emulated within a carefully regulated and socially approved context. Thus, on the nineteenth-century stage, English and American white minstrels could publicly display the extent to which they had mastered Negro cultural forms and behaviours, and could for a short time at least participate in what they conceived of as Negro life. (Pleasantly complicating this process was the fact that before the Negro was mimicked on the stage the Irishman had served the same purpose; in fact, in the transition period in America, Negro speech was simply grafted on to Irish tunes.)[25] That these minstrels and their later followers – Al Jolson, Amos and Andy, Eddie Cantor *et al.* – became the most popular entertainers in the United States within their time underscores the mass participation in the minstrelization process. And the fact that, say, a Mick Jagger can today perform in the same tradition without blackface simply marks the detachment of culture from race and the almost full absorption of a black tradition into white culture. This form of 'passing' is distinctly different from that available to the stigmatized racial group. Where the low-status member must first possess a physique at least marginally similar to the dominant group's and must additionally master the high-status group's cultural devices, always risking discrediting, the high-status minstrelizer has only to learn a minimal number of cultural techniques and *temporarily* mask himself as a subordinate – literally a Negro *manqué* in this case.

A recent example illustrates how rapidly the same process can take place artifactually. A South African wine, 'Rock 'n' Roll Sherry', carries on its label an exact reproduction of a 1923 photograph of King Oliver's New Orleans jazz band with Louis Armstrong – except that the faces are shown to be white![26]

Although such examples are dramatic and grand in scope, the cultural plagiarism process is essentially one of everyday occurrence and in many cases a part of the normal educational process of an élite. Willie Morris, in speaking of his childhood in Yazoo, Mississippi, said:

> There was a stage, when we were about thirteen, in which we 'went Negro'. We tried to broaden our accents to sound like Negroes, as if there were not enough similarity already. We consciously walked like young Negroes, mocking their swinging gait, moving our arms the way they did, cracking our knuckles and whistling between our teeth. We tried to use some of the same expressions, as closely as possible to the way they said them, like: 'Hey, m-a-a-n, what you *do*in' theah!,' the sounds rolled out and clipped sharply at the end for the hell of it.[27]

Morris further documents the way in which other stages of

growing up are identified with Negroes, perhaps the most profound of which is the pre-adolescent understanding of sexual intercourse as something one does with Negro women only.[28]

Both individually and collectively then, the high group becomes intimately involved with the low.

In our very lives, we have to come to repeat this pattern, individual biography recapitulating cultural history. Born theoretically white, we are permitted to pass our childhood as imaginary Indians, our adolescence as imaginary Negroes, and only then are expected to settle down to being what we really are: white once more.[29]

What makes this kind of cultural borrowing different from that across national lines is the paradoxical denial of the existence of low culture by the high. Often in history this has been accomplished by the simple argument that the low are not quite human. During the earlier years of New World slavery such a paradox was in full flower: slaveholders and travellers wrote extensive journals documenting the beliefs, attitudes, habits and behaviours of slaves all to demonstrate by their 'differences' their non-human, or at best 'savage' status. Indeed the more carefully the observers noted what we would today easily recognize as a coherent, viable human culture, the more likely they were to use it as negative evidence.

Although such crude readings of human behaviour are less likely today, the tendency to treat minority or low status peoples as lacking culture turns up in different guises, especially in history and the social sciences. The Pygmies of the Congo, for example, were initially understood to lack indigenous song, language and ritual – simply because the dominant Negro peoples in contact with them used the same forms, and the direction of influence was assumed to be one-way; but recent research has shown the process of influence to be just the reverse.[30] Again, Frank M. Snowden's research on blacks in ancient Greek and Roman art turned up abundant proof that Africans regularly performed the roles of jugglers, wrestlers, servants, jesters and the like, all of which he took as evidence that Africans were acculturated and integrated into these societies.[31] But his assumption that the Africans had lost their cultures is unproved, and it could equally be argued that certain roles, and thus the Greek and Roman societies themselves, had become 'Africanized' to some degree through the cultural styles and skills of their alien occupants.

What is more remarkable is that the strategies of the anti-racists among social scientists in the West show a peculiar similarity to the ideologies of the racists. As I suggested in the beginning, early scientific anti-racists in the United States addressed the folk equation of race and culture by specifying and delimiting the concept of race so as to discredit or at least transvalue what they conceived to be the everyday stereotypes of races. All the more strange, then, was their response to the other side of the folk equation. Though anthropologists such as Franz Boas understood that culture needed to be described and reinterpreted so that their alien qualities could be understood as human responses to universal human problems, and though Boas did such a translation of the culture of the Eskimos, he and other anthropologists took a different approach to American Negroes. So, instead of historical studies and descriptive accounts of cultural practices, anthropologists chose to either completely deny the cultural practices of American Negroes or to treat them as stereotyped fantasies of white people.[32] That is, they attempted to dispel the negative Euro-American *readings* and *valuings* of culturally different behaviour of Afro-Americans by denying the existence of the behaviour itself. This meant that they were forced to treat black dialects, music, dance, interpersonal style and the like as non-existent just at the point where these phenomena were beginning to flood the country through the mass media, when they were in fact becoming the basis of an American vernacular culture.

Strange as it appears on the surface, this anti-racist strategy was perfectly in tune with the liberal politics of the times. Since liberals assumed that America was a successful cultural melting-pot, they saw variations in culture to be the results of poverty and racism. All that remained was for barriers against racial inter-marriage to be removed for racial distinctions to disappear. So, like the racists they hoped to rebut, anthropologists very early fell into the habit of confusing equality with sameness and inequality with difference. Faith in the equality of all people was not inconsistent with a disrespect for unassimilated peoples in our midst, a disrespect that assumed that they would not be different from us had we not prevented them from being like us.[33] How unlike the anthropological brief for Negroes was G. K. Chesterton's forthright plea for the Irish:

The tendency of [Yeats' Celtic] argument is to represent the Irish or the Celts as a strange and separate race, as a tribe of eccentrics in the modern world immersed in dim legends and fruitless dreams. Its tendency is to see the Irish as odd, because they see the fairies. Its trend is to make the Irish seem weird and wild because they sing old songs and join in strange dances. But this is quite an error; indeed it is the opposite of the truth. It is the English who are odd because they do not see the fairies. It is the inhabitants of Kensington who are weird and wild because they do not sing old songs and join in strange dances . . . In all this the Irish are simply an ordinary sensible nation, living the life of any other ordinary and sensible nation which has not been either sodden with smoke or oppressed by money-lenders, or otherwise corrupted with wealth and science . . . It is not Ireland which is mad and mystic; it is Manchester which is mad and mystic, which is incredible, which is a wild exception among human things. Ireland has no need to pretend to be a tribe of visionaries apart. In the matter of visions, Ireland is more than a nation, it is a model nation.[34]

To sum up, then, in arguing against the equation of race and culture, social scientists have properly refuted several notions: that race determines culture; that there is a natural affinity between the two categories or between any particular race and any particular culture; and that there is thus a cultural means of determining what an 'inferior' race might be. But at the same time, having denied any capacity for developing viable culture to peoples amongst us whose physiques happen to be different, they leave them with only stigmatized bodies, since it appears difficult to transvalue race without transvaluing culture. Now, American social science finds itself facing a people identifiable by body, but having no 'real' culture. Is it any wonder, then, that we have recently begun to see race re-enter social science research as a variable with explanatory power? Now, again, race, not culture, is being argued to be the source of low I.Q. scores.

But social scientists are not alone in having become confused by racist interpretations of body and culture. Marxists, too, have encountered difficulties with the notions of ethnicity and culture, since they conceive of them as false consciousness and as smoke-screens of class (though this theoretical distinction did not keep Engels or the Webbs from detesting the Irish and seeing them as 'degrading' influences on the English workingman!).[35] What strikes me as so curious about the Marxists is that although ostensibly concerned with the exploitation of workers, they have failed to notice that the cultural products of the lower classes have also been pooled and in turn exploited. At once limited in the variety and forms of occupation open to them and at the same time isolated from the central resources of the society, often ghettoized or kept on the margins, the low-status groups live largely on their own cultural resources. The irony of the situation is obvious: the low-status group, though cut off from the sources of power and production in the larger society, is at the same time less alienated from its own cultural productions. The twist is that the élite of the society is free to draw on the lower group's cultural pool. Were there ever more massive examples of the conversion of community life and culture into commodity than those in which black folk-life has been turned into national culture in the United States, Brazil or Cuba? Or where an entire people has been made the entertainers and bearers of another people's folk-art, as with the tinkers of Scotland or the gypsies of Europe?

Finally, the circle comes round: in their efforts to demystify race, social scientists and revolutionaries have abandoned culture and grouped the stigmatized and excluded peoples of many races and cultures together in a concept larger than race, one variably called the *lumpenproletariat*, the 'wretched of the earth', members of the 'cultures of poverty' or simply 'the masses'. One more cynical than I might recognize these as moral characterizations based on lacks, and thus as classical stereotypes.

3.

To many, I fear, the anecdotal history I have sketchily drawn here will appear to be a gratuitous exercise in irony. In a world hell-bent on the destruction of cultural variety and integrity through industrialization, 'wars of pacification', the Common Market, revolution, and the like, the niceties of racial and cultural definition look academic and madly out of touch. But there is also an odd sense in which these questions are taking on critical significance.

It is customary to regard the development and spread of racist ideology in the nineteenth and twentieth centuries as simply an élitist ploy in the effort to maintain and establish control over workers and slaves. Certainly the rationales of racist thought tell us as much. But was it not also this very period which witnessed the rise of assertive racial and ethnic consciousness and cultural revitalization on the part of the peoples who were massively dislocated and dispossessed? And was this also not the period in which these outcast groups had their greatest influence? As the native and the peasant began to tentatively abandon aspects of traditional identity for whatever cultural forms industry, city and the 'West' might provide, those who ran the industries and metropolises began to search out alternatives, not from their own severed and truncated pasts, but among those workers, peasants and slaves in their midsts. As Roger Bastide has said of the spread of African and Afro-American cuisine, dance, music, art forms, religion and speech in the Americas:

> That spiritual void which the city creates at the heart of each human individual is resented, naturally, just as much by the European as by the Negro. As a result the European turns increasingly to Africa or Black America for the satisfaction of those vital needs which industrial society can no longer answer.[36]

There is something pathetic and perhaps ill-fated about the spectacle of Euro-America 'Africanizing' and England 'Celticizing' under industrialization, but what was the choice? As we have increasingly come to discover that our own past was as dislocated and discontinuous as those very 'traditional' societies which we have observed in the throes of 'modernization', we have thrashed about in the search for some kind of meaning and identity that will at least last us for even one generation.

If we are to survive in an age in which technology has freed man from the necessity of enslaving other men in order to progress, then (as Claude Lévi-Strauss has suggested)[37] we must unlearn much of what we have accepted since the dawn of the Neolithic and look elsewhere for our models of salvation. Perhaps we are the butt of our own historical joke: we now find ourselves desperately studying the discredited and displaced, and stumbling nakedly into a pastoral of ludicrous dimensions.

Acknowledgement is gratefully expressed for support from the United States Public Health Service, National Institute for Mental Health grant MH 17,216, which aided preparation of this essay.

1. For a short overview of scientific anti-racism, see Thomas F. Gossett, *Race: The History of an Idea in America*, Schocken Books, New York, 1965, pp. 409–30.

2. Fynes Moryson, *An Itinerary*, 4 vols. (London, 1617); quoted in David Beers Quinn, *The Elizabethans and the Irish*, Cornell University Press, Ithaca, New York, pp. 71–2.

3. ibid., p. 63.

4. Edmund Spenser, *Faerie Queene*, Macmillan, 1970, *passim*.

5. William Camden, *Britain, or a Chorographicall Description of . . . England, Scotland, and Ireland*, trans. Philemon Holland (London, 1610).

6. Christine Bolt, *Victorian Attitudes to Race*, Routledge & Kegan Paul, 1971, pp. 136–51.

7. Quinn, op. cit., pp. 25–6.

8. James Redfield, *Comparative Physiognomy or Resemblances Between Men and Animals* (New York, 1852), pp. 253–8; quoted in L. Perry Curtis, Jr, *Apes and Angels: The Irishman in Victorian Caricature*, David & Charles, Newton Abbott, Smithsonian Institution Press, Washington, D.C., 1971, p. 12.

9. Curtis, op. cit., *passim*.

10. John Beddoe, *The Races of Britain* (London, 1885); quote in Curtis, op. cit., pp. 119–21.

11. Much of the following is indebted to Roger Abrahams, 'Stereotyping and Beyond' in Roger D. Abrahams and Rudolph C. Troike, eds., *Language and Cultural Diversity in American Education*, Prentice-Hall, Englewood Cliffs, New Jersey, 1972, pp. 19–29.

12. ibid., p. 25.

13. Cf. the quotes and references throughout Felix N. Okoye, *The American Image of Africa: Myth and Reality*, Black Academy Press, Buffalo, New York, 1971.

14. Sidney Mintz, foreword to Norman E. Whitten, Jr and John F. Szwed, eds., *Afro-American Anthropology: Contemporary Perspectives*, Collier-Macmillan, 1970; New York: Free Press, 1970, pp. 4–5.

15. Ray L. Birdwhistell, *Kinesics and Context: Essays in Body-Motion Communication*, Allen Lane The Penguin Press, 1971; University of Pennsylvania Press, Philadelphia, 1971.

16. Alan Lomax, *Folksong Style and Culture*, American Association for the Advancement of Science, Washington, D.C., 1968.

17. ibid., pp. 170–203.

18. Marvin Harris, *Patterns of Race in the Americas*, Walker, New York, 1964, p. 56.

19. William Camden, *Britain*, 2nd edn (London, 1722), vol. 2, p. 1423.

20. Statutes of Kilkenny (1366), quoted in David H. Greene, ed., *An Anthology of Irish Literature*, University of London Press, 1971; Modern Library, New York, 1954, p. 298.

21. *The London Magazine*, 1746; quoted in Allen Walker Read, 'British Recognition of American Speech in the Eighteenth Century', *Dialect Notes*, vol. 6, 1933, p. 329.

22. B. Carradine, *Mississippi Stories*, The Christian Witness Co., Chicago and Boston, 1904, pp. 98–9. I am grateful to William Stewart for calling this reference and the one of the preceding footnote to my attention.

23. Matthew Gregory Lewis, *Journal of a West India Proprietor*, London, 1834.

24. For a novel that develops the background for *Jane Eyre*, see Jean Rhys, *Wide Sargasso Sea*, Penguin Books, 1970; Norton, New York, 1966.

25. Carl Wittke, *Tambo and Bones*, Duke University Press, Durham, N.C., 1930, *passim*.

26. Steve Voce, 'It Don't Mean a Thing', *Jazz Journal*, vol. 24, no. 1, January 1971, p. 16.

27. Willie Morris, *North Toward Home*, Houghton Mifflin, Boston, 1967, p. 81.

28. ibid., p. 79.

29. Leslie A. Fiedler, *Waiting for the End*, Penguin Books, 1967; Stein & Day, New York, 1964, p. 134.

30. Colin M. Turnbull, 'The Mbuti Pygmies of the Congo' in James L. Gibbs, Jr, ed., *Peoples of Africa*, Holt, Rinehart & Winston, New York, 1965, *passim*.

31. Frank M. Snowden, Jr, *Blacks in Antiquity*, Harvard University Press, Cambridge, Mass., 1970, *passim*.

32. For further development of this argument, see John F. Szwed, 'An American Anthropological Dilemma: The Politics of Afro-American Culture' in Dell Hymes, ed., *Reinventing Anthropology*, Pantheon Books, New York, 1973, *passim*.

33. Paul Riesman, 'Review of Carlos Castaneda, Journey to Ixtlan', *New York Times Book Review*, 22 October 1972, p. 7.

34. G. K. Chesterton, 'Celts and Celtophiles' in *Heretics*, Bodley Head, 1905, pp. 176–7.

35. Friedrich Engels, *The Condition of the Working Class in England in 1844*, quoted in Patrick O'Farrell, *Ireland's British Question*, Batsford, 1971; Schocken Books, New York, 1971, p. 144; Sidney and Beatrice Webb, 1892, quoted in Janet Beveridge, *An Epic of Clare Market*, G. Bell, London, 1960, p. 9.

36. Roger Bastide, *African Civilizations in the New World*, C. Hurst, London, 1971, p. 224.

37. Claude Lévi-Strauss, 'The Scope of Anthropology', *Current Anthropology*, vol. 7, no. 2, 1966, p. 122.

Philip S. Rawson

The Body in Tantra

Tantra is an Indian tradition and cult of ecstasy, which cuts across the boundaries of all the Indian religions. But this is an essay neither on Tantra as such, nor on its Art. The exhibition I organized at the Hayward Gallery, London, in autumn 1971 was meant to lay down the basic knowledge. Its catalogue has been converted into two books.[1] I don't want to repeat myself, nor do I want to give a straight academic account from the outside of one of the many traditions of Indian Tantra. Instead I shall take cues that Tantra offers, and try first of all to illustrate the way Tantra radically attacks conventional attitudes and beliefs. Then I shall try and show what validity Tantra's cult of the body may have for *us*, taking a stand *within* Tantra. Above all, I want to talk in English terms, not in sub-Sanskrit, because the whole subject is difficult enough anyway.

It has become a journalist's cliché that our body is an instrument in and by which the universe of molecules knows itself. In a sense we, as men, are one of the universe's organs of knowledge. From whatever point of view we begin, this remains true, even at the level of the basest scientist materialism (which is, of course, a simplifying idealism that forgets its own roots in mathematical axioms intuited from experience and in some rigid object as criterion of measurement). Those things we identify and call 'atoms', and those we call 'chemical compounds', are cycled from what we call an inorganic cosmos into these bodies of ours, within which 'knowledge' is somehow secreted, like a pearl in the unconscious flesh of the oyster.

Each of us, as he grows up from being a baby, learns to structure his world at two levels. He first uses, then integrates and co-ordinates. It is rather like the activity of a settler creating an estate, physical and mental, out of primeval jungle. He uses the trees to make his tools, then trims the fringes into manageable groves; the bulk he turns into farm and parkland, where everything is identi-fied by markers and where he knows more or less what the land will do. Nearer home he neatly lays out gardens, with walks, avenues, shrubberies, flowerbeds and lawns, arranged in clearly intelligible patterns. Around these he knows his way thoroughly. He can name every part and object. His 'home' is at the centre, his house, the same as the others laid out in neat rows; and in his house, his body. In his body, himself. Or so the Western image has it. Between the self and unintelligible primeval jungle each man interposes patterns of knowledge, frameworks of sense, customary acts and images. As he becomes aware of these he forgets what they really are. He locates himself inside a framework of projected space, with its three co-ordinates, and of his time, with its single co-ordinate of succession. He comes to believe he is a self, moving about along these co-ordinates, encountering other selves; he con-structs images of relationship, such as cause and effect, or classifi-cation systems among things; he acts, expresses his subjective choices, experiences reactions. He creates fictional worlds to which he resorts for entertainment. All these he sets up before his own eyes like cheerful billboards around his estate.

But there is a threat: an ultimate, never-eliminated threat. He is never allowed quite to forget the primeval jungle. For the earth has a claim on him. His body betrays him; his house crumbles; the chemical compounds in his blood and flesh are being steadily reclaimed by the great cycles of the world. And because he has taken such pains to locate, settle and identify himself, he has, in the process, created for that self a whole universe of 'others'. And they, because they are not subject to his individual will, can them-selves seem to threaten him. He will hate them. The threats they offer always share the force of the ultimate threat. The 'final demand' that arrives when he has no money; the nasty encounter in the street; the girl who spits at him and won't; all these – to change the image – are small waves that lap on his beach from an ultimate typhoon out there in the ocean, that will never go away. Here ocean and primeval forest are images for the same reality.

Men and women spend their lives, especially their young lives, winning symbolic victories over that ultimate threat. They 'conquer' the mountains, give themselves to causes out of a mixture of motives; they multiply their orgasms in embroidered nests of sensual illusion. They labour to hear friendly voices, recognize them, and maybe headlines yelling 'He's the greatest'; when they are older they look for status in the hierarchy, a country squireship and the glossy body of a car. Then the threat can scarcely be heard.

Tantra says, 'Look! You *are* the ocean and its typhoon! You *are no different* from the forest!' That sounds easy, but each man and woman, cocooned at the centre of his or her comfortable estate, cannot see past the billboards and hoardings they have put up. They stare at the brilliant commercials they themselves designed, which offer the human race dreams of a stainless-steel-and-formica paradise, forever free from smelly breath; and they dream of some kind of ultimate victory for an ultimate mind over the 'threat', in a vastly remote science-fiction future. They can't even see the forest or the ocean any more.

Tantra says, 'Look at your hands! Your dirty pants! and understand *them*. Every visible object is a divinity, whose real nature is the Supreme Principle.' But that is really hard to know. Some people try, by taking acid. Some try to express 'themselves', extending the energies of their bodies in streams of symbolism. They dispatch endless flows of committed action into space and time. But each one's eyes look out only along his lines of action. As each one chops out his private estate from the primeval jungle, he is totally absorbed in the chopping and trimming. To change the image back again, each one is like a man working a raft on a stormy sea, shouting to others in the same situation, keeping company with some, maybe, till they sink or vanish: always working, quite unaware of what the sea is, or who the man is who is struggling with the sea.

Some Indian religions say, 'All this is mere illusion! Hate it and let it go!' Not Tantra. Tantra says, 'None of this can possibly be without significance!' And it asks, 'Why do you think it seems to have extent in Time? Have you ever known a true beginning and end, which were not mere changes of state?' Time is the key. The Indians named the chief powers of their Tantra 'Mahākāla', the

Great Time, and 'Kālī', the Goddess as Time personified. She is the material substance, the continuum in expression. All that we feel and see and know is a tiny fragment of Her: a section, so to speak, through her immense unity. And everything that happens *She is enjoying*! That means *you*! We in the West stick to a strangely simple and narrow view of time. This is probably because we are committed to believing that only what we can count and calculate is real. Calculation takes time. Even when it goes very fast, as in the computer, it is a time-process; and so time is absorbed into the calculating out of what is being calculated and becomes 'invisible'. Our science – and our science-fiction – still work within a framework of time which assumes a remote beginning and some distant end, with the irreversible processes of entropy operating between.

The view of time taken by Indian philosophy – linked as it is with linguistics – is quite different. Tantra especially demonstrates that there is a platform of experience from which the processes of time can be seen as the single matrix of the universe and its inhabitants, not as their abstract cause or condition. The sea which the rowers on their rafts are afloat on is a direct function of their efforts. The original gardener who hacked out his gardens from the primeval jungle is a function of the same reality as the jungle; the appearance of the jungle over him is produced by an original and sustained, because timeless, act of creation; and that consists of a kind of separation within the aboriginal whole of nameless Nature. The split between knower and known, between seer and seen, between man and what he struggles with, are an essential part of creative process; and *that* Tantra identifies as a perceptual spasm, narrowing our view to the slit of the passing moment. Together the two aspects diffract the whole. There are all kinds of images to indicate the nature of this dual process of creation by limitation. The chief one is sex. For all the dialectical divisions by which creation takes place work as couples. Object and subject; time and space; man and world; to be and not to be.

Tantra offers the platform from which all this can be seen as clear fact. Just as no one can tell you what the taste of a lemon is if you've never sucked one, so no one can tell you what it is like to occupy that Tantrik platform unless you have. And Tantra has no interest at all in *persuading* you, or proving its position true. You will only know if you try. It has no interest in intellectual argument.

That belongs to the lower levels of dialectic. Tantra, with its different schools and texts, embodies a continuously developing version of a unified vision and tradition which have an unbroken history stretching back into the most distant reaches of our human 'past'. It has adapted itself to many different kinds of society, and could to ours.

The basic image embodying that vision is that the human body itself is the womb of its own world. What we know as this lump of bone and flesh is in fact an instrument, imbued with an infinity of possible forms, wealthy beyond our understanding. It is the envelope for a complex system of channels and knots; through these the energy flowing into creation is dispersed, filtered, narrowed and divided, so as to elaborate images of objective universes spread out in space and time 'beyond' our senses, in furious turmoil. Part of that turmoil and separation consists in shoal upon shoal of selves, who stare at each other, imagining themselves distinct. Each one 'generates' (the word is apt) its own estate upon what it believes to be its own private primeval space. Through a subtle map of narrower and narrower channels in each body the energy is distributed, like water through an irrigation system, to feed each person's experience. And each sees laid out before him a world, strung on the four co-ordinate lines of up-and-down, left-and-right, to-and-fro and irreversible past–present–future. The last co-ordinate, time, is the weak point in the imprisoning circle of our obsessions and beliefs. Our body's functions always and forever outstrip any intellectual understanding we may have of them. In all the comfortable – or uncomfortable – patterns of our lives the body's movements and apprehensions, with all their reflected patterns in time for which we have no words or concepts, are left to wither unrecognized, unused – except, perhaps, in certain kinds of art.

None of us, not even the most esoteric physicist, can ever know anything else but his own 'idea' of the world. This idea can never *be* the world, and can never contain the dimension of passing time. Furthermore, the 'idea' itself owes its validity, in the last resort, to the creative profusion offered by the senses and their imagery. We, however, are the victims of a tightly organized communal belief in an external 'dead-nature', which has become deeply embedded in all our culture-habits, and has laid a blight on our whole personal and social life. Our language, our journalism, even our dedication to various kinds of photography as art-forms, all persuade us that there is (or was a moment ago) a separate 'thing' out there somewhere beyond our lens or sense-mechanisms of which we can take 'true' snapshots, and that we ourselves are, in some unexplained way, made up of the same stuff as it is. It somehow 'gives' us all we are allowed to know.

When you come down to it, all that we actually know is memory. Without memory neither you nor I would know we exist. The world that our senses give us changes and shifts. Its vibrations and their interwoven patterns last – like ripples on a pond or cloud-shapes – only for a longer or a shorter moment. Mountains are just a form of clouds that we say last longer, that is, change more slowly. The mental snapshots of that flux which we are able to fix and repeat give us our illusions of permanence. Tantra, however, sees the entire flux and pattern of vibrations as already complete in its infinite variety within the womb of the universe. The processes of time only filter it out through our bodies and senses, phase by successive and continuous phase, item by item. But we *can* identify in ourselves the source through which the Whole is feeding us our experience; and if we learn, so to speak, to face upstream towards that source, we can see the dialectical process within the perspective of ourselves as a total unity in multitudinous flower. At any single moment of our time everything is already there; though normally we cannot see it because our attention is facing the other way, intent on following our sense-experiences outward along the creative energy-flows. Creation, or Genesis, as a unity, already complete at this very moment, is waiting for us to discover it just beyond the top of our subtle skulls. The reality we are now all seeing is limited by the fact of our being human. But to reach the Tantrik platform enables us to see the whole like seeing the street. Even an idea of the remoteness of stellar events is part of the filter-pattern of our universe.

The source of the flows Tantra identifies as the womb and body of a Great Goddess. Her *hole* is the *whole*, which is the cause and origin of all its parts. The body of each of us is a subsidiary of this cosmic genital mechanism. Within it is embedded a seminal male, the seed of Being, invisible and totally unintelligible. But without it there would be nothing. To be is positive. The Goddess distributes that positive Being into all that is. The male seed is both what she is and distributes. So within each person the original sexual division is also present. The seed, together with its functional distribution into things-that-are, co-exist in each person; and each, to gain the Tantrik platform, needs to reconstitute in him or herself the original undivided state of the cosmic sexes, upstream of the projection of time and space. There, where everything, as I said, exists at once, where the whole is an instantaneous reality, all that is happening can be known in a single thought. It is not understood by calculation or reasoning – that would be to downgrade it to merely mental function – but intuited as a unified, all-at-once *gestalt*, figure, image, form. It is not a matter of extending our memory-interpretation of sense-experience so as to cover a longer reach of time-eternity even – but of making the continual movement of perception into perception not of things but of the principle of things; where you are – NOW.

Again, it is easy to talk. But how can one reach the Tantrik platform? One of the important things about Indian thought and religion is that it has carefully preserved not only words but actual techniques. There are plenty of religions and philosophies which survive as words and pious formulae. But India knows actually what to *do*. Of course, the Indian techniques were devised for Indians, and for us simply to adopt them wholesale and in a general way just does not work. But there is no doubt that they can be adapted. The important thing is to get down to brass tacks. Deeds and powerful images can change a person far more effectively than reading acres of print. And Tantra is full of powerful images which amplify and complement each other, and connect up with systems of effective act. The act involves the body and all its functions, which the images co-ordinate and control. Tantra shows people first how to look at their experiences of the world, in *all* its aspects, not only the aspect of numerical calculation; then how to vitalize and amplify them; next how to contain them in images which are not mere general ideas, so as to harness the energies which normally flow into them; then finally how to condense those energies still further into a force which can be driven back up against the stream, to the point where they enter into the status of the physical. All of this demands the use of the body in special ways. To guide the process there are maps, useful just as maps of city streets are useful, to help you find your way. They are not meant to be 'art treasures' for 'art-tourists'.

All the books one can read about Tantra, and about Indian philosophy in general, leave out an absolutely vital first stage. They all jump straight to exalted general thought and theory. They have therefore deceived generations of well-meaning people into vague, unfocused fantasies. Tantra recognizes that practice must come before any rumination. But before one can even begin to practise seriously one needs to develop the capacity for a special kind of thinking which has never been properly explained. It is the key to the whole matter. It has sometimes been summed up and neatly packaged as 'concentration', 'yogic meditation', and so on. Many people, especially those inclined to Buddhism, have been misled into believing that they must cultivate a kind of still, blank, but restful emptiness of mind, mistaking this for what is technically called 'the Void'. But the basis of all *Tantrik* work is to develop the faculty of holding a 'field-image' in the mind. The yantras, which figure so largely in Tantrik art (see Plate 33), are visual illustrations of such field-images; mantras, these groups of powerful syllables, sometimes related to actual words, sometimes not, are audible analogues: 'Om Klīṁ Strīṁ Hūṁ'. Tantra differs from many orthodox Indian religious doctrines – at any rate as they are interpreted nowadays – in holding that all the body's past experiences and memories must be *turned to account*, not simply suppressed. This is as true of the Tantrik Buddhism of Tibet as of the Hindu Tantra of Bengal and Rajasthān. It means that sensuous experience, along with the intuitions it nourishes, is fundamentally *useful* – not just something to be avoided; and that Tantra is more like art than abstract philosophy.

It does, however, have its own kinds of Philosophy. Figure 1 summarizes one school. The structure of sexual dialectic creation, by separating object from subject (continuously in progress down its different levels), is shown in the upper stages. It is a process of limiting and degrading through the Kañchukas. But we, poor mortals, inhabit the bottom stage. And that is where we have to begin, with our body and its world. We must never divorce ourselves from them. Any realization we may set out to achieve can only work if we are prepared to bring the whole metaphysical structure to life, beginning with and including the foundations.

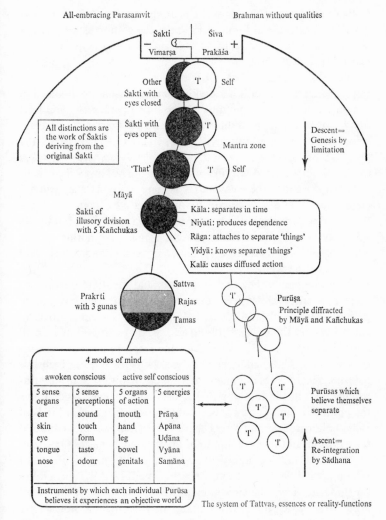

Figure 1

When we sit to begin our long ascent to the Tantrik platform we can only start with ourselves; not with anything we have read or fancied someone else might have done. Our world is that which spreads out around us, that we can move about in, smell and hear. Our own psychological classifications may not be the same, quite, as those shown here, but they are near enough. The set of notions in the bottom circle of Figure 1 indicates the complete spectrum of our experience of the world. The column on the left lists the sense-organs; the next the fields of experience covered by those sense organs. Then there are the five organs of action; and finally, on the right, there are a set of inner bodily energies which are involved in the action of the corresponding organs – line by line. As you read them, you are understanding them in an abstract way, as categories of information. But here is the real crux of the matter – the point where the body comes into it – completely – where yoga takes over and our Western notions of meaning shrivel away into shadows. For if we take these categories as mere thoughts, they will not change us. We can ruminate to our heart's content about the higher principles on the diagram, Māyā, Śakti and Śiva, but unless we have started with the foundations, which have nothing to do with intellectual rumination, we will never get a glimmer of the real meaning of the whole system.

Tantra demands that each person should meditate on each of these categories of his own experience, one by one, over long periods of time, totally focused. What he or she must do is to concentrate in the mind 'field-images' of the reality implicit in all these different functions, filled with the memory-traces of experience in time. Then, later, he will be able to form more inclusive field-images of these images. Art-made symbols and mantra-sounds help in the focusing of the first field-images. And this is the point at which Tantra specifically diverges from other kinds of Indian philosophy and yoga. The others all hold that in meditation the 'motions of the mind' are to be abandoned as meaningless and empty, and totally extinguished. Different traditions, Buddhist and Hindu, give different methods for achieving this. But Tantra takes the opposite view. The various categories of 'motions of the mind' are treated as a precious raw material; they include not simply motions of what *we* would call the *mind*, but all traces and patterns of sensuous–sensual experience. This is the selfsame fund of material which the arts draw upon; and I have pointed out elsewhere that India's greatest writer on aesthetics and artistic meaning was an advanced Tantrik master, called Abhinavagupta (*ca* A.D. 1000); and that Indian art owes an unacknowledged debt to the Tantrik attitude. All the arts – music and painting especially –

were dear to Tantrikas because of the way they stimulate and co-ordinate sensuous traces.

The Tantrik point is that yogic meditation consists first in going carefully over and over the contents of each of these categories of experience in one's mind, evoking every memory and echo of the body's life which can be found. Take the related categories of 'skin' and 'sense of touch'. What of these has your own body known? Remember them all: stroking, pressing, squeezing, concrete, fur, feathers, wet clay; feeling water dripping, running; the acts of crushing, smacking, catching. All these extend horizontally across the diagram to the 'hand' as organ of action, and into the kind of inner energy which it expresses: explore your own memory fund of the active 'feel' of bodies, of the tactile space created by handling furniture, pottery, by stroking grass, hugging a tree, bunching leaves together, pulling hair; exploring the shape of areas, of crowded human bodies, of bundles of cloth, of whole tactile regions, like the Indian kitchen and sitting-space in front of a peasant house, or a verandah floor entirely pressed out of cow-dung plaster by hand; the spaces you roll in, hang from, squeeze into. All of these will have echoes and re-echoes in the memory. And then you will begin to know what Tantra means by a whole 'field' of contents. Controlling your attention so that it is not captivated by any single one of these touch sensations, you can form of the whole what I called a 'field-image'. And this field-image is actually a condensation of space and time, known directly and inwardly. Once the scope of the field has been recognized consciously, all the external events with which it is connected will reveal themselves as instances or punctuations defining the field itself, which can then be identified by a certain symbol. And you will find that, with practice, the field can be made ready to spring into the mind when the symbol is presented. Our whole field of touch, for example, can be evoked when we offer a symbolic cloth to an image of the supreme deity in ritual pūjā.

All of the various possible such fields, with their energies, must be explored in meditation, distinguished and correlated with all the others in the lists. Then at the *top* of the lowest circle in Figure 1 are the four modes of mind, along with each of which the fields will operate. They too are a special kind of field which each person must explore or realize for himself. To be aware, to experience clearly each of these modes of mind as a sustained inward phenomenon is a difficult and infinitely rewarding task. No one can tell you if you are right, except maybe a guru who has himself 'got there'. If you think you can find others, not mentioned in the lists, please do. The important thing, however, is to be able to maintain each field awake as a field, and not to let any actual external event impinge so much as to capture and draw away your whole attention to itself.

And now, with all your fields of sense and body-memory twanging, so to speak, resonating in sympathetic vibrations with each other, raise the issue of the 'I' involved; where and what is it? There is not any answer yet; except, perhaps, that what we have on the right of the diagram is that 'field of separate I's', the shoals of selves that believe themselves separate both from each other and from their functional fields. Once you get to this point you realize that the experiencing of the fields, and then of the things they contain as *separate*, is a kind of limitation or diffraction, within the scope of a higher field. Something, somehow, is surveying all these fields – a 'subject', an 'I' in some sense; not the old habitual 'I', but a much more remote and unidentifiable unity.

There is still present, therefore, a residual sense of objective and subjective running through experience of all these fields. And this can have, if one examines the field of fields intently, a set of three 'layers of density' (called guṇas) running up from the lowest, downward-sinking inertia of the static; through the state of vibrating energy and motion, to the condition of shining, pure being, the presence which absolutely distinguishes something that is, and our knowledge of it, from something which is not. The three have other names, and appear as goddesses: Desire, Activity and Knowledge. When we have realised fully how the fields and fields of fields are extended by this triple polarity, coloured with those three primaries, we become able to perform the action (which is indescribable) of turning around within our own organism and confronting the womb of time, the source from which our whole field of fields radiates, the yonì of Māyā Śakti, she who measures out the world and us (see Plate 40). Gazing into that womb we see what looks like an erupting volcano, the processes which result in separations, divisions, layings out in sequence, the creation of objects and causes. This state of awareness is not a blank empti-

ness. But it can only be reached when we have dammed up and
turned back on itself the downward and outward current which we
might call (with deference to Schopenhauer) the torrent of the
active will, which creates, divides and then grasps at what it
creates. It can no longer escape into individual experiences.
Instead it 'pools out', so to speak, in those vibrating fields of fields
at the summit and centre of which our new state of consciousness
is born. This can never happen, according to Tantra, by pure
elimination, by a negative tranquillity, but only as the culmination
of extreme fullness, a fullness so extreme as to seem Void; in fact
by transformation of all the body's echoes and energies.

Transformation is the key. It suggests an alchemy by which the
base metals of the body are all converted into a new and un-
analysable gold. No gold appears, though, without the baser
metals. What these last are, and what the physical processes are by
which they are transmuted, is the substance of Tantra. One essential factor is that the whole mass of the body's energies and recollections, in consummated form, may be experienced as a female
principle of motion, called in Buddhist Tantra Dakinī.

First of all, however, there are several complementary systems
which can be used and have developed from different lines of
thought. They all originate outside the religious orthodoxies, and
are certainly far older than Hinduism, Buddhism and Jainism.
These religions made their own use of the older traditions, and
modified them to fit in with their own verbal and philosophical
theories. So there are now Hindu and Buddhist Tantras which
differ in their interpretations of practices and ideas. The Tantrik
Buddhism of Tibet has made a monumental effort at scholastic
elaboration and synthesis. But it is always necessary to remember
that, in Tantra, *practices come first*. It is because they *work* that
they have been preserved. And they work because they are based
on what one can call inner facts, which everyone observes who
attempts any Tantrik action. Different peoples and different sects
may register these facts in different terms; but there can be no
doubt that there is a common basis of inner experience behind the
different sets of terms used.

The first and fundamental image which reflects inner facts is the
'subtle body' (see Plate 35). This is shared by all Indian traditions,
as well as by Indian medicine. It is experienced as that immense

ramification of channels of energy mentioned earlier, which flows through the entire body, at the level not of physical flesh, but of function and field. Surgery and dissection do not discover it. Its main trunk is in the spine, its branches run to those organs of sense-perception, of action and the mind's faculties we have already seen; and the twigs run out to all the nervous terminals. The human body is thus like a plant which is fed by sap along its system of veins. But this sap is not something merely physical, like blood, lymph or hormones. It is something directly experienced as 'vitality', that which makes the mere physique continue to *be*. Some of its transformations are those 'energies' listed in the right-hand column of our diagram. Descriptions given in many texts attempt to 'pictorialize' it in the form of a kind of liquid light or breath – something which is only experienced as function, rhythm and flow. In a sense it is the image of the totality of field-images mentioned earlier. This transcendent energy infuses into the world system through a point identified with the crown of the person's head; there it is transformed from its original pure nature. A radiant subtle thread, the main trunk-channel, running down the spine, terminates between the genitals and anus. At different levels down this channel are strung a series of radiating 'wheels' or 'lotuses'. Some traditions give six or more. Some give four. Each of these represents the human entity in a state of progressively lower awareness. Tantrik Buddhism refers to them as 'knots'. When the inflowing energy radiates out at the lowest level, the ordinary world of common reality spreads out its fields around the person, who imagines himself as a separate centre for it, and sees it, so to speak, projected 'over against' himself. When he is able to perform the meditations described earlier on, together with certain other practices, his consciousness can be made to climb back up along the system towards the summit, to the place of original light, the thousand-petalled lotus in the crown of the head. The knots are progressively loosened, and at each lotus the inner condition of awareness becomes more comprehensive, less limited by individual fact and history.

Those other practices include, of course, yoga. Everyone nowadays is familiar with the athletic postures, twists and pulls which make up Hatha yoga – the basis of Tantrik yogas. There are, of course, many customs included in yoga which have a medical significance, promoting the general health of the body, though properly with Tantrik ends in view. Such are the washings of bowel and stomach. The first can be done drawing the long bowel out through the anus and washing it in water; the second by swallowing thin muslin and pulling it up again. But most of the many other contractions and postures (that I haven't space to describe here) are directed to stirring up one or other of these inner fields and channels of energy, especially by working on the spine. Without a realized sense of these fields and channels, such yoga is no more than a game.

One major component is the set of breathing exercises, 'restraint of the breath', in Sanskrit Prāṇayama. They, again, are not at all purely physical; but they are shared with non-Tantrik yoga. Some traditions of the latter use them for 'suppressing' those 'movements of the mind' mentioned earlier. But the essential point is that the Prāṇa, usually translated 'breath', which is to be controlled, is *not* the physical breath. It is the subtle energy itself. All the inhalations and exhalations of the *actual* breath, through right and left nostrils, are designed sympathetically to stabilize the *subtle* breath: which is sometimes called 'the rhythm of the universe'. The second crucial activity is a joint contraction and posture which is used for a very special purpose. This both presses on and squeezes the region of perineum, between the legs. It is meant to stimulate into vivid life the psychosomatic root energy which, in the ordinary man, sleeps in the lowest of those lotuses. This Hindus call the famous Kuṇḍalinī, the tiny brilliant snake, who coils three and a half times round a lingam in that lotus; this phallic form constitutes the bottom end of the central channel of the spine. Kuṇḍalinī covers its aperture with her own mouth. She can be heard, when one begins Tantrik work, constantly making an indistinct humming, like a swarm of bees; and her coilings, here imaged as static, *are* your dynamic universe. The yogic pressures are meant first to wake her up. Then she may be imbued with all the previously dispersed fields of energy, gathered and concentrated by mantras and field-images. By further yogic devices she is persuaded to straighten and force her way into that central channel to begin the ascent, withdrawing with her all the experiences of the person from his particularized world. She is herself the 'presentation image' of the psychic and cosmic energy of the universe particularized for each individual. When she enters the lower end of the central channel, the yogī's world is suddenly spiritualized; the first stage of transformation occurs.

In the complexes of ritual, described in many of the texts called Tantras, mudra or hand-gesture plays a part, often combined with stylized dance posture. This bears the same relationship to the clear and elaborate hand and position language of the Indian dance as the condensed syllables of spoken mantra do to the verbal language. These bodily acts condense particular fields of significance, and then realize them as the inner property of the person who performs. They are symbols of personal altitudes, which, when they are practised and performed, induce in the performer the content they symbolize. So each gesture does not 'express' a subjective state or urge it out to a spectator. Instead it 'impresses', inwards, upon the performer himself the field of which it is the vehicle. This is a crucial distinction. For all the higher states known to Tantra are, so to speak, 'already there'. The body, in assimilating the formula, coaxes its meaning awake in the subtle organism.

Another most important – perhaps ultimately the most important of the control systems for the creative energy – is the sexual act itself.

Sexual yoga is a very important part of Tantra, which of course has not been much publicized until recently. India shares with Europe a tradition which identifies sexual enjoyment as a drastic stimulation and sudden 'outflow' of the psychocosmic creative energy. The sexual juices of men and women are the visible forms of that energy – white and red, respectively; and sexual desire is direct evidence of its presence in an awoken state. What Tantrik yoga requires is that the sexual energies of man and woman be vigorously aroused; that then they should not be wasted in mere momentary pleasure, but 'turned back up', and reconverted into their original substance, adding their force to the field-images. That subtle snake Kuṇḍalinī takes them into herself, to supplement her radiance and the power of her ascent. Especially significant is the fact that truly Tantrik yoga needs to be performed, certainly in the early stages, by a sexual couple, not by a solitary person (some puritan sects do hold that sex is only ever symbolic). The postures of real sexual yoga work on the body's subtle energies in the same way as those of Hatha yoga – but perhaps more effectively. The point is that each individual seems to need his or her own sexual energy complemented by that of a member of the opposite sex. Thus the outflows of each partner are, so to speak, capped off and fed back into an inner circuit. Mutual orgasm, as the sacrificial terminus of a long rite, may thus be a sacramental exchange. (There are also traditions which hold that orgasm must never occur.) After a period of practice man and woman will gradually discover that each on their own contain their complement. Outer woman and man then become unnecessary to man and woman. Each discovers within themselves an inner counterpart. In fact it 'was' always so. The habit of 'projecting' had made each feel that the energy of the opposite sex actually resided *in* a member of the opposite sex. But once the field of counter-sex experience is awoken and realized, it can be discovered, so to speak, at inner source; and the state of double-sexed inner arousal will become a part of each one's meditative realization. This is the reason why so many Tantrik figures appear in art as couples. So far as the male Tantrika is concerned, well-endowed female yoginīs are the most important people in his life; and the social environment which makes Tantrik yoga and rituals possible is highly valued. In India the Kula family system supplied an excellent framework. Today it still survives. The cákrapūjā (or 'circular rite'), in its various forms, is the focal centre. During this ritual, a kind of Eucharist, performed on auspicious occasions, a circle of couples exchange partners and partake of four other normally forbidden indulgences expressly to increase its efficiency.

There is no space to pursue the details here.

To return to the body itself, Tantra takes sex to be the highest condition of awareness of the originating energy. And sex has therefore been treated as itself symbolic of the whole aim of Tantra. It becomes the raw material for an unbelievably sacral function. Once the state of inner mutual sexuality has been achieved, and the psychosomatic energy Kuṇḍalinī has been set on her inward ascent up the spinal channel, there are stages to be passed through at the level of each lotus wheel when knots are loosened and the vistas expand. And at each of them the inner sexual complement – female or male – changes its character. The less advanced Tantrika only reaches, say, the third or fourth lotus every now and then; he falls back afterwards, in everyday life, to the everyday condition. But the advanced Tantrika will succeed in living at ever higher stages of awareness, not losing his ground. The consciousness of the most advanced of all does not ever descend below the heart. And it is only at the levels below the heart that outer rites, outer realities and outer sexual partners can operate. Above the heart lotus they have no relevance.

When the sexual internalization is first achieved during sexual intercourse the bodily energy rises, naturally, to the level of the lotus behind the genitals. The first transformation there of the sexual counterpart is into the purified essence of erotic feeling, the deities of love, liquid and beautiful, radiant like the moon.

It is at the level of the navel, the belly lotus, the region of fire, that the most drastic purging of consciousness has to take place. Again, outer facts need to be internalized. The outer facts are all those drastic demonstrations that time, as we believe it to be, can only mean to us death and destruction. The outer symbols are those connected with the obliteration of the individual and his significance – the graveyard with its funeral pyres. The ultimate threat, the destroying typhoon mentioned earlier on, has to be faced out in the body and then itself transformed. Tantrikas, men and women, are initiated and meditate in fact in the cemetery, among the dying fires and charred bones. They feed the jackals with symbols of their own bodies, setting themselves totally beyond the pale of the caste system, defiled beyond any purifying. They meditate in sexual intercourse, sitting on decaying corpses. Their yoga *realises* the stench and nastiness of decaying flesh, and assimilates its personal meaning. Most people find this exceedingly revolting. It is meant to be. You are no Tantrika if you have not come out of the other side of disgust and dread, so that your personal preferences have been dissolved in the universal pattern. The inner sexual counterpart at this lotus level becomes the black essence of destroying time, hideous of face, everyone's nightmare of their scarecrow Death (see Plate 37). But when this sexual union is consummated into an inner condition, the fire of the graveyard becomes the consuming fire of achievement; the gateway to success the ring which protects the reality of Tantrik achievement from the mere fantasy enjoyments of the dilettante; it is also the fire that transmutes the baser metals into the first stage of alchemical gold.

Once the inner energies ascend to the heart, words become

irrelevant. The outer world falls away and its realities become like distant echoes woven into the vibrations of cosmic history. But the inner sexuality moves on to a new plane. By the time the upper levels of lotuses are reached the spine has become like a vast and hollow crystal tube, resonating with vibrant light and sound, touch scent and taste. It extends upwards, out of and beyond the human sphere. Only the gods know what further lotuses it may pierce.

The final terms which we may apply to the remotest, all-embracing creative movements, can only remain sexual. The divine Names which Tantra applies to the ultimate principles of the universe are sexual. Our human sex is a kind of blurred mirror-image, or pale reflection, of the bliss the double God feels in creating. Knowledge, in the sense of ordinary discrimination and reckoning, simply evaporates. For from 'above' flows down the milk of enlightenment, flooding the whole bodily organism, which then experiences itself as the original unitary field, in which every instant of time is implicit at once. The greatest of the meditative yantra-diagrams, the Srī yantra (see Plate 40) is a direct image of this state. The meaning of the yantra, worked on and developed over a long period of time, can dawn on the experienced meditator as he surveys and worships it. It is not – absolutely not – an abstraction. It is an image of the utmost fullness; it means the completest realization of every fact at every level of possibility: from the molecule to the nebula, from the tread of every gnat's foot to the total history of human folly. It becomes a matter of direct perception that each incident of these implies every other.

The sexual dialectic can be pursued to the point of total dissolution. All that anyone can experience is an energy-function of the Goddess, the female of the creative pair. There is a dot at the centre of those interlaced male (upward-pointing) and female (downward-pointing) triangles of the Srī yantra. It is meant to represent the seminal male, the principle of Being, without which nothing exists. It is actually present in all the triangles, everywhere. It traced out the first. If we look at the dot itself in close-up, it becomes a field again, with a small male organ buried in it. And that male organ, as any kind of fact, or any thought, must be, is itself a function of the Goddess, the female. There is no point at which we can step beyond Her.

And so back to the human body. Its sensual experience and

sexual bliss are the raw material for its own transformation. Inner and outer are combined in one; feeling and knowledge marry; the male and female components of individual and cosmos are inwardly transfigured by their own mutuality. The Tantrika then experiences the universe in blissful sexual intercourse with itself, without beginning or end for every single instant. What is always the last mystery remains inexplicable – the true nature of the individuality, change and difference the Goddess so strenuously creates. Tantra demonstrates their infinite value by recognizing that they are the actual substance of Her timeless sexual joy.

1. P. S. Rawson, *The Art of Tantra* (Thames & Hudson, 1973; New York: Graphic, 1973).
— *Tantra: The Indian Cult of Ecstasy* (Thames & Hudson, 1973; Avon, 1973).

John O'Neill

Gay Technology and the Body Politic

My purpose is to view contemporary political events, demonstrations, student–police clashes, festivals, sit-ins and love-ins as a
renewal of the mythological substructure of political knowledge
and organization. This is an exercise which deliberately seeks the
limits of our present knowledge by confronting our sense of political realism with its pathos of scepticism about the renewal of the
body politic.[1] By the same token, it is an exercise at the poetic
limit of the Western tradition of rationality and the invention of a
wild sociology.

Many observers have dismissed the phenomena I shall be concerned with as regressive or else purely expressive behaviour. In
general, they regard the political process as immune to the antics of
the cultural revolution and its mode of internal revolt. The appeal
to the poetry of life as the basis of a new politics arouses the
cynicism if not the despair of political observers. The three-day
nation founded on the rock of Woodstock is surely an irrelevance
to the stability of corporate America and an affront to the revolutionary endurance of its soul brothers in Algeria and Vietnam. The
reality which dominates our political life is the production of
corporate and state practices governed by a conception of rationality which represses any relation to life and nature other than the
exercise of domination. This reality is manufactured through the
sub-rationality of science and the institutions, language and
images which foster the assumption that the good life is only
achievable through, or else the same thing as, an expansionist
practicality.

In order to grasp the everyday sense of these connections we need to consider technology as revelation, as an instrument of appearances and the construction of truth in the assertions of cathedrals, skyscrapers, noise and theatre. It is then possible to see that the meaning of our everyday lives in the urban industrial world is a construction of what it is we are trying to say, how we are trying to live among telephones, typewriters, films, television, automobiles, aeroplanes, refrigerators and contraceptives.

To envision these things, however, is to rely upon the conversation of machines which reveal the 'mechanical' as the forgetfulness of the presence and absence of man in the technological world. Such is the achievement of Charlie Chaplin's films, the theatre of Brecht, Marx's *Capital* and the music of our times. The machine-paced world is revealed through the films of Charlie Chaplin, whose shuffle reverses the scenarios of assembly and falling grace, turning a pratfall into a political act. In this way capitalism as the life-form of things is dramatized and the absence of man implicit in Marx's analytic of *Capital* is brought to expression and reversal through art. For this reason the body politic is dependent upon art for revealing evil as the construct of a rule (a machine) for the accumulation of knowledge (*Faust*) or of power (*Capital*) and the forgetfulness of alternate social orders. Edmund Burke's *Reflections On the Revolution in France*, for example, is therefore an essay in political poetry because it sings of the goodness of the great national prejudice of family order and its struggle with the 'mathematical' rules of the Revolution. What is at issue here is not the conservative pathos of Burkean order any more than the Utopian pathos of socialism. It is the insistence upon the principle that the production of social order cannot start from Hobbes's or Mandeville's asocial rules for the transformation of evil but is the historical work of human recognition and reciprocity.

We are in search, then, of an *aesthetics* of technology to serve as the basis of the modern connection between art and politics and the dissolution of the mind–body dualism which determines the orders of reality and illusion in our political life. Our task is to recover our forgetfulness of the 'mechanical', which has always served as the metaphor for the complex and remote organization of the social and political institutions that arose with the power of machines. The machine, as Carlyle saw it, is the 'sign' of modern times, the dominant symbol of our sensibility, knowledge and power. It is in terms of the machine that we conceive our own bodies, society and government, reducing the values peculiar to each of those forms of life to the utilities which result from technique.

Men are grown mechanical in head and in heart, as well as in hand. They have lost faith in individual endeavour, and in natural force, of any kind. Not for internal perfection, but for external combinations and arrangements, for institutions, constitution – for Mechanism of one sort or other, do they hope and struggle. Their whole efforts, attachments, opinions, turn on mechanism, and are of a mechanical character.[2]

Thus it happens that the machine alters the ratio between the human senses as well as between society and nature. In what I shall call *gay technology* I believe we may discern a variety of social forms which return the industrial and political 'machine' to the rhythm of life and the body politic. My examples are, of course, as precarious as is the tendency of hope.[3]

Consider first the new unisex mode and its implications for the redefinition of the relation between identity and the occupational world. It is a paradox of the Women's Liberation Movement that this seeks entry into a work world already 'abandoned'. The W.L.M. demand for the equality of the sexes actually extends the normative asexuality of the division of labour required but never so consistently practised in industrial society. More important still, it accepts a new reduction of the female body to the standards of the machine rigorously internalized in private techniques of orgasm which re-energize the chastity of capitalism beyond anything achieved by the Protestant ethic. This combination of equality and mechanical chastity[4] is seriously advanced as the springboard of women's liberation precisely at a time when the post-male abandonment of the world of technology has reinvented a diffuse, polymorphous and non-focused sexuality which transcends the genital definition of male and female roles. Feminists to the contrary, the male body image is threatened not merely by the prospect of insatiable vaginas or the semi-automatic clitoris. However threatening the female weapon, the basic source of male anxiety derives from man's emasculation by the machine world which no longer projects masculine scenarios in any great number. This process is, of course, much more in evidence in the professional and bureaucratic occupations, including war, and it is precisely because of their lack of masculine prerequisites that women are seen as a competitive threat in these areas.[5] Added to this, there is the difficulty the organization man has in projecting an adequate male image as the oedipal centre of his own family. Masculinity is increasingly the pose of male models lasciviously sucking on a Marlboro or else a game of astro-cowboys carefully watched over back home by mum and the kids.

Gay technology transcends the old-order hangups of occupational identity and the standards of decorum dictated in the presence of machines. Thus rock music, its artists and audiences dissolve the sterility of technology into the convulsive, sweat-drenched improvizations of violence, love, care and community. Rock expresses the joyful embrace of life and technology that is the driving vision of the modern world as well as its own nightmare. The arousal of rock reveals the world as desire, the body as environment, caught between order and chaos, invoking community, flirting with self-destruction and infantile disorders.

The conventional technological congregation demands decorum in the presence of machines, engines, typewriters, microphones and television sets. To fart in the face of a T.V. set, or to piss on a car, is not nearly as acceptable as to lie naked on the bonnet of a Ford or to murder, rape and thieve on a T.V. set. For these reasons rock is especially revolting. Its standards of technological decorum are flirtatious, cajoling, argumentative, burlesque and destructive. Its instruments are dissolved into a whirl of boogies, minces, struts, leaps and swaggers in which they are transcended as sound-conveyors to become flesh, pain, laughter, tears and joy. By the same token the artist–audience relation ordinarily staged by the technological medium is made into a community of experience which is intimate and hopeful, enraged but essentially political in its connections – even where these fail.

Observers of rock concerts typically evaluate performances from the standpoint of adult linear conceptions of sound, movement, sense and value. They listen while the kids love and scream. They writhe at seeing performers who neither sing nor walk. They are affronted by the crying, the prancing and the leaping. They see no place for genital or anal display, for tears, laughter, sweat and destruction – still believing, as they do, in the power of the uncorrupted word and the trained voice to reveal its message. In all this they ignore the body and soul of music, and its incantation of a fundamental humanity which in all its misery and through all its joys seeks a community that is no less real for remaining a hope. But the critics reduce this incipient community to their own fearfulness of mass hysteria, by the very same token through which they separate mind and body, reason and the human passions. Thus their rejection of the world of rock fulfils their own denial of the symbiosis between the degradation of modern political life and its delinquent consequences

The critics fear the power of the artist to move thousands of people, while overlooking that their minds are subject to the mass violations of a commercialism that is predicated upon instinctual levels below anything Hobbes or even Freud might have contemplated. Indeed, commercialism is the naked lunch of millions who could never understand the significance of Billie Holiday's remark that 'I knew I'd really licked it one morning when I couldn't stand television any more. When I was high I wanted to stay that way, I could watch T.V. by the hour and loved it . . . if you've beaten the habit again and kicked T.V., no jail on earth can worry you too much.'[6] Even when they recognize the anti-war, peace, love and non-competitive ethic which pervades rock (though in tension with its more violent values), the critics content themselves with sceptical evaluations of the chances of such values against the reality of the major corporate and governmental institutions which they challenge. In this they choose death against Eros – unaware, however, that they have chosen against their own youth and their own future. Thus they construct out of the present discontents the grounds of lasting injustice. Moreover, the linear reviewers of rock, folk, bikes and pop for the most part overlook the general *crisis* of art, language and culture which has prevailed for a century now. Their disgust at the confusion of art and life has, however, no solid basis. Does it arise from a contempt for the reality of human life from which art is our only preservation? Or is it rather a disgust at the contamination of life by the futility and madness of art? What is the ground of this confrontation between the sacramental and the demonic in which we hold together the world's flesh, and the mind's word, making of noise a deep interior silence? The answer to these questions lies only in its felt absence invoked in the wild prayers of rock, in its ecstasy of gratuity and the stringency of its saints.

Walter Ong has argued for a certain parallelism between the sequences of communication processes and the Freudian stages of psychosexual development.[7] There are, of course, huge problems in such comparisons, not to speak of the initial abstraction of such a schema. But what is of value in these constructions is the notion that the human sensorium is a structurally and historically produced producer of its own acoustic, visual, tactile, libidinal and social environment. If this is so, then the literary laments over the passing of the syntactic basis of the classical doctrine of knowledge and art into the 'speechlessness' of the 'stoned' is not clearly a collapse of common language or of 'our central habits of consciousness'.[8] The new musical culture rejects equally the sphincters of print and bullshit. It shares the awareness that our linguistic environment is violent, exploitative and a basic tool of social manipulation. In rock and folk lyrics there is an enormous sensitivity to being verbally 'fucked over' by the elders' literate culture. They sing instead of the responsible impregnation of holy interiors.

It may be objected that what I am saying is itself an example of the way poetry beguiles the *polis*, it being subject to no rule of understanding by which we can resist its charm and estimate its true knowledge. The problem here is one of political education and our understanding of its tasks. Is there, as some would argue, nothing to be learned from the claims of Woodstock nation or the May Revolution? To hold such a view is to accept that the synapses of character and political order are destroyed in modern society. But this in turn is as much an expression of an alleged reality which escapes us as the yearning for Utopia. The truth is that the realities – religion, politics, sociology, economics and psychology – are no longer ordered in any evident way, or any way that cannot be challenged. And so they are in competition with alchemy, magic, apocalypse and mysticism.

The children of Woodstock are unsure of their own generation. They grew up in the concentration camps of suburbia and highschool, blowing their minds on rice crispies and graduation. They were asked to love a land with a shopping centre for its heart. They were raised on the little white lies in the average births, deaths, dreams and killings that hold to no centre but scream around the insides of the brain like a police siren. Woodstock is a response to the hypocrisy of North American life which has made Truth *the* political issue of the day and vulgarity its connection of grace and the gift of life. Woodstock, as Abbie Hoffman has said, was an attempt to land a man on earth. The immediate failure of Woodstock does not appear only at Altamont. It is already present in its uninhabitable launching-site, determined by its own uses and its cycle as a corporate satellite, advertising local American troubles as universal events. The symbol of Woodstock's self-entrapment is its helicopters lifting in its road casualties (the organizers) and lifting off its speedy wounded. The music of Woodstock is the song of Vietnam employing the same resources of American youth and technology, imploding a simple society with its autistic efforts to attract world attention with America's awkward attempts to make humanity out of hunger, cold, fatigue, shit, piss and nudity, whereas these were nothing more than the organizational problems of America's largest temporary amusement corporation.

Woodstock is a presentiment of American technology gone gay – a launching-pad for its mind–body tripped out as corporate folly, recklessly spawning itself as a disaster area, tricking the lifeworld for its own needs. Is it nothing more? Are we to ignore its claims to be a *polis*, its celebration of birth, communal feeding, love and self-policing – or dismiss it as a country fair, as pretentious as American pie? If we do this, we exceed the contradictions of Woodstock and of the latrine-cleaner at Woodstock who had one son in Vietnam and another somewhere 'out' in the crowd. This man had a certain beauty of integrity which withers any talk of generation-gap politics and turns the question of unity back upon the society in which his experience is common and without recognition of its enduring strength.

Like Plato's *Republic*, Woodstock nation is a persuasion of the cave beset by its own guardian angels and fought over by its poets and philosophers. The failures of Woodstock are the same failures of the society whose imagination is turned towards the sun without any knowledge of the choice between good and evil. Woodstock is a collage of the society to which it appears and to which it fails to make itself alien except as a limit. Altamont is therefore neither the sequel nor the end of Woodstock, but simply the result of the American way of externalizing the experience of good and evil as part of growing up and thereby abandoning innocence with its children.

The question of the relation between the cultural revolution and political revolution is one which appears to divide us into realists and dreamers. Here, however, appearances are not deceptive, that is to say, the options of political theory are indeed orders of character. The cultural revolution is avowedly Utopian. It is inventive of character and society. In this, however, it is rejected as inadequate knowledge, evidently innocent of sociology, economics and politics. But the implicit realism of those social sciences is analytically nothing else than their own immaturity. It is their lack of design, their neglect of Utopia which is the mark of their peculiar authority. But this authority is predicated upon an unconscious ideal of character and social order as the material of expert but unplanned knowledge.

The issue here is not between the totalitarianism of Utopia and the liberal fancy of piecemeal social science. What is at stake is the unborn sociology of a society which is reflexively aware of its notions of order and character. In making this issue plain, the improvisations of the cultural revolution invite the dissolution of professional social science and its expert lay organization of knowledge. It reveals the distance between 'sociologists' and a sociology aware of itself as work with people. Such a sociology dreams of an end to the hierarchy of knowledge suspended in a genuine collectivity of social work. It is a *wild sociology* – not in the sense that it is prehistorical sociology, but precisely because within the very history which wild sociology presupposes, it dares to be utopian. The ignorance which determines professional sociology, on the other hand, is precisely its unhistorical knowledge of the present – modified, to be sure, by its construction of history as the past but never illuminated by a projection of history as Utopia. Where establishment sociology is concerned with the administration of existing social order, wild sociology is free to project scenarios of alternative orders. This is what is at issue in the crisis of Western sociology and the society that it reflects. It is for these reasons that individual awareness of the quality of everyday life – its objects, language, space, time and needs – erupts into the meaninglessness of the corporate agenda. The politics of experience represents the insurgency of human values at the low points of everyday life in the urban industrial world: what Henri Lefebvre calls the 'zero point' of social experience, where a kind of irrational asceticism is discernible under the apparent affluence and rationality which dominate our lives, but never so completely as to make counter-cultural response impossible.[9]

This is not to argue that the cultural revolution is the only way of revolution today. However, that is not because there is some intrinsically 'political' strategy of revolution. I mean rather to remark upon the poverty of our culture as a resource for revolutionary transformation. This is to weigh its failure, its class bias, its fragmentation and frivolity. It is to feel the nervelessness of a culture that is expert property, prostituted and destructive of the very style of life which is the underlying promise of all culture. At the same time, it is to touch at this very zero-point of culture its promise of the transfiguration of everyday life, not as a canvas to be wiped clean but as the natural light of man.

This potential for transfiguration is not at all obvious amidst the vulgarity and garbage of Woodstock or the May revolution. But this is the way of wild sociology into the world; it can enter only through self-mockery, nihilistic flirtations and the very self-violence which it seeks to avoid. Its way is profane because its resources are nothing else than the world and its people struggling for improvement. It is easy to be cynical about the organizational and promotional features of 'rock-ins' and 'maybe's', to dissolve them in a phrase, to empty their *logos* into the waste-bin of fashion. Indeed, the spontaneity, festivity and refusals which constitute these events make it inevitable that the participants will 'blow it', will be unable to sustain their enthusiasm and disintegrate as at Altamont, in Paris and elsewhere. The critics will observe failure and speak wisely of what is to be done within the limits of an untransfigured world which lives without fancy and avoids enthusiasm in favour of the pigeon-holes of politics, history and sociology.[10]

Woodstock is the story of the machine in the garden – a musical machine this time, to be sure, yet still caught in the rape and the promise of the land.[11] Like the railroad and the telegraph which are the background to *The Education of Henry Adams*, the rock machines of Woodstock are the dynamos of a new pastoral and the medium of those 'two hostile lives' which still rule the summers and winters of American youth as they did when Henry Adams was a boy.

Winter and summer, then, were two hostile lives, and bred two separate natures. Winter was always the effort to live; summer was tropical licence. Whether the children rolled in the grass, or waded in the brook, or swam in the salt ocean, or sailed in the bay, or fished for smelts in the creeks, or netted minnows in the salt-marshes, or took to the pine-woods and the granite quarries, or chased muskrats and hunted snapping-turtles in the swamps, or mushrooms or nuts on the autumn hills, summer and country were always sensual living, while winter was always compulsory learning. Summer was the multiplicity of nature; winter was school.

The bearing of the two seasons on the education of Henry Adams was no fancy; it was the most decisive force he ever knew; it ran through life, and made the division between its perplexing, enduring, irreconcilable problems irreducible opposites, with growing emphasis to the last year of study. From earliest childhood the boy was accustomed to feel that, for him, life was double. Winter and summer, town and country, law and liberty, were hostile, and the man who pretended they were not was in his eyes a schoolmaster, that is, a man employed to tell lies to little boys.[12]

In North America the land and its seasons are as divided as its Republic. They are elemental to the expression of the conflicts in its political life and thus we cannot ignore the music and songs in which this land becomes the figure of the renewal of political dialogue. The struggle of reason in our times is the struggle to reconnect the private and public domains of experience which have been separated into the orders of sensate and rational discourse. As Marcuse writes:

The fight will be won when the obscene symbiosis of opposites is broken – the symbiosis between the erotic play of the sea (its waves rolling in as advancing males, breaking by their own grace, turning female: caressing each other, and licking the rocks) and the booming death industries at its shores, between the flight of the white birds and that of the gray air force jets, between the silence of the night and the vicious farts of the motorcycles ... Only then will men and women be free to resolve the conflict between the Fifth Avenues and the ghettos, between procreation and genocide. In the long range, the political dimension can no longer be divorced from the aesthetic, reason from sensibility, the gesture of the barricade from that of love. To be sure, the former spells hatred – but the hatred of all that which is inhuman, and this 'gut hatred' is an essential ingredient of the cultural revolution.[13]

In this task the poet and artist are mediators in the renewal of dialogue between the mythic archetypes of man's place in the world and the Platonic ordering of the archetypes of truth, beauty and justice under the philosophical rule of the instrumental good.[14] The privatization of experience which shapes modern society derives essentially from the nature of its labouring and intellect processes. Ancient knowledge was intrinsically tied to the realm of politics, to the field of action and historical glory. It was nourished by the connections of myth and memory. But these bonds are broken in the self-infinitizing labour of the modern man of culture and capital. Today, poetry and politics, just as art and technology, can no longer be separated if we to are remake the connections of mind and body, to restore the community of the senses which is the foundation of our political life. All politics therefore is ultimately a matter of *education* and all education a mode of *political* education. It is for this reason that there is a long-standing quarrel between poetry and philosophy over the true nature of the body politic.

1. I am therefore extending the direction of two previous essays – 'Authority, Knowledge and the Body Politic' and 'Violence, Language and the Body Politic' – in my *Sociology as a Skin Trade: Essays Towards a Reflexive Sociology*, Heinemann, 1972; Harper & Row, New York, 1972.
2. Thomas Carlyle, 'Signs of the Times' in *Critical and Miscellaneous Essays*, Chapman & Hall, 1894, vol. 1, p. 476.
3. 'It is fair, then, that before returning from exile poetry should publish her defence in lyric verse or some other measure; and I suppose we should allow her champions who love poetry but are not poets to plead for her in prose, that she is no mere source of pleasure but a benefit to society and to human life. We shall listen favourably: for we shall clearly be the gainers, if that can be proved.' Plato, *The Republic*, X, 607.
4. Midge Decter, 'Toward the New Chastity', *The Atlantic*, vol. 230, no. 2, August 1972, pp. 42–55.
5. Karl Bednarik, *The Male in Crisis*, Secker & Warburg, 1970; Alfred A. Knopf, New York, 1970.
6. Dan Wakefield, ed., *The Addict*, Fawcett World Library, New York, 1963, p. 9.
7. Walter J. Ong, s.j., *The Presence of the Word: Some Prolegomena for Cultural and Religious History*, Yale University Press, London and New Haven, Conn., 1967, pp. 92–110.

8. George Steiner, *In Bluebeard's Castle: Some Notes towards the Redefinition of Culture*, Faber & Faber, 1971; Yale University Press, New Haven, Conn., 1971, p. 128.

9. Henri Lefebvre, *Everyday Life in the Modern World*, trans. Sacha Rabinovitch, Allen Lane The Penguin Press, 1971, p. 185.

10. Alfred Willener, *The Action-Image of Society: On Cultural Politicization*, trans. A. M. Sheridan Smith, Tavistock Publications, 1970.

11. Leo Marx, *The Machine in the Garden: Technology and the Pastoral Ideal in America*, Oxford University Press, New York, 1964.

12. *The Education of Henry Adams: An Autogiography*, intro. D. W. Brogan, Constable, 1971; Houghton Mifflin, Boston, 1961, p. 9.

13. Herbert Marcuse, *Counterrevolution and Revolt*, Allen Lane The Penguin Press, 1972, p. 130.

14. O'Neill, 'Authority, Knowledge and the Body Politic'.

John Broadbent

The Image of God, or Two Yards of Skin

We are agreed that the dumb can speak through the body, and the illiterate read it like a book: 'For there are mystically in our faces certain characters which carry in them the motto of our souls, wherein he that cannot read ABC may read our natures.' (Thomas Browne, *Religio Medici*, 1642)

'A good painter has two chief objects to paint: man, and the intention of his soul. The former is easy, the latter hard because he has to represent it by the attitude and movements of the limbs. The knowledge of these should be acquired by observing the dumb, because their movements are more natural than those of any other class of person.' (Leonardo da Vinci, *Notebooks*)

Browne and Leonardo agree with McLuhan that there is something unnatural about reading, even about speaking: 'Phonetic culture endows men with the means of repressing their feelings and emotions when engaged in action. To act without *re*acting, without involvement, is the peculiar advantage of Western literate man.' (Marshall McLuhan, *Understanding Media*, 1964, ch. 9)

But for the seventeenth century, to be inarticulate, and naked, was to be unnatural in the other direction – less than human. It is when King Lear goes mad that language fails him and he rips off his clothes; and when Edgar pretends to be mad that he rips off *his* clothes and pretends to be dumb. Lear had to pass through these storms to be restored to a better nature; but inarticulacy, nakedness, illiteracy were states of purgation, not states good in themselves; they belonged to tragedy. The victories of living were celebrated in comedy in terms of various kinds of doubleness that require alert speech and careful clothing – repartee, girls disguised as boys, twins disguised as strangers. Normally, language and upright posture were seen as the characteristics of being human, and of being divine. When God punishes Satan in *Paradise Lost* he turns him into what he had disguised himself as, a snake – no longer heavenly but autochthonous:

> he would have spoke,
> But hiss for hiss returned with forkèd tongue
> To forkèd tongue
>
> (Milton, *Paradise Lost*, 1667, Book x)

'He would have spoke': to lose your speech and your shape was to lose the signs that delimited your boundary as human.

We agree too about the larger notion, that the grammar of the body corresponds to the grammar of the cosmos. The body took its meaning from the world; the microcosm and the macrocosm made sense of each other: 'That great wise disposer of all things in heaven and earth, who makes twins in the little continent of their mother's womb to lie at ease and peace, and the eccentric motions of the orbs, and the regular and irregular progressions of the stars, not to cross or hinder one another . . .' (Jeremy Taylor, *Doctor Dubitantium*, 1660)

Taylor moves in a clause from the sphere of the uterus to the spheres of the planets and of the fixed stars. His easy syntax is a magic for ensuring that the universe will not thwart itself. It's smug; but it deserves some of its assurance about the universe, by being so sure about the body. Bishops could talk about the uterus without affecting candour. Sir Thomas Browne called it 'the truest microcosm, the womb of our mother'. Donne and Webster both called the body a lump of curdled milk. That is an example of the contempt they felt for the body, as well as admiration; but the contempt is bodily too: it is based on the sense that we feed at the breast, and we decay. They hold pregnancy in the same register as cosmology; they are less likely to be idolatrous, or trivial, about either breasts or the galaxy.

One of *our* motives for attending to the human body is that the heavenly bodies are now too far away. We can land on the moon but we can't relate it to twins in the little continent of their mother's womb. We know too much; so much that the truth has become unknowable in its quantity and complexity, and unrelated to anything else. Donne saw the beginnings of this:

> As new philosophy arrests the sun
> And bids the passive earth about it run,
> So we have dulled our mind, it hath no ends:
> Only the body's busy, and pretends.
>
> *(To Lady Bedford* ('To have written then . . .'))

There seems nothing left for the imagination to create; our mind 'hath no ends', so we close in on the body, like a tortoise. The cosmos is expanding at the speed of light, and will collapse again. Civilization is growing exponentially, and will collapse again. The scale of quite familiar and diurnal things has suddenly enlarged – even in England, counties have supernova'd into regions; lorries and planes swell into juggernauts, jumbo jets, supertankers; and their noise drowns the churchbells which, as Peter Laslett noted, used to be the loudest noise in England. Unable to register these expansions, we turn in to the one thing whose boundaries we can still define, the body.

What is the body a medium *for*? In the seventeenth century it was a medium for the expression of soul. It was in fact the manifestation *of* the soul, rather as Christ was the incarnation of the godhead:

> For of the soul the body form doth take;
> For soul is form, and doth the body make.
>
> (Spenser, *An hymn in honour of Beauty*, 1596)

Spenser was referring to the Christian doctrine of incarnation, and also to Platonism: the soul is like the Platonic 'form' or paradigm of identity; the body is the ectype of it which our senses are aware of down in this shadowy world. In one aspect, the body cannot but express the soul: greedy men behave greedily, the actions of noble men are 'clear' and so on. In another aspect, though, the body is seen as *hindering* what the soul wants to express, or wants to be.

This view of the body as a hindrance to the soul was particularly acute in the early seventeenth century. Here is Donne addressing his own soul on the disadvantages of being born into a body:

> Think further on thyself, my soul, and think
> How thou at first wast made but in a sink

. . . . .

This curded milk, this poor unlittered whelp,
My body, could, beyond escape or help,
Infect thee with original sin and thou
Couldst neither then refuse, nor leave it now.
Think that no stubborn sullen anchorite
Which fixed to a pillar or a grave doth sit
Bedded and bathed in all his ordures, dwells
So foully as our souls in their first-built cells.
Think in how poor a prison thou didst lie
After, enabled but to suck and cry.
Think when 'twas grown to most 'twas a poor inn,
A province packed up in two yards of skin,
And that usurped or threatened with the rage
Of sicknesses, or their true mother, age.

(*Second Anniversary*, 1612)

This raises two problems. First, where is the self? Is it in the soul,
or soul and body together? Second, isn't this disgust for the body
and its functions, even for the vagina that gave it birth, patho-
logical?

I think it was in the sixteenth and seventeenth centuries that
the first question, where to locate identity, came to have a more
than philosophical interest. It is what the soliloquies of tragic
heroes are about. Donne did not give a single answer. In one poem
he rejects all the qualities that poets and theologians might attribute to a good woman, and insists on her body as her self:

Can men more injure women than to say
They love them for that by which they're not they?
Makes virtue woman? Must I cool my blood
Till I both be, and find one, wise and good?
May barren angels love so! But if we
Make love to woman, virtue is not she,
As beauty's not, nor wealth: he that strays thus
From her to hers is more adulterous
Than if he took her maid.

(*Elegy* XVIII)

It's playful, but it makes a post-Freudian point: that to love the
attribute is to evade the identity, and so in effect to withhold love.
Donne goes on to use the macro–microcosm link:

> Although we see celestial bodies move
> Above the earth, the earth we till, and love:
> So we her airs contémplate, words, and heart,
> And virtues; but we love the centric part.
> Nor is the soul more worthy or more fit
> For love than this – as infinite as it.

The pronouns have found their nouns: the *they* and *she* of women do not subsist in adjectives like 'virtuous' and 'beautiful', but in the body and especially the body's centre, the vulva, the womb, which is also the centre of the universe. So Donne dismisses the orthodox centre of being, the soul. The vulva, he says, is as infinite as the soul – she has such an enormous vagina; but he also means that the body is as infinite as the soul because in the womb it too offers immortality, as in the vulva it offers love. The body warrants selfhood.

Nietzsche made the same point: 'the awakened and knowing say: body am I entirely, and nothing else; and soul is only a word for something about the body . . . Behind your thoughts and feelings, my brother, there stands a mighty ruler, an unknown sage – whose name is self. In your body he dwells; he is your body.' (*Thus spoke Zarathustra*, Part 1, 1883, trans. W. Kaufmann) But he says it with the solemnity of dogma; so we respond with scepticism; while Donne's wit, and his location of the discussion in bed, encourage us to play with these notions, not debate them.

You can only make Donne's kind of joke, only assert his kind of positive, if you have two poles to work between – soul as well as body, heaven and earth. It is that distension between poles that gave the seventeenth century its wit. Hamlet saw men staggering about halfway between heaven and the lair of animals. Sir Thomas Browne described man as 'that great and true amphibian whose nature is disposed to live, not only like other creatures in divers elements, but in divided and distinguished worlds' (*Religio Medici*) – the worlds of body and soul, heaven and earth. I don't think it was a question of their sensibilities being more unified than ours, so that they could hold the poles closer together, but rather that they were more aware of the *dis*unities, the *dis*continuities; or perhaps that they were more playful with them, or took more risks. For them the whole universe hung on a paradox, *verbum caro factum est*, the word made flesh; that religious metaphor could become the language of a poem or a farce. It is because they saw the soul as *different* from the body, heaven *separated* from earth, that they were able to see human beings as mediators across those boundaries.

Our tendency is to dissolve the boundaries; theirs was to work along them. In a poem called 'Angel wings' Brian Patten finds a pair of angel's wings in a cupboard, but

> I was not naïve enough to believe them real.
>
> Nowadays even the mention of the word angel
> embarrasses me.

('The irrelevant song', *The Irrelevant Song*, Allen and Unwin, 1971)

But the seventeenth century did believe in angels, and used them as the apotheosis of that totality which we experience briefly in love. When the archangel Raphael tells Adam how angels make love, he bases his account on the human body:

> Whatever pure thou in the body enjoy'st
> (And pure thou wert created) we enjoy
> In eminence, and obstacle find none
> Of membrane, joint, or limb, exclusive bars;
> Easier than air with air, if spirits embrace,
> Total they mix, union of pure with pure
> Desiring; nor restrained conveyance need
> As flesh to mix with flesh, or soul with soul.
>
> (Milton, *Paradise Lost*, Book VIII)

The totality is expressed in that dislocated present participle, 'Desiring'. Because they were so conscious of the margins between states of being, the body–soul and man–angel margins were often used as models for the I–you boundary that we cross in love. In other words, their divided world, and their definition of man as an amphibian, gave them a set of metaphors for thinking about love as relational, and as cosmic, at the same time:

> we by a love so much refined
> That our selves know not what it is,
> Inter-assurèd of the mind
> Care less eyes, lips and hands to miss.
>
> Our two souls, therefore, which are one,
> Though I must go, endure not yet
> A breach but an expansïon
> Like gold to airy thinness beat.
>
> (Donne, *A Valediction forbidding Mourning*)

At this stage I want to draw a contrast between Donne's language of the loving body about 1600, and Henry Miller's in 1962. Donne's dominant words are pronouns, words of relationship; his imagery is drawn from precious metals with symbolic value, from physiology, astronomy, theology; and his images hang on a scale that is continuous from heavengate to vulva. Here are some phrases from Miller's *Sexus*: 'old rubber bands . . . pushing a piece of stiff suet down a drainpipe . . . gall . . . worms . . . pus . . . there wasn't another charge in the battery . . . cheese . . . hammer . . . implement . . . it looked disgustingly like a cheap gadget . . . the chopped sirloin, the mashed potatoes, the gravy and all the spices . . . jolted her like an electric charge . . .' (London, 1962, pp. 142, 227) The categories of this language are food, decay, disease; and electrical engineering. There is no scale up or down, no reference across a boundary. The body is being used merely as a machine for galvanizing despair or for treating famine. It's easy to beat the present with the past. The point is, what is the nature of the difference? In this case you might say that Donne enjoyed a world-view which encouraged complexity, relationship, mobility; while Miller seems caught in a degraded environment, some kind of motorway service-area, or a torture-chamber.

Donne had no motorways but his age did have torture-chambers; and of course he can be disgusted, and aggressive; so can all the Jacobeans. But his aggression and disgust are usually not total; like the love, the commitments to soul or to body, they are ambivalent, games played with the frontier. He has a poem called 'The comparison' which is a ritual of disgust and idealization defined by each other:

> Are not your kisses then as filthy and more
> As a worm sucking an envenomed sore?

That is the insult to his enemy; then he pays his own love a compliment:

> So kiss good turtles, so devoutly nice
> Are priests in handling reverent sacrifice
> And such in searching wounds the surgeon is
> As we when we embrace and touch and kiss.

Another comparison, from Brian Patten. Like Donne, he rejects the pretty Petrarchanism of the teen magazines:

> some descriptions of peacocks, of sunsets,
> some fat little tears,
> something to hold to chubby breasts,
> something to put down,
> something to sigh about,
> I don't want to give you these things.
> I want to give you meat,

– and, like Donne in a certain mood, he offers the body, the phallus, as final:

> the splendid meat,
> the blemished meat.
> Say, here it is,
> here is the active ingredient,
> the thing that bothers history,
> that bothers priest and financier.
> Here is the meat.

And (still like Donne), the genital has two values: splendour and blemish. Towards the end of the poem, though, he separates from Donne:

> The sirens wailing on police-cars,
> the ambulances alert with pain,
> the bricks falling on the young
> queens in night-parks
> demand meat
> the real thing.
>
> I want to give you something
> that bleeds as it leaves my hand
> and enters yours,
> something that by its rawness,
> that by its bleeding
> demands to be called real . . .
> ('Meat,' *The Irrelevant Song*, Allen and Unwin, 1971)

Or, as it said on the women's page of the *Sunday Times* for 16 July 1972, 'Not to mince words, he's pure beefcake.' Patten separates from Donne in offering *pure* minced beef. His meat does not relate to anything else (as Donne's body relates to the sky); nothing else has any identity, so the lines too drift on without rhythm or distinction, demotic mutters. The only identity lies in the meat, and in meat alone; and its realness is guaranteed by its suffering, its being raw and bleeding. Donne's priest and surgeon have given way to a butcher.

Politicians who profess to know what the people feel should consider what it means if that is a true record, or even a true prophecy, of how you may feel in London now.

Of course the seventeenth century was aware also of disintegration, rawness, blood, bricks, policemen; Shakespeare saw death as a policeman – 'For that fell sergeant, Death, is swift in his arrest'. But, once again, I think they saw death in relation to life, as a frontier transaction, as they saw body and soul, love and disgust in terms of each other; while we tend to see each in isolation. It's a cliché that we have draped death in the veils we pulled off sex. But the cliché isn't quite true. No generation has seen so much death as ours has, but we've seen it only in books and pictures. We forget that watching television is not seeing, and not reading, but only watching. Our experience therefore is appalling, but illusory. We have watched all the dead bodies in the world but we don't know what they are saying.

An actual dead body transmits a message, has meaning; so has a dead body in a work of art; but a dead body in the 'news' is without meaning. There is an extraordinary scene about this in *Titus Andronicus*: the heroine Lavinia has been raped and had her tongue and hands cut off so that she can't tell what happened to her. Back with her family, she uses the stumps of her arms to turn over the pages of a copy of Ovid's *Metamorphoses* to show them Book VI, where Philomela suffered the same fate (Lavinia being, so to speak, the real-life Philomela). Then with her handless wrists and her feet she scratches a stick in the sand to write the names of her ravishers. When the body fails as a medium of expression, we revert to writing.

What I am getting at here is our tendency to idolatry of the body as if it were always beautiful, whole, painless and successful. I think this is because we are inured to merely watching death and torture. The day I started to write this essay, there was a review in the *Guardian* of the Documenta art exhibition at Kassel on the nature of reality. The review was headed 'Document of a dead end', but it was precisely death that artists had excluded from reality. 'The human body,' the reviewer wrote, 'preferably naked and fairly sexy', was a prime ingredient of the exhibition. Sometimes it was in a painting or sculpture, sometimes a photograph; or it might be a living model. At the top of this hierarchy of reality, it might be the artist himself posing as a work of art. Behind most of these exhibits, the reviewer reported 'predominantly blue skies'. A dead end, but no death.

I want now to present and analyse part of a speech from Shakespeare's *Cymbeline* (IV, ii). The heroine, Imogen, is a young bride; she is separated from her husband, and trying to find him. She wakes up from a drugged coma in the wilds of Wales, forgetting where she is, still dreaming of travel. She finds herself beside a headless body: they have both been assumed dead, and buried together under flowers. Imogen is disguised in boy's clothes; the corpse is disguised in the clothes of her husband. Actually it is the body of an enemy who was trying to rape her. As usual, the plot is intolerably complicated but the patterns are clear: the rapist has suffered the final emasculation; the girl must accept her masculinity – put on boy's clothes – before she can be really married; another, that she must come to terms with the body, and the blood inside it.

> Yes sir, to Milford Haven, which is the way?
> I thank you. By yond bush? Pray, how far thither?
> Od's pittikins! can it be six mile yet?
> I have gone all night. Faith, I'll lie down and sleep.
> But soft! no bedfellow! O gods and goddesses!
> These flowers are like the pleasures of the world;
> This bloody man the care on't. I hope I dream:
> For so I thought I was a cave-keeper
> And cook to honest creatures. But 'tis not so:
> 'Twas but a bolt of nothing, shot at nothing,
> Which the brain makes of fumes. Our very eyes
> Are sometimes like our judgements, blind. Good faith.
> I tremble still with fear; but if there be
> Yet left in heaven as small a drop of pity
> As a wren's eye, feared gods, a part of it!
> The dream's here still: even when I wake it is
> Without me, as within me; not imagined, felt.
> A headless man? The garments of Posthumus?
> I know the shape of's leg; this is his hand;
> His foot Mercurial; his Martial thigh;

The brawns of Hercules; but his Jovial face –
Murder in heaven! How ...? 'Tis gone! ...
                                        O Posthumus, alas!
Where is thy head? where's that? Ay me! where's that? ...
                        O!
Give colour to my pale cheek with thy blood,
That we the horrider may seem to those
Which chance to find us. O my lord, my lord!

She is not watching the telly. Her experience of death is 'not
imagined, felt'. She discovers that blood is a component of death
as well as life, of war as well as sex. (The word 'blood' meant
virility and lust as well as ordinary blood in the seventeenth century, so that when she smears it on her face to disguise herself
Imogen accepts the roles of man, soldier and corpse, as well as
living woman and bride and boy.) She talks about the body as if it
were divine, using the name of a god for each part; but she learns
that the body is also merely a corpse dressed in familiar clothes. In
short, she registers that we live in a dual world in which flowers are
the pleasure of it, and this bloody man the care of it.

When Donne was Dean of St Paul's he came to preach the
funeral sermon of Mrs Magdalen Herbert, who had been his loved
patroness and the mother of lifelong friends of his. He evoked her
actual deadness: 'That body upon which you tread now, that
which now, whilst I speak, is mouldering, and crumbling into less
and less dust, and so hath some motion, though no life ...' Our
ritual for the dead is opposite. We would travolate the dead body
through black curtains into cleansing fire like a funeral rush-hour;
but for the seventeenth century, to realise the dead body was to
realise its majesty and hope of resurrection: 'that body which was
the tabernacle of a holy soul, and a temple of the Holy Ghost ...
that body at last shall have her last expectation satisfied, and dwell
bodily with that Righteousness in these new heavens and new earth
for ever and ever and ever and infinite and super-infinite evers.'

To 'have her last expectation satisfied' is to reverse the cliché
that orgasm is a little death: death is the great orgasm. Donne
meant it, for he goes on to quote the *Song of Solomon*, the words
between Christ and his bride the church: 'We end all with this
valediction of the spouse to Christ: "His left hand is under my
head, and his right embraces me" was the spouse's valediction and

goodnight to Christ then when she laid herself down to sleep . . .
Beloved, every good soul is the spouse of Christ.' (Chelsea, 1 July
1627.)

This is what our own prophets are now offering, in secular terms,
as the only hope for mankind: the resurrection of the body into
erotic relationship with the sources of life. Here is Norman O.
Brown in *Life Against Death*:

> If we can imagine an unrepressed man – a man strong enough to live
> and therefore strong enough to die . . . such a man would have a body
> freed from unconscious oral, anal and genital fantasies of return to the
> maternal womb . . . In such a man would be fulfilled on earth the mystic
> hope of Christianity, the resurrection of the body . . . With such a trans-
> figured body the human soul can be reconciled, and the human ego
> become once more what it was designed to be in the first place, a body-
> ego and the surface of a body, sensing that communication between
> body and body which is life.
> *Life Against Death: The Psychoanalytical Meaning of History* (Sphere
> Books, 1968), p. 255

If that sounds extravagant, here is Marcuse suggesting what would
happen if society relinquished its neurotic obsession with growth
and performance and adhered to a different reality principle, based
on the body's values:

> No longer used as a fulltime instrument of labor, the body would be
> resexualized. The regression involved in this spread of the libido would
> first manifest itself in a reactivation of all erotogenic zones and, conse-
> quently, in a resurgence of pregenital polymorphous sexuality and in a
> decline of genital supremacy. The body in its entirety would become an
> object of cathexis, a thing to be enjoyed – an instrument of pleasure.
> *Eros and Civilization: A Philosophical Inquiry into Freud* (Allen Lane The
> Penguin Press, 1969), p. 201.

In 1967, Marcuse reviewed Brown's anthology *Love's Body* and
censured it for being mystical, mystifying, ahistorical and therefore apolitical, unpractical. He relates Brown's ideas to the
seventeenth century via the Fall: '[Brown's] solution, the end of
the drama of history, is the restoration of original and total unity
. . . subject and object, body and soul – abolition of the self . . .
abolition of the reality principle, of all boundaries . . . But such
fusion would be the end of human life.' ('Love Mystified: A

Critique' in *Commentary*, 1967, reproduced in his *Negations: Essays in Critical Theory*, Cape, 1968)

I believe it is vital to reflect on the divergence of these two minds in our generation. To adjudicate between them would be an exercise set in all our university departments of history, had history not abandoned its claims on education. Of course it is difficult to adjudicate, or mediate, between poet and historian, visionary and political economist, if you start by not believing in either dreams or politics. All I can do myself at present is to suspect under the difference of 'mythical' Brown and 'political' Marcuse an American identity. When the English colonized the Atlantic coast of North America in the sixteenth and seventeenth centuries, it was partly to rediscover paradise, to get back behind the Fall – not only to fruitfulness but also to purity:

In New England, described as resembling the Garden of Eden, partridges were supposedly so big that they could no longer fly . . . This American flair for the grandiose, likewise religious in origin, is shared even more by the most lucid minds . . . the first explorers were conscious of playing an important role in the history of salvation . . . the certainty of the eschatological mission, and especially of attaining once again the perfection of early Christianity and restoring Paradise to earth, is not likely to be forgotten easily . . . the paradisaical elements . . . are now more or less repressed, but we find the yearning for, and the exaltation of, a new beginning, an 'Adamic' innocence, a beatific plenitude which precedes history.

(Mircea Éliade, *The Quest: History and Meaning in Religion*, Chicago University Press, 1969, 'Paradise and Utopia')

And Éliade goes on of course to quote Whitman singing 'the body electric'.

So the drive to get back behind the Fall is something the twentieth century shares with the seventeenth; but I want to bring to bear on our version some of the criticisms that the seventeenth century made of it. In paradise as seen by the seventeenth century, Adam and Eve were like this in part: they were innocent as children, naked as prehistoric men; and created in the image of God:

> Two of far nobler shape erect and tall,
> Godlike erect, with native honour clad
> In naked majesty seemed lords of all,

And worthy seemed, for in their looks divine
The image of their glorious maker shone,
Truth, wisdom, sanctitude severe and pure,
Severe but in true filial freedom placed;

.   .   .   .   .

Nor those mysterious parts were then concealed,
Then was not guilty shame, dishonest shame
Of nature's works, honour dishonourable,
Sin-bred, how have ye troubled all mankind
With shows instead, mere shows of seeming pure,
And banished from man's life his happiest life,
Simplicity and spotless innocence.
So passed they naked on, nor shunned the sight
Of God or angel, for they thought no ill;
So hand in hand they passed, the loveliest pair
That ever yet in love's embraces met,
Adam the goodliest man of men since born
His sons, the fairest of her daughters Eve.

(Milton, *Paradise Lost*, Book IV)

But all these qualities – of innocence and happy nakedness and
majesty and freely expressed love and the likeness to God – were
seen as having been lost at the Fall. And the Fall consisted precisely in trying to actually become a god, in breaking the boundaries of human life. Satan says to Eve,

And what are gods that man may not become
As they, participating godlike food?

Eve is impressed by the fact that he can speak – he has already
broken the limitations of his nature, it seems; so she eats the forbidden fruit and finds herself indeed in a state of

dilated spirits, ampler heart,
And growing up to godhead   (Book IX)

Adam follows her. They make love; but wake to shame, and
eventual death. Later in the poem, the archangel Michael shows
Adam, in a vision, a hospital for the dying. Adam is appalled: it
seems to make nonsense of the image of God theory, even after
the Fall:

Can thus
The image of God in man created once
So goodly and erect, though faulty since,

To such unsightly sufferings be debased
Under inhuman pains? Why should not man,
Retaining still divine similitude
In part from such deformities be free
And for his maker's image sake exempt?
　Their maker's image, answered Michael, then
Forsook them, when themselves they vilified
To serve ungoverned appetite . . .　　　　　　　(Book xi)

Michael goes on rather hesitantly, not sure himself how the image of God, once created in man, can be so deformed; but he is consistent in blaming man himself, not God or nature, 'since they God's image did not reverence in themselves'.

There are plenty of answers to that seventeenth-century view. One is that our failure to reverence God's image in ourselves does not belong to myth but to the present, and that it is the established order, often the Church, always the censors, who blaspheme it; only by breaking their bonds might we restore God's image in our bodies. This could happen in a quite literal and local way if, for instance, our schools educated potential mothers out of a scrubbing response to the body, instead of into it. Another reply to the seventeenth century is that our minds, apparently, can fix a time and place for cancer; so perhaps those people in Milton's hospital would not be dying so cruelly if they had been able to love their bodies.

In practice, we oscillate. Within each of us, and within each epoch, there is a sense that our troubles come from transgressing the limits of human existence: we should expect less, obey the rule of 'not too much', draw in our horns lest a vulture peck them off. But there is also a sense, which may be felt even by the same person, that, faced with all those other closed-down people, and the inertia of institutions, and the brevity of life, we must follow Blake – 'The road of excess leads to the palace of wisdom.' And in between there are those, and those parts of us, who work along the margins, within the oscillations, committed to neither pole.

During discussion at the I.C.A. after the lecture on which this essay is based, I said I belonged on the margin and called myself a trimmer. The audience objected that this stood for a pessimism which is itself reactionary. I think this argument rather sterile: it assumes that one can will oneself to be a kind of person, or to cross a boundary. It seems to me that the area in which Norman Brown meets Marcuse, where emotions become political and yet remain felt, is itself essentially a boundary; but that few inhabit it. Perhaps a social-worker and her client do when they consider her eligibility for a supplementary grant, and how best to apply the rules of the Department of Health and Social Security to the benefit of a child. Some of us live in another such area – the boundary between generations – when we teach and learn. Often in these circumstances we fall back onto one side or the other. As teachers we clench ourselves into those academic sneers that shield us from the vitality of pupils; as pupils we assert that only we are virile. Or we pretend to wear each other's protective clothing. To inhabit the boundary you have to be fairly naked. It is the ability to drop the defences a little, to survive unaccommodated in the danger-area, that's important. It is rare. The defences are so multiplex – the appeal to authority, tradition; the anecdote or giggle that leads one away; the shapeless drift of indecision that blots all other people and ideas to vague foam. Ultimately, I have only one political hope: that we may break the vicious generations, and the vicious education, 'loveless, unendeared', that force us to spend most of our lives talking about things other than what we feel. I do not see diving into 'the body', or any other single area, as a way to achieve that. To support the case for working the margins I want to bring one or two myths, finally, to bear.

Characteristically, Brown and Marcuse see the affirmation of bodily life in terms of Narcissus as opposed to Prometheus: not will and energy, rebellion and invention and their punishment, but gazing with love at the world until the self is oceanically at one with all: 'Fusion: the distinction between inner self and outside world . . . overcome. To the enlightened man, the universe becomes his body.' (Norman O. Brown, *Love's body* (New York, 1966) pp. 253–4) 'The libidinal cathexis of the ego (one's own body) may become the source and reservoir for a new libidinal cathexis of the objective world – transforming this world into a new mode of being.' (Marcuse, *Eros and Civilization*, p. 169) But in the myth, the gratification of Narcissus is achieved at the expense of relationship. Intent on his own reflection in a pool, he failed to answer the nymph Echo, who loved him; she pined till her body faded away and there was nothing left but her voice. Contrariwise,

Prometheus, hard-edged and wilful, was man's champion against the gods.

In terms of another myth, the prophecy is to reject Apollo for Dionysus, Apollo as god of light and art and control for Dionysus as god of wine and ecstasy: 'The consciousness strong enough to endure full life would be no longer Apollonian but Dionysian – consciousness which does not observe the limit, but overflows; consciousness which *does not negate any more*.' (Brown, *Life Against Death*, p. 270) Yet Apollo is also god of healing; while on the other hand it was under the influence of Dionysus that Augauë ate her son Pentheus. Euripides dramatized that event in *The Bacchae*. I saw a version of it in Cambridge recently, in which the characters were naked during the orgy scene when Pentheus is dismembered and eaten by the Bacchantes, his mother among them. But it was characteristic that the production quite failed to get across the violence that imbues any group activity, let alone a cannibal orgy; here were nice girls frolicking with body-paints; and when Augauë came to eat her son the stage was strewn with polyurethane gizzards as if, again, it was the meat that mattered rather than the emotion.

Sometimes the prophetic future is stated as a playing with the world instead of a Promethean striving. In this case the cult hero is Orpheus, who conquered death with his enchanting lyre. Orpheus could play the lyre so that stones and trees moved and wild animals were stilled; his music drew iron tears down Pluto's cheek – yet he failed to bring back his wife Eurydice from hell, and he too turned into a disembodied voice: he neglected the Thracian women so they tore him apart and threw his head, still singing, into the river.

One lesson of these myths is that he who seeks his body shall lose it, and probably lose somebody else's body for them as well. He who transgresses the limits of existence shall be *un*limited, *dis*-membered. This is also the religious, hence the seventeenth-century view: the ambition of men to be gods in *Genesis* is met with loss of the *imago dei*, expulsion from the garden, with the Tower of Babel, the flood. If you try to merge, to fuse, you will be *sub*merged, *con*fused. If you try to become a god, you become two yards of skin. On the other hand, the myths make it clear that transgression, submergence, confusion, playing, are necessary to life; and the man who always resists them, who never lets go, who cannot play, will also be destroyed, let go and played with.

Brown declares:

> The resurrection of the body is a social project facing mankind as a whole, and it will become a practical political problem when the statesmen of the world are called upon to deliver happiness instead of power ... In the face of this tremendous human problem, contemporary social theory, both capitalist and socialist, has nothing to say.
>
> (*Life Against Death*, p. 277)

Fisher and Cleveland, in their work *Body Image and Personality*, have something to say which may be relevant. In the unstructured environment of a T-group, it was the high-Barrier people – that is, the people with a stronger sense of their bodies' boundaries, who are also the power-seekers as opposed to the love-seekers – who emerge as more open, and as less authoritarian, than the low-Barrier:

> Each person sought to express his views and no one individual emerged as a definite leader ... there was a good deal of kidding and joking. Themes of hostility or sex ... were discussed in an open and relaxed manner. On the other hand, the groups comprising individuals with less definite body boundaries behaved differently. In these groups the members tended to sit passively and wait for one individual to take the lead ... talk was limited ... Joking about sexual topics or discussion of hostile behavior was absent.
>
> (Seymour Fisher and S. E. Cleveland, *Body Image and Personality*, New York, 1958; rev. edn, 1968, ch. 7.)

It must be admitted from signs elsewhere in their work that Fisher and Cleveland may have a somewhat more locker-room norm than Brown and Marcuse; but the point of my reference to them here remains, that the image of Narcissus is inadequate as an ideal: it may involve a dependency that leads to tyranny, or cannot produce revolt and change. In this it is similar to the ideal image of trance-inducing drugs. L.S.D. can induce

> an increased preoccupation with the body. It seemed as if the body were charged with energy ... The body seemed to lose its symmetry and to become amazingly plastic ... The body might seem to become separ-

ated from the individual so that he could feel himself as being at some distant point or behind himself. It might seem to come apart and there would be a sensation that the head could be removed . . . The individual finds it hard to tell where his body leaves off and the rest of the world begins.

(Fisher and Cleveland, op. cit., p. 26.)

Narcissistic prophecy, and narcotic trances, are both symptoms of the mystical anarchism that flourishes on the alienated verges of society: 'the cult of the Free Spirit . . . the ideal of a total emancipation of the individual from society, even from external reality itself – the ideal, if one will, of self-divinization . . .' (Norman Cohn, *The Pursuit of the Millennium: Revolutionary Millennarians and Mystical Anarchists of the Middle Ages*, London, 1957, ch. 13)

So in the Adam-cult of the fourteenth century, 'the lost Paradise was recreated and at the same time the advent of the Millennium was affirmed. Primitive innocence and blessedness were restored to the world by living gods in whom Creation was felt to have attained its perfection and to be transcended.' (ibid., ch. 9) We indulge in this kind of cult partly because we feel weak, childish, alienated, unable to get any further by Promethean action; but partly also, I think, because we have lost a sense of pain. In both cases, you might say, we have been reduced by Western hyperculture to the status of a dreaming child.

What we forget is that this reduction is only for the fortunate, for the white Omnipotent Administrator of Eldridge Cleaver's myth: 'a most weird and complex dialectic of inversion is established in Class Society. The Omnipotent Administrator is launched on a perpetual search for his alienated body, for the affirmation of his unstable masculinity.' (*Soul On Ice* (1968), 'The primeval mitosis') But what is the point of offering the resurrection of 'the body' to the people at the other end of that colour or class scale, the Supermasculine Menials? 'The chip on the Supermasculine Menial's shoulder is the fact that he has been robbed of his mind . . . the society in which he lives has assumed in its very structure that he, minus a mind, is the embodiment of Brute Power.'

This is not only slavery, but hell. In Book IV of the *Metamorphoses*, Ovid staged a descent into hell. It is peopled by Supermasculine Menials, mindlessly enduring the pangs of their mighty bodies:

                                   there Tityos
Gave his liver to the birds as he lay flat across
Nine plots of land; there Tantalus reached lips
Toward water while the trees above him swayed
Fruit beyond his grasp; there Sisyphus heaved
Great rocks uphill or as they plunged down slope
Ran after them; there Ixion revolved
Within his wheel, himself pursuer and
Pursued . . .

                       (trans. Horace Gregory, New York, 1958).

In 1548 Titian painted these four tortured beings for Mary of
Hungary. In 1556 the paintings were removed to a special 'room
of the damned' in the royal palace in Madrid – Tityos and Sisyphus facing Tantalus and Ixion. Later, Tantalus and Ixion were
destroyed but the other two survive in the Prado. Along with these
four, the supremely punished in Greek mythology were the
Danaïds, who have to carry water in leaking pots. For the Renaissance range of hell we must add Marsyas, also painted by
Titian, and Prometheus.

   This is what was done to them all:

Prometheus	chained to a rock	liver eaten by vultures
Tityos	pegged out over 9 acres	liver eaten by 2 vultures
Marsyas	tied upside-down to a pine-tree	flayed
Tantalus	tied to a fruit tree in a marsh	the water keeps rising to his chin but he cannot drink it, nor eat the fruit of the tree
Ixion	chained to a wheel of fire	the wheel never stops rolling
Sisyphus	required to roll a boulder uphill	the boulder keeps rolling down again
The Danaïds	required to fill a well with pots	the pots leak

All these tortures recur in fairy-tales, and have been recorded in
historical times; some of them are still used in prisons and by
interrogators. If we structure them, we get something like this:
the body is immobilized (Prometheus, Tityos, Marsyas, Tantalus)
                                   and
attached to an inanimate natural object (the same and Sisyphus)
or
the body is kept perpetually in motion (Ixion, Sisyphus, Danaïds)
                                   and
is attached to a cultural object (Ixion, Danaïds)

That is, all their bodies are treated as if they were either food animals (pegged out like skins, flayed), or food machines (wheel, irrigation). Either their own essential bodily needs for water and food are denied, or they are turned into the food of other creatures. From this we may conclude that the unpunished body would be (1) unattached; (2) able to rest; (3) able to eat and drink at will; (4) not itself eaten, dismembered, disrupted or on the other hand automatized. This seems obvious but they are not conditions enjoyed by babies, schoolchildren, machine-minders, drivers, to say nothing of patients, soldiers, prisoners. In general, the conditions of various kinds of 'work', as well as of acknowledged suffering, in industrial society, approximate more to the punishments than to the ideals of which they are the reverse. Camus actually called Sisyphus the 'proletarian of the gods' (*Le mythe de Sisyphe*, Paris, 1942). Erving Goffman defines proper demeanour, and its opposite, profanation of the self, in these terms:

He must have access to the eating utensils which his society defines as appropriate ones for use . . . he must be able to decline certain kinds of work . . . which his social group considers *infra dignitatem*. When the individual is subject to extreme constraint he is automatically forced from the circle of the proper. The sign vehicles or physical tokens through which the customary cermonies are performed are unavailable to him. Others may show ceremonial regard for him, but it becomes impossible for him to reciprocate the show or to act in such a way as to make himself worthy of receiving it. The only ceremonial statements that are possible for him are improper ones . . . The use of these [constricting] devices provides significant data on the ways in which the ceremonial grounds of selfhood can be taken away. By implication we can obtain information from this history about the conditions that must be satisfied if individuals are to have selves.
'Where the action is', *Interaction Ritual: Essays on Face-to-Face Behaviour*, Allen Lane The Penguin Press, 1972.

But Goffman was writing about psychiatric hospitals, not Hades.

With Ixion and Lear, many of us are 'bound upon a wheel of fire' – though the continuity of the image of being eaten is more significant these days. It is in accordance with the logic of myth that in a consumer society the consumer should be consumed. You can see it happening in supermarkets, where the customer–consumers are passed through the turnstiles like the animals whose parts they have just bought being driven through the abattoir. So the song 'Melting pot', which tries to jump over the sexual problems of racism, talks about our bodies in terms of cooking:

> WOMAN   Take a pinch of white man,
> Wrap it up in black skin,
> Add a touch of blue blood
> And a little bitty bit of Red Indian boy.
> MAN   Curl it up in king-kies,
> Mix with yellow Chinkies,
> If you lump it all together,
> Well you get a recipe for a getalong scene:
> O what a beautiful dream!
> CHORUS   If it could only come true,
> You know, you know.
> What we need is a great big melting/American pot,
> Big enough to take the world and all it's got,
> Keep it stirring for a hundred years or more,
> Turn out coffee-coloured people by the score,
> Yeah Lord! . . .
> (Cookaway Music Ltd, 'Melting pot', 1969.)

Would a Body Programme gratify us at so deep and simple a level that we could dispense with exploiting and polluting luxuries – and with aggression? There is no evidence in myth or literature that people stay content with deep and simple pleasures. We have invented the technological opposite of the rack in the pleasure-machine of *Barbarella*. Henry Miller's lover uses the electrodes of our torturers. We are all guilty of gluttony and cruelty: the businessman who drives his car at you like a charging hog, the teenage football hooligan, the picket, the nuclear button-presser. All of us are guilty of suppression and censorship: however radical, we with Stalin silence our wives or our pupils or our critics because they don't understand us. We make hell for other people by projecting on to them fantasies of what we hate within ourselves. The problem is how to acknowledge that we do all do that; and yet not just wallow helplessly in the guilt of it. (In discussion after the lecture on which this essay is based, my assertion that hatred is natural was received with shock, although one member of the audience said to another, 'What I feel for you is bloodlust.' It is as though the virtue of aggression – the ability of Prometheus to save us from the dependence – were totally contaminate. We have been, that is to say, not just flayed, but un-livered. By whom?) This accounts I think for Marcuse's warning: 'Even the ultimate advent of freedom cannot redeem those who died in pain. It is the remembrance of them, and the accumulated guilt of mankind, that darken the prospect of a civilization without repression.' (*Eros and Civilization*) As in Shakespeare's history plays, each generation wants to rip the skin off its forebears in reverse:

'Yes!' replied the Eunuch. 'I'm thirsty for blood – white man's blood . . . I want to drink for every black man, woman or child dragged to the slaughter from the shores of Africa, for every one of my brothers and sisters who suffered helplessly in the rotten holds of the damned slave ships . . . and for every one slaughtered and lynched in the mire of the New South . . .' 'No,' said the Infidel. 'No. More blood will only add crime upon crime . . . Blood upon blood; crime upon crime; brick of blood upon brick of blood of a new mad Tower of Babel which, too, will fall . . . There can be no triumph in blood.'

(Cleaver, op. cit., 'The allegory of the black eunuchs'.)

Blood is virtuous only when it is seen double, as Imogen saw it: we spill it when we love, and when we kill. The body alone, or seen as merely a glistening delight, or only in punishment, is an illusion. It has virtue when we notice the god inside it, and when we admit that it will wrinkle into two yards of skin and die. These transactions are the dynamic of Renaissance mythology, and seventeenth-century art. Even in England Sir Peter Lely celebrated the body with nymphs at a fountain (Plate 41). But only one of them is a Bacchanalian pin-up; one is growing old, and thinking about it; one is sad; one is rather plain and disordered; in the foreground are a beautiful bottom and feet, but the feet are dirty, and though you may think her left hand is playing with her genitals, it may have been scratching her piles.

Also at Dulwich is a painting by Poussin (Plate 42). The man is visually related to the goat's horns, the woman to its hindquarters. The baby ignores the woman's breast and sucks the goat's udder instead. So far, the painting declares our kinship with the animal world, the violence and the fecundity of two yards of skin; but the baby, his bottom between a woman's knees and his head between the knees of a goat, is the infant Zeus, king of the gods. However, we are men.

Here is a modern motto:

fall in

Sang eagle ox ferret and emerald arch.
O we, too, must learn to live here;
To use what we are.

(Kenneth Patchen, 'Because my hands hear the
   flowers thinking', *Because It Is*, Laurence Pollinger
   Ltd and New Directions Publishing Corporation,
   1960.)

Index